30.-

D1564721

Ancestor Worship
in Contemporary Japan

Ancestor Worship in Contemporary Japan

ROBERT J. SMITH

STANFORD UNIVERSITY PRESS

1974 *Stanford, California*

Ancestor worship — Japan

Stanford University Press
Stanford, California
© 1974 by the Board of Trustees of the
Leland Stanford Junior University
Printed in the United States of America
ISBN 0-8047-0873-8   LC 74-82780

Published with the assistance of
the Andrew W. Mellon Foundation

For Kazuko

Preface

At the outset I would like to acknowledge my immense debt to four men whose work on the subject of ancestor worship in Japan must be the starting point for any scholar in that field: Yanagita Kunio, Ariga Kizaemon, Hori Ichirō, and Takeda Chōshū. The full extent of that debt will be immediately apparent to those familiar with their writings, which unhappily remain largely untranslated.

By and large, the work of early European and North American scholars in this area of Japanese culture can safely be ignored. It exhibits little feeling for the profound differences between the practice of ancestor worship in China and Japan and a marked tendency to portray the latter as a kind of warped version of the orthodox Confucian pattern. Its focus was on theological and doctrinal issues, rather than on popular belief and practice; its approach was descriptive rather than analytic. Despite the length of the bibliography at the end of this book, only in the past twenty years or so has there been any great amount of research into the actual practice of ancestor worship in Japan (Dore 1958; Maeda 1965; Ooms 1967; Plath 1964; Smith 1966).

Why this paucity of information? I must confess that the reason is not clear to me. More Japanese participate in the rites marking memorial observances for the spirits of the dead than in all other rites combined. Were this alone not sufficient to stimulate their investigation, it might be thought that the intimate connection between the conception of the household—whose character a great number of scholars have been at pains to investigate—and that of the ancestors would have made the subject popular with social scientists. Yet this has not been so.

The situation with respect to the established religions is also peculiar. Although the Shintoists have long claimed that their faith rests squarely on the worship of the gods and the ancestors, Buddhist scholarship has been largely silent on the subject, even though for the most part Japanese Buddhism *is* ancestor worship. I find this reticence on the part of the Buddhists less puzzling by far than the almost total neglect on the part of the social scientists, for the orthodox Buddhist can only be dismayed by the implications of most of what he finds in popular ancestor worship in Japan. To begin with, it reveals what he is likely to interpret as fundamental misunderstandings of doctrine; in addition, the manner of dealing with the ancestral spirits strongly implies a rejection of the basic idea of karma, a lack of interest in the doctrine of reincarnation, and a profound transformation of the Mahayana view of the nature of heaven and hell. It never fails to surprise students of Buddhism that in Japan alone a person who has died is at once accorded the status of a buddha irrespective of the qualities he exhibited in life.

The foreigner conducting research in Japan is inevitably the recipient of assistance that he can seldom repay but must acknowledge as essential to whatever degree of success his endeavors enjoy. I can only hope the many people who have helped me so generously will find something here to suggest that their confidence in me was not misplaced. In the hamlet of Kurusu in the village of Yasuhara, the late Takao Hōen—for what was to be the last of many times—served as a helpful and interested participant in the collection of data on the memorial tablets of the households of his community. His son Kazuyoshi will place a copy of this book on the altar where his father's tablet now rests. In Takane, Nasukawa Ichirō made possible the census of the tablets, not without obvious bemusement. What he thought of the undertaking I cannot be sure, but he made the arrangements and carried off the occasion with high good humor. In Sone, Kubo Hiromichi, priest of the Anjōji, threw himself into the project with characteristic energy. Without his help little of substance would have come from my visit. In this community, Muratake Seiichi of Tokyo Metropolitan University and two of his students, Hirose Tōru and Watanabe Kichiji, were extraordinarily helpful in introducing me to people and in assisting with the tablet census.

Among the many people who have stimulated my thinking about the ancestors, I must mention especially Keith Brown, who was living in Takane at the time of my visit and on whose warm relations with the community my success depended; Harumi Befu, who has offered many useful comments over the years; and Arthur P. Wolf, whose work on the ancestors in rural Taiwan has long provided much material so sharply at variance with my own from Japan that I have been forced many times to reconsider my analysis. David W. Plath has been good enough to read the entire manuscript in draft form, and I hope he finds in this final revision signs of the many ways I have profited from his perceptive comments. Richard K. Beardsley, Bernard Bernier, and Emiko Ohnuki-Tierney kindly checked portions of the manuscript for me.

For support of the research that forms the basis of this book I am indebted to the American Council of Learned Societies for an Area Studies Grant (Asia) and to the China-Japan Program of Cornell University for a Faculty Research Grant. During the academic year 1962–63 I held a Fulbright Teaching Award at Tokyo Metropolitan University, where I received from faculty and students alike much helpful criticism and advice in the early stages of the planning of my research. In carrying out the tablet censuses in the cities I was given invaluable assistance by Koitabashi Tōichirō and Kuchiba Noriko. In the spring of 1971, while I was a visiting professor in the Department of Anthropology of the University of Arizona, Mr. Larry Manire gave me patient and expert help in coding and programming my data; for the funding of the computer operation I am indebted to the department.

I have used some of the data from my research in preparing a paper, "Who Are 'the Ancestors' in Japan?," to appear in the forthcoming *Ancestors*, edited by William H. Newell (The Hague, Mouton & Co.). I would like to thank the copyright holder for permission to use selected materials from that paper in this book.

I owe special thanks to J. G. Bell and Peter J. Kahn of Stanford University Press for skilled and incisive editorial work.

Most of all, to my wife Kazuko I must once again record an unrepayable debt. Had it not been for her unfailing support when it was most needed and her perceptive criticism when I was most wrongheaded, this entire undertaking would have foundered long since.

R.J.S.

PHOTO CREDITS

In the photo section following p. 122, photos 8, 9, 10, 13, 15, 16, 17, and 21 were taken by Professor Herman Ooms of the University of Illinois, Chicago Circle, in Nagasawa, near Kawasaki City, in 1965. In addition, photo 1, of the Kōanji temple in Tokyo, is from the Ooms collection. Photo 17 is reprinted by permission of the International Institute for the Study of Religions.

Photo 2 is from the author's collection, as are photos 3, 4, 5, 6, 11, and 12, taken in Yasuhara in 1952. Photos 4 and 11 are reprinted by permission of the Center for Japanese Studies, University of Michigan.

Professor Takeda Chōshū of Dōshisha University, Kyoto, has generously permitted me to use five photographs. Photo 7, taken in Yamaguni-mura, Kyoto Prefecture, in 1969, appeared in Takeda Chōshū, *Kyoto Prefecture Folk Customs* (Tokyo, 1973), and is reprinted by permission of the publisher, Daiichi Hokki. Photo 14 was taken in Ibusuki City, Kagoshima Prefecture, in 1970; photo 18 was taken in Mikata-chō, Fukui Prefecture, in 1953; and photos 19 and 20 were taken in Kyoto in 1964 and 1974, respectively.

Contents

Tables

Author's Note

Two comments must be made concerning the materials discussed in this book. First, I have deliberately omitted any reference to practices reported from the Ryukyu Islands, and I have made no use of the extensive literature on the outlying islands such as Sado and Tsushima, with the single exception of one study done in the Izu Islands. Second, I have referred repeatedly to several main-island communities for which a great deal of material is available in English: Sone, Mie Prefecture (Bernier 1970); Takane, Iwate Prefecture (K. Brown 1964); Yasuhara, Kagawa Prefecture (Smith 1956); Niike, Okayama Prefecture (Beardsley, Hall & Ward 1959); Shitayama-chō, Tokyo (Dore 1958); Nagasawa, Kawasaki City (Ooms 1967, 1974); Suye, Kumamoto Prefecture (Embree 1939); and Takashima, Okayama Prefecture (Norbeck 1954).

Although there is considerable Japanese-language material on many of these places, and a great deal more on literally hundreds of other communities, I have deliberately attempted to confine my references to sources in Western languages, primarily English. I have hoped by this means to make it possible for readers without access to Japanese-language materials to check the sources cited and expose them to critical rereading and possible reanalysis. If a Japanese work has been translated, the translation is cited in preference to the original. Where a Japanese author has written on a subject in both a Western language and Japanese, I have referred the reader to the Western-language work. What is thereby lost in esoteric impact will be offset, I hope, by the possibility of independent assessment of at least some of the materials.

For the same reason that I have tried to keep the number of references to Japanese-language sources to a minimum, I have used very few Japanese words in the text. This will cause some pain to my colleagues whose specialty is the study of Japanese society and culture, and I can only hope that they will adjust easily to the English words I have used to translate terms ordinarily given in romanized transliteration. I have also decided against including in the Glossary the characters with which the Japanese entries are ordinarily written. With all due respect to yet another group of specialists, those whose field is Chinese society and culture, I have taken this unorthodox step deliberately in order to prevent the confusion of Japanese and Chinese concepts that often arises when too much attention is given to written characters. When a specialist on China sees the Japanese characters for words like *uji-gami* (tutelary deity), *gaki* (hungry ghost), and *kami* (god), he is likely to be misled in one of two directions. On the one hand, if a word is written with a familiar Chinese character, he may incorrectly assume that both the word and the concept have been borrowed. On the other hand, if an unfamiliar character is used, he may mistakenly assume that the Japanese have got the whole thing wrong and distorted the original Chinese concept. Should he wish to discover what characters are used, any good dictionary will provide them. Let me warn him that he is in for some surprises.

Perhaps most important of all, I have avoided technical terminology so far as possible. During the past hundred years Japanese folklorists and social scientists have worked to build a vocabulary of generic terms for social units and customs that are known by a great variety of popular and regional terms. Though precision is desirable, it would be wrong to let it obscure the meaning of terms in current popular usage, particularly in the case of a society like Japan where the past fifteen years have seen the collapse of most of the structures and the sharp decline of many of the beliefs and practices that the terms once denoted. I have therefore used technical terms sparingly, preferring wherever possible to employ a close English equivalent for most kin units, arrangements, and relations—main house, branch house, successor, nonsuccessor, natal house, adopted couple, household head, etc.

Since I mean these terms to be understood in their popular sense, rather than in any technical meaning, a word of explanation is in order. When in the course of a conversation in his apartment in Osaka a man tells you that his is a branch house and that his main house is in Shiga Prefecture, he will very likely use the words *bunke* (branch house) and *honke* (main house). Ordinarily he will mean by this no more than that he is a second or third son who is the head of a neolocal family, and that his father or his elder brother is the head of what he calls his main house, the house where he was born. If his father has died, he will refer to his elder brother as the successor, using the term *ato-tsugi* or *kōkeisha*, or he may simply say that his brother is the *chōnan* (first son) and by implication the heir. He may call the house where he was born *chichi-no-uchi* (my father's house) or *ani-no-uchi* (my elder brother's house), or, because he himself has moved to the city, *chihō-no-uchi* or *inaka-no-uchi* (the house back in the country). He is unlikely to refer to it as his *jikka* (natal house), the word a woman most often uses for the house out of which she has married.

If your conversation about these matters is with a woman in these same circumstances, she may explain that her husband is a *jinan* (second son) or *sannan* (third son) and that this house is the branch house of his main house. She seldom refers to the house into which she was born as her main house, for she has cut most of her ties to it by marrying out. Her natal house will have been continued through her brother or through a sister who has taken an adopted husband (*muko-yōshi*). In either case the child of the household head who serves as the link through which continuity has been guaranteed is called *ato-tsugi*. In fact, if the daughter of the house takes an adopted husband, he becomes the head of the house (*kachō*) into which he has married even though she is the link in the succession.

In popular usage, then, when a man or woman tells you that this is a branch house, the implication is that it has inherited no property from the main house and has neither the responsibility nor the right to venerate the ancestors. It is usually referred to as a "new house." But in many rural areas all these terms have much more specific meanings, or did until very recently. Not all new houses are branch houses by any means. Much more is implied, but how much more, and precisely what, are matters of bitter dispute among Japanese social scientists that are unlikely ever to be resolved. Frequently there are status differentials accompanied by economic and ritual obligations between main and branch houses. Often, to become a branch house a new house headed by a second or third son must be formally so designated by its main house; but evidence abounds to show that the relationships between houses are not always so clearly defined, even in areas where the distinction is said to be an important one. In one of my interviews in a village, I was told something that seemed at variance with information I had just been given in another household. I protested, "But over there they say that you are one of their branch houses. Aren't you?" The man I was talking with grinned and said, "Oh, they like to say that. We don't mind. It doesn't do anyone any harm after all."

This conversation occurred in a community where a form of kinship unit usually called the *dōzoku* is found. Perhaps no other single entity has so captured the imagination of Japanese ethnologists or so stirred the passions of generations of scholars. In my opinion the study of dōzoku has been overdone, and emphasis on it has led to serious misunderstandings of the character of modern Japanese kinship and social organization. In fact, millions of Japanese are born, live, and die without ever being members of any such grouping of linked households—for that is what the dōzoku really is. For these millions the largest kinship unit is the household, and, as we shall see, the ancestors in Japan are the members of the household who are dead and who are cared for by the living.

The households in which the Japanese live can be divided usefully into two types. One is what Koyama (1966) has called "succeeded houses," i.e. houses headed by a successor to the previous head. In such a household, it is one of the duties of the successor to venerate the ancestors of preceding generations, for with the property he has inherited the ancestral altar as well. The second type is "created houses," headed by a nonsuccessor such as a second or third son. Such a man, the first-generation head of a newly established house, inherits neither property nor the right and duty to care for the ancestors of his natal house, although he may pay his respects to them when he visits. When he dies he becomes the first ancestor of the house he created, and his soul will be cared for by his successor. As we shall see, the memorial tablets for any given house begin with those of its founder and his wife. It is obvious, then, why most people speak of a "created house"—whether a formally recognized branch house or simply a neolocal one—as having no ancestors of its own for whose care it alone is responsible.

A final word on some of the common terms of Buddhism and Shinto that appear so frequently in the first three chapters. Although I do not find the following translations for common words entirely satisfactory, I have been unable to improve on them:

BUDDHISM	SHINTO
temple *tera, -ji*	shrine *jinja, miya, -gū*
altar *butsudan*	god shelf *kamidana*
tablet *ihai*	god *kami*
buddha *hotoke*	tutelary deity *uji-gami*

Where full names have been used in citing works by Japanese authors and in referring to individuals, I have followed Japanese practice in giving the surname first.

Ancestor Worship
in Contemporary Japan

Introduction

THERE MUST always remain some uncertainty about the origins of ancestor worship in Japan. To some it has seemed obviously a cult imported from China; but they have been unable to show how a phenomenon so thoroughly bound up with lineage principles could operate in a society lacking lineage organization altogether. To others it is equally apparent that ancestor worship lies at the heart of the indigenous belief system of Japan and thus predates the introduction of Buddhism and Confucianism. Still others argue that although the Japanese practices resemble ancestor worship they fall short of the full-fledged development to be seen in China or in some African societies. We cannot finally know which of these positions comes closest to the truth, but we can be certain that insofar as the practice of ancestor worship in Japan owes anything at all to continental sources, it has not unexpectedly taken on emphases without analogue in any other Buddhist country of Asia. In this respect ancestor worship is like all other features of Japanese culture that are wholly or partially of alien derivation—the transformations wrought by the Japanese have been profound.

In the course of dealing with the historical materials I shall first discuss the earliest manifestations of ancestor veneration in the indigenous, pre-Buddhist tradition, in part for the light they throw on the character of the syncretic practices of later centuries. These early forms are important in another way as well, for by A.D. 400 at the latest there evidently had become established an indigenous view of ancestry and descent that despite all the later amalgamations of Buddhism, Taoism, and Confucianism persists to the present day in the peculiar institution of the imperial house. This same view of ancestry and descent persists also among many lesser ancient families, and by extension among all Japanese. The conception of the ancestry of the imperial house found in the early chronicles has exerted a profound influence at every level of Japanese social organization, from the patrilineal household to the nation as a whole. Indeed, that influence was particularly felt in the development of the idea of a national polity, an idea that dominated the thinking of the oligarchs of the Meiji period.

My second historical concern will be with the consequences of the introduction of Buddhism into Japan through China and Korea, with particular reference to its effect on the conceptualization of gods and ancestors. In particular, I shall deal specifically with the Buddhist *urabon-e*, or *bon*, the midsummer Festival of the Dead. Although it is true that there has since been a considerable accretion of indigenous elements, bon was already by the early seventh century, when its first observance in Japan is reported, a complex of elements of a heavily syncretic character. At the time of its introduction it must have exerted an irresistible appeal, for it had already become in China the major vehicle for the fusion of Buddhism and ancestor worship. It remains to this day the single great Buddhist festival of Japan, the perfect counterpoint to the Shinto emphasis of celebrations marking the New Year. Over time the association of ancestral rites with institutionalized Buddhism became so complete that for most Japanese today Buddhism has come to mean ancestor worship and little more. In tracing the course of this development, I shall necessarily touch on the complex relationship between Buddhist and non-Buddhist beliefs and practices that reveals on the one hand important continuities with Japan's past and on the other the surprisingly recent development of practices that are ordinarily taken to be of great antiquity.

At this point, a word about religious syncretism in Japan. For some purposes it is clearly not fruitful to ask if a given term, concept, or deity is of Buddhist, Shinto, Taoist, or Confucian origin. Yet it is by no means true that the blending of all these elements with indigenous folk beliefs is so complete that the ordinary Japanese draws no distinctions whatsoever among them. Innumerable instances may be cited of a clear separation of ritual universes roughly along the line of demarcation between Shinto and Buddhism, among them the common practice of marking a dead forebear's change in status from buddha to god. The occasion on which this shift is said to occur is the final memorial service for the individual soul, which is held after a long period of purification of the spirit. The memorial tablet is removed from the Buddhist altar in the house, and some substitute for it is placed on the god shelf or in the community's Shinto shrine. For ordinary people this happens at the thirty-third or fiftieth anniversary of death; for Shinto priests in some areas it is thought to happen in a shorter time, usually six or thirteen years after death.

The separation of ritual universes is a constant theme in those villages called shrine-communities (*miyaza*), where the responsibility for carrying out rites at the local Shinto shrine falls in turn to the heads of certain households. During a man's period of service, he is called by the ordinary word for a Shinto priest, and the Buddhist altar containing the ancestral tablets of his house is sealed and removed from his dwelling (Hori 1969: 300–301). The intent of this practice is obviously to prevent pollution of the Shinto shrine through even indirect contact with death and the dead. On a more general level, in the ordinary Japanese dwelling the gods and buddhas are separately enshrined. The god shelf is high up on the wall of the room, often above a door, and is made of untreated wood. It contains no images, for the gods are not anthropomorphized. The worshiper stands before it. The Buddhist altar, by contrast, is usually an ornately lacquered and gilded cabinet set into or against a wall. It may contain a representation of the Buddha; it almost invariably contains memorial tablets of the dead. Ordinarily the worshiper sits before it. When there is severe illness or a death in the household, it is still today the common practice to seal off the god shelf lest the pollution offend the gods and bring harm to the members of the family.

Clearly, firm distinctions are regularly drawn between Shinto and Buddhism. Of even greater significance in my opinion is the obvious, if often neglected, point that these two systems of belief have different histories in Japan in the course of which they have been variously and differently exploited, promoted, or suppressed. Such experiences have altered their content to some extent, have shifted the focus of their rites and ceremonies, and not infrequently have done great violence to orthodoxy. The veneration of ancestors, whether in the form of memorialism or of worship, has been shaped in large part by high-level policy decisions throughout recorded Japanese history, and popular "folk" beliefs and practices have been made periodically to serve some larger political purpose. By the eighth century the Nara court could already build on a well-established policy that linked reverence for the imperial ancestors with political control. The fusion of the indigenous gods and the alien buddhas simply strengthened the central role of ancestor veneration in the theory of the state. However, we know far less about the developments in that early period than we do about the two outstanding instances of the exploitation of ancestor worship, which occurred toward the middle of the seventeenth century and in the closing decades of the nineteenth.

In the first instance, as a means of ensuring that no Christians had survived the vigorous suppression of their faith, the central government required of every domain lord that all households in his territories register as parishioners of a Buddhist temple. Although a few lords opted for registration at Shinto shrines instead, the vast majority followed the clear intent of the government. This step had a profound effect on both Buddhism and the ancestral rites. A little more than two hundred years later, following the Meiji Restoration of 1868 and the early failure of the new government to establish Shinto as the national religion, official efforts to link Shinto emperor worship (*tennō sūhai*) with "Buddhist" ancestor worship (*sosen sūhai*) proved dazzlingly successful.

Thus it can be argued that for three hundred years, from the mid-seventeenth century to 1945, ancestor worship was tied in a variety of ways to the policies and objectives of the state. That this has not been so for the past thirty years marks a fundamental change. Those thirty years have seen the breakup of tens of thousands of small corporate rural hamlets and the increasing concentration of the population in urban centers. The household, focus of the ancestral rites for centuries, is itself vanishing. The conjugal family has emerged as the primary domestic group, and the increasing numbers of neolocal families owe no obligation to the ancestors based in any degree on the inheritance of property or long-term coresidence.

The opening chapter deals with these issues and others, with special emphasis on the history of ancestor worship. Succeeding chapters discuss the nature of deities, the various kinds of spirits, the line of demarcation between human and god, and the timing and character of memorialism and veneration. Much of the last two chapters is based on data collected in 1963 (Smith 1966, 1974) concerning the location of tablets and the identity of those represented by them. In the Conclusion I return to the issue of the disappearance of the household and the rise of the neolocal conjugal family, a development that seriously threatens the continued existence of ancestor worship in its familiar form. It now seems to me that if ancestor worship in any form has a future in Japan, it will necessarily be defined in terms of the rights and duties of the members of a family rather than of a household. This shift alone signals major changes in the conceptualization of the ancestors and will surely bring about marked attenuation of the rites directed to them.

One. *The Historical Perspective*

> I would like to point out some common tendencies manifested in the major
> Japanese religions as well as in the folk beliefs ... (1) emphasis on filial
> piety (*kō*) and ancestor worship connected with the Japanese family system
> and agriculture from ancient times; (2) deep-seated and common beliefs in
> spirits of the dead in connection with ancestor-worship, as well as with
> more animistic conceptions of malevolent or benevolent spirit-activities;
> (3) emphasis on *on* (debts or favors given by superiors, human or super-
> human) and *hōon* (the return of *on*); (4) continuity between man and deity,
> or ease in deification of human beings; (5) mutual borrowing and mixing
> of different religious traditions, in other words, a syncretic character;
> (6) coexistence of heterogeneous religions in one family or in one person.
>
> —*Hori 1967: 214*

I N   T H E protohistoric period before Buddhism entered Japan, there must
have existed a set of beliefs and practices having to do with the relationship between the living and the dead (D. Brown 1968; Inoguchi
1954). We have almost no direct evidence about these conceptions, nor
do we know a great deal about the conception of the relationship between human beings and the supernatural. What evidence there is all
suggests that in ancient Japan the dead were treated with fear and respect as a category of men whose life had ceased, whereas the gods were
for the most part beings who either had always existed or had existed
for incalculable eons when they first became known to man.

No single feature of this early belief system stands out more clearly
than the preoccupation with pollution and taboo. Abhorrence of the
corpse apparently extended to the building in which death occurred,
which was abandoned, and to the kinsmen of the deceased, who were
placed temporarily under severe restrictions of movement and contact
both with the living and with such sacred phenomena as fire and the
light of the sun. It was thought that every living being had both a phys-
ical and a spiritual component, so that though the corpse was both
frightful and polluting, even more potentially dangerous was the spirit,
which was called by such various names as *tamashī, mitama,* and *hito-*
dama. Now a corpse can be disposed of by a variety of means, all cal-

culated to assure the survivors that it is permanently out of the way. It can be interred, cremated, or exposed in a remote spot far from human traffic. But that other aspect of a person, his spirit, which was thought to have the capacity to leave the body even in life, was after death not to be disposed of so easily. Understandably it was thought possible that some spirits might try to linger in the world of the living. Such spirits, unwilling or unable so suddenly to take leave of this world, and perhaps even vindictive toward those who retained the gift of life, were objects of fear. It became important, then, to see to it that such spirits were removed from the world of men as expeditiously as possible. This much is clear enough, but it is far less clear whether the spirits of the dead were conceived to be ancestors in this early period of Japanese history and venerated as such.

There are several conflicting views of the nature of Japanese society in the fifth and sixth centuries, before the centralization of the Yamato imperial polity in the seventh century. In what follows I shall be dealing with the most generally accepted interpretation of the rise of the Japanese imperial line, but I should point out that the entire issue has been opened for closer scrutiny since World War II (see Kiley 1973). The Yamato regime itself seems clearly to have been established by the middle of the fifth century, but it is not until A.D. 645 that the emperor is referred to as a "manifest god" (*akitsu-kami*) and succession set through the senior male line. Both of these developments are clearly part of the general process of political centralization.

The origins of the Yamato dynasty are also less than clear, but the orthodox view has long been, of course, that its history is coterminous with that of the state itself, making Japan unique in its unbroken line of imperial succession. In this view, early Japanese society appears to have been composed of many kinship units called *uji*, whose leaders (*uji-no-kami*) led their members in the worship of the group's tutelary deity (*uji-gami*). Although the precise nature of this kinship unit is unclear, uji has traditionally been translated as "clan." This translation is surely incorrect, and has recently given way to terms such as "familistic grouping," "alliance of families," and "extended kin group." Whether the tutelary deity was a deified common ancestor or a deity claimed to be ancestral will never be resolved (see Kamstra 1967: 72–110). The orthodox claim that the Yamato emperor was merely the head of an uji whose hegemony over similar units was early established is also in dispute, but there is one view of the matter that I find sufficiently compelling to justify summarizing here (see Ariga 1959, 1967).

Clearly the uji originated as some kind of localized kinship group with a tutelary deity and a leader responsible for maintaining territorial boundaries and protecting the group's members. As the power of some groups increased, they extended their territories. In time the uji became increasingly political in character, and membership in them became less and less dependent on kin ties as powerful uji conquered nonkinsmen or offered them protection. In this early period, Ariga believes, the tutelary deity was probably the actual lineal ascendant of the head of the uji, but not necessarily the ancestor of other members of the group. This deity was the protector of the land and all the people of the uji. The shift of focus from kinship to territoriality undoubtedly occurred quite early; it remains today central to the conception of each Shinto shrine as the locus of the tutelary deity of the residents of a given community. By whatever term these gods are called today—uji-gami, *ji-gami, chinju, jichin, ubusuna-gami*—all are the defenders and protectors of the people who live within the compass of their power, whether or not those people are bound by ties of kinship.

Clearly the conceptualization of the nature of ancestry and descent was important in this early period, for the head of the uji apparently owed his position to the supposed close relationship between his first ancestor, the founder of the group, and the tutelary deity (Reischauer 1937: A, 9). What was the character of this relationship? By way of reply, Ariga considers in some detail the ancestral reckoning of the imperial house. Briefly the argument is this. In the reigns of the Emperor Temmu (673–86) and the Empress Jitō (690–97), the shrine at Ise was designated the seat of the tutelary deity of the imperial house. Enshrined there is Amaterasu-ō-mikami, the Sun Goddess, from whom the imperial house claimed direct descent. "Direct descent" as used here must be taken in a very special sense, for all the lineal ancestors of the imperial house are named in the early chronicles in an unbroken line back to the first ancestor, the legendary Emperor Jimmu. We can only assume, Ariga argues, that well before the compilation and editing of the early chronicles, the *Kojiki (Record of Ancient Matters)* in 712 and the *Nihon-shoki (Chronicles of Japan)* in 720, there had developed a very special con-

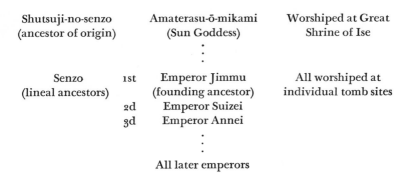

Shutsuji-no-senzo (ancestor of origin)		Amaterasu-ō-mikami (Sun Goddess)	Worshiped at Great Shrine of Ise
		:	
Senzo (lineal ancestors)	1st	Emperor Jimmu (founding ancestor)	All worshiped at individual tomb sites
	2d	Emperor Suizei	
	3d	Emperor Annei	
		:	
		All later emperors	

Fig. 1. Ancestry of the imperial house.

ception of the nature of ancestry and descent. He draws a distinction between lineal ancestors (*senzo*), of whom the first generation—the founding ancestor—is always regarded as the most important of all ascendants, and the ancestor of origin (*shutsuji-no-senzo*), the person or house from which the founding ancestor is believed to have derived.

The lineal ancestors of the imperial house, all of whom can be traced back generation by generation to the founding ancestor Jimmu, are worshiped individually at their tombs. No matter that the early emperors are mythical in character, there is, or could be, a tomb for each of them. But the ancestor of origin is worshiped not at a tomb but at a shrine. For the imperial house at the time of Temmu, the ancestors can be represented as shown in Figure 1. According to legend, Amaterasu gave the three imperial regalia (sword, jewel, and mirror) to her grandson Ninigi, who descended to earth with them in the company of some other gods; it was Ninigi's great-grandson Kan-yamato-iware-hiko-no-mikoto who became the first emperor of Japan, Jimmu (see Ellwood 1973: 65–68, 95).

It seems likely that every uji in early Japan had its own ancestral cult and myth; only with the emergence of the hegemony of the imperial house were these disparate cults consolidated into a single system. As a result of the rise to preeminence of the uji of the imperial house, Amaterasu, its ancestor of origin, was made the prime deity of the pantheon. The emperor became in effect the high priest who alone could approach the tutelary deity of the country. As her descendant, he became the supreme guardian of the nation and its people (J. W. Hall 1968: 28).

Both Ise and the imperial house itself were to pass through many vicissitudes before the Meiji Restoration in 1868. However, it would be a great mistake to imagine, as many have, that neither was of much real importance during the thousand years when imperial power was slight. For example, during the Kamakura period the military rulers tried to give some coherence to Shinto worship on the national level by exalting the imperial ancestress and encouraging worship at Ise. With the decline of imperial fortunes the Ise priesthoods had formed great landed estates that yielded large incomes, considerable portions of which the military houses began to divert to their own uses. This diversion of their income led the priesthoods to seek other means of support. One result was the promotion of what came to be known as Ise Shinto and the Ise pilgrimage, with its attendant votive offerings to the deity. The Ise shrine never lost its hold on the popular imagination and for centuries remained easily the favored place of pilgrimage. There were other shrines that may be said to have been "national" in character, in contradistinction to the vast majority of local shrines whose protective influence extended only to the narrow boundaries of each local community, and these other national shrines were also objects of pilgrimage; however, only Ise could claim to be the seat of the imperial ancestress. There can be little doubt that on the folk level the continued reverence for Amaterasu and the popularity of her shrine combined to prepare the way for the acceptance of the nineteenth-century restorationists' theory of reverence for the emperor (*sonnō-ron*) (Kishimoto & Wakimoto 1956: 28–29).

The consolidation of imperial power in the early period was of no long duration, but even though the uji system declined rapidly throughout the sixth century the symbolic importance of the uji-gami endured, albeit greatly altered in character. In Ariga's phrase, where originally both kin and territorial ties bound the people of the uji together, with the decay of the system only territorial ties were left as the basis of affiliation with the group. Thus it is not hard to understand the alteration of the term uji-gami into a great variety of other terms combining the meaning of protector or guardian with the meaning of land or earth.

Let us return for a moment to Ariga's distinction between lineal ancestors and the ancestor of origin, for it is an important one for understanding the political uses that have been made of ancestor worship in recent Japanese history. Of course, any family may claim that its ancestor of origin is a given deity, and a god is often claimed by more than one house or line as ancestor of origin. Only the imperial house, however, can claim direct descent from the Sun Goddess. Where a deity is claimed as ancestor of origin by more than one house, it is enshrined in as many places as have chosen to claim the protective presence and is worshiped at each of the shrines by the respective group of descendants. However, a lineal ancestor is another matter entirely, for he is exclusively the ascendant of one house and is usually associated with one grave and a single altar.

The foregoing discussion is straightforward enough, but it does not touch on ancestors of origin of another derivation, that is, those who are not gods but deified humans. The deification of men and women, a very common and very old practice in Japanese religion (see Chapter 2), is greatly bound up with ideas of ancestry and descent. No better illustration of this connection can be found than when one or another uji or, in more recent times, great military or priestly house has deified an emperor and claimed him as ancestor of origin. Thus one branch of the Minamoto family, the Seiwa Genji, took as its ancestor of origin the apotheosis of the Emperor Seiwa (858–76), whose fourth son was in fact the founding ancestor of the line. The emperor was not in fact, and could not have been in theory, the founding ancestor, for he was after all a lineal ancestor of the imperial house who had succeeded the Emperor Montoku (850–58) and had in turn been succeeded by his son, the Emperor Yōzei (876–84), eldest brother of the founder of the line of the Seiwa Genji. Having enshrined the deified emperor, the Seiwa Genji worshiped him at his shrine. But to the members of the imperial house itself, he remains a lineal ancestor, properly worshiped at his tomb and not at a shrine. The ancestor of origin is never the object of Buddhist rites, but only of Shinto ones, for he is a god. On the other hand, worship of the lineal ancestors for the most part occurs exclusively in the Buddhist idiom. This distinction obtained even in the imperial house until the decision of the early Meiji government to convert all imperial ancestral rites from the Buddhist mode to the Shinto.

What are the implications of this clear separation of ritual universes? Shinto ritual places heavy emphasis on the purity of the object of veneration, the gods, and can be conducted only by those who have purified themselves and are free of pollution. Buddhist ritual, on the other hand, may be seen as a means of overcoming the ultimately polluting condition of death. The subject of the rites, itself impure, can be removed from that state only through a lengthy ritual process. Except under extraordinary circumstances, much time and ritual effort are needed to purify the spirit of the dead. The ultimate effect of the rituals of Buddhism is to transform the spirit of the dead into a god.

The Influence of Buddhism

Whatever its early form and development, Japanese ancestor worship obviously owes much to Chinese influence, but I shall argue that Buddhism as it came from China had a far greater direct impact in this regard than Confucianism. By the time the Japanese sought out the sources of Buddhism in China, it had long since incorporated Confucian ancestral rites and the concept of filial piety in which they were rooted. Indeed, the Japanese were particularly beguiled by the whole array of what Nakamura (1964: 421) calls pseudosutras of Chinese origin, most of which, like the eagerly promoted *Bumō-onjū-kyō* (Sutra of Parental Benefits), placed heavy emphasis on the virtues of filial piety (see Ch'en 1973: 36–42).

Buddhism was to make a major contribution to the "multilayered, coexistent and syncretistic beliefs" (Hori 1959b: 405) by which the Japanese conceptualize the world of man and the world of gods and spirits. The introduction of Buddhism did not lead to a repudiation of the native gods, for Buddhism lacks such doctrinal requirements. In Europe the introduction of Christianity produced converts on the one hand and pagans on the other (Nakamura 1964: 391). In Japan, by contrast, all beliefs coalesced. There have been no pagans.

A major concern when Buddhism was introduced, and one that has been reemphasized periodically, was to account for the coexistence of the indigenous gods and the buddhas of the alien religion. The solution lay in the Buddhist doctrine of *honji-suijaku* (archetype–transient manifestation) and in the Japanese concept of *shinbutsu-shūgō* (unification of gods and buddhas). The idea of honji-suijaku is often mistakenly assumed to be a Japanese innovation (Matsunaga 1969: 3). In fact, the practice of absorbing native gods into Buddhism had begun in India and was simply continued as the religion spread through Central Asia, China, Korea, and Japan. In Japan, as elsewhere, the native gods were identified as the transient manifestations of the archetypal buddhas. As a consequence, the Buddhism of the sixth century was a "vast conglomeration of cults and faiths" (Sakamaki 1967: 27).

Like all else in this syncretic universe of buddhas and gods, the identifications and equivalences shift, merge, fade, and blur from one historical period to the next, from temple to temple, from shrine to shrine, and from region to region. The more popular an archetype, the more numerous its transient manifestations were likely to be. The bodhisattva Jizō (Kṣitigarbha) is the archetype of at least 25 indigenous gods (Matsunaga 1969: 237). The bodhisattva Kannon (Avalokiteśvara) takes 33 different forms, each of them identified with one or more gods as its transient manifestations. From the perspective of the gods the situation is equally fluid, for depending on time and place each has been identified with any number of buddhas and bodhisattvas, not infrequently as manifestations of several archetypes simultaneously.

Throughout the Nara and Heian periods (710–1184), the dominant theory of honji-suijaku relegated the gods to the distinctly secondary position of avatars of the buddhas. Here the Japanese Buddhists had ample precedent, for in early Indian Buddhist texts there are references to the conversion of the *deva* kings to the religion, and in later texts the lesser deities are routinely identified as avatars of Buddha and the bodhisattvas (Tsunoda et al. 1958: 268). The Chinese had certainly made use of the concept by the middle of the T'ang period (618–907), and in what appears to be one of the earliest surviving references to the practice a Chinese text notes that "the spirits and gods were avatars of Vairochana" (*ibid.*: 269). The image in the great hall of the Tōdaiji in Nara is the Vairochana Buddha. He is called in Japanese Roshana or Dainichi-nyorai (Great Sun Buddha), and there is evidence that at an early period this Buddha and the Sun Goddess were identified as *honji* and *suijaku*, respectively (Hori 1967: 206; Ponsonby Fane 1962: 220–22). This identification suggests that the Tōdaiji was conceived to be the "clan temple" (*uji-dera*) of the imperial house, since it housed the archetype of the tutelary deity Amaterasu. Such temples, "established by patricians, were not meant to propagate Buddhism to the general public. Their purpose lay in praying for the successive [continued or eternal] happiness" of their donors (Takeda 1965: 595).

Ariga (1967: 180) sees yet another connection between the Tōdaiji, which was designated *sō-kokubunji* (principal protector temple of the land) and had many branch temples all over the country, and the already well-established and hierarchically ranked shrines of the tutelary deities of the great houses. These shrines and the kokubunji temples, which mutually reinforced one another, clearly symbolized the power of the imperial house by concentrating in its hands the primary responsibility for conducting rites before both the most powerful gods and the most powerful buddhas—all defined as protectors of the country. Despite the subsequent vicissitudes of the imperial house itself, the core of the worship of the tutelary deities remained closely connected with the political hierarchy. Much later, in the eighteenth and nineteenth centuries, the schools of Mito and the nativist scholars were to reaffirm this principle, and the Meiji government was to exploit its potential brilliantly in its program for the revival of "pure Shinto" (Ariga 1967: 182).

Yet not all the Buddhist sects promoted the theory of the identity of the gods and buddhas. Shinran (1173–1262), founder of the Jōdo-shin sect, denounced the union of Shinto and Buddhism that had proceeded apace for centuries before his time and disavowed the popular interpretation of Buddhism as the protector of the state. At the other end of the spectrum, as early as the fifteenth century there emerged a revivalist movement, *yui-itsu-shintō* (primal Shinto), whose major proponent was Yoshida Kanetomo (1435–1511). His interpretation of honji-suijaku, a concept he endorsed wholeheartedly, was the exact reverse of that promoted by the Buddhists up to that time (Sakamaki 1967: 28). It was the gods who were the archetypes, he asserted, and the buddhas the transient manifestations. Similar interpretations had developed in India, where the Brahmans came to identify the Buddha as the ninth avatar of Vishnu, and in China, where the Taoists were proclaiming him the avatar of Lao Tzu.

In Japan, though, these and related developments had little effect on the preeminence of Buddhism. The Tendai and Shingon sects in particular encouraged the amalgamation of Buddhism with Shinto through the respective doctrines of *ichi-jitsu-shintō* (one-reality Shinto) and *ryōbu-shintō* (dual Shinto). Although these doctrines are traditionally ascribed to the founders of these sects, Saichō (767–822) and Kūkai (774–835), it was probably not until the Kamakura period (1185–1338) that they were first systematized—the culmination of centuries of efforts to unify the gods and buddhas (Morrell 1973). The Shingon formulation, which equated the two realms of the sect's central deity, the Mahavairochana Buddha, with the Inner and Outer Shrines of Ise, was particularly ingenious. The two Tendai monasteries of Hiei and Miidera eventually took as their respective tutelary deities the mountain god Sannō and the Korean goddess Shiragi *myōjin* (Tsunoda et al. 1958: 269–70). Buddhist-inspired syncretism of this sort remained dominant in Japanese popular religion for centuries. Indeed, so firmly entrenched was the identification of the gods with the buddhas that the efforts of the Meiji government to separate them—for the obviously political purpose of making a state cult of the purified Shinto practices—never achieved more than partial success at best. The Meiji regime was able to sort out the names by which places of worship were designated, so that the clan temples (uji-dera) and shrine temples (jingū-ji) disappeared. But in most of the popular pilgrimage sites the syncretic mode is still in flower, as evidenced not only in the compound identity of the deity but also in the mixture of architectural styles, forms of ritual, and powers attributed to the deity by the pilgrims themselves.

Bon

Known in English as the Festival of the Dead, the Feast of Lanterns, the Feast of All Souls, or the midsummer festival, bon is Japan's great popular Buddhist holy day (Ashikaga 1951). Its focus is ancestor worship. Today it is observed on August 13–15 by most people, somewhere close to the 13th to 15th days of the seventh month by the lunar calendar. The first reference to it in the Japanese chronicles occurs in the *Nihon-shoki* (Aston 1896: II, 134), which reports that in 606 the Empress Suiko (554–628) ordered its observance in all the temples of the country.

The cornerstone of the festival is the sutra known in Japanese as the *urabon-kyō* (from the Sanskrit *Ullambana sūtra*), which also is first referred to by name in the *Nihon-shoki* (*ibid.*: 263) at the order of the Empress Saimei (655–661) in 659 that it be expounded in all the temples of the capital and "requital made to the ancestors for seven generations." Requital to the ancestors and to the souls of the dead generally took such forms as dedicating images, building chapels and temples, and copying and reciting sutras (Takeda 1965: 594). Of course, this was not ancestor worship (*sosen-sūhai*) but *sosen-kuyō*, offerings and prayers on behalf of the spirits of the dead (Anesaki 1938: 79).

Whatever the Japanese may have added to this festival during the past 1,300 years, it is clear that by the time they first encountered bon it was already of a highly syncretic character. The sutra on which it is based is not even Indian in origin (see Reichelt 1934: 100–104 for a summary; and Ch'en 1973: 61–64 for a review of its history) and appears to have been written in Sanskrit and translated into Chinese sometime between 266 and 313 by Dharmaraksha I (Hōgo in Japanese), a native of a Central Asian kingdom, who arrived in the city of Loyang in 266. The sutra concerns the offering of food to the Buddha and the priests on behalf of the *preta*, which the Japanese, following the Chinese, have called *gaki* (hungry ghosts) (see De Visser 1935: 66–67).

It may well be that the Chinese is unfaithful to the original sense of the word preta, which refers only to a spirit who suffers hunger and thirst because of misdeeds in past lives (Kazama & Kino 1965: 592). Gifts could not be given directly to the suffering spirit, but had to be offered to a holy or virtuous person on behalf of the soul of the deceased. The merit thus gained by the donor was transferred to the preta. Of the six planes of existence of the World of Desire (Sanskrit *kama-loka*; Japanese *rokudō*), one is the *preta-loka* (Japanese *gaki-dō*), where souls with no posterity to offer them food go after death. Only dwellers on this plane are believed to benefit indirectly from offerings made on their behalf (Matsunaga 1969: 50). There is a story in which a Brahman asks the Buddha whether merit can be transferred to departed kinsmen through rites and ceremonies and whether the spirits of the dead can actually enjoy the things offered to them. The Buddha replies that the preta alone can benefit from nourishing gifts of food, and that the offerings made to the priests on their behalf come to them in the same form in which they are given (Weeraratne 1965: 748). The popular version of the origins of bon tells of Mokuren, disciple of the Buddha, who sees his mother's tormented ghost in a dream. She pleads for his help in effecting her deliverance, and he beseeches the Buddha to tell him how to assist her spirit. He is overjoyed when he learns that he may indirectly provide her with food (see Iwamoto 1968).

Clearly there is much to be said for the view that the Chinese took the sutra as a canon of filial piety (Shioiri 1965: 584–85), and that it had attained great popularity by the sixth century. Indeed, the ceremony of bon came to be the most important Buddhist rite in China, its appeal being that through offerings to priests one could assure the deliverance and repose of the souls of one's parents and ancestors (see Ch'en 1973: 31–34). In China, then, by the sixth or seventh century at the latest, heavy infusions of Taoism and Confucianism had produced something that can only be called Buddhist ancestor worship (Reichelt 1934: 67–111; Shioiri 1965: 586–89; Züchert 1959). This is, of course, precisely the period when Buddhism was adopted by the Yamato court. By the eighth century Buddhism had emerged "fully and triumphantly established throughout China" (Wright 1959: 82), partly as a result of the active incorporation of the Confucian virtues into the heart of the religion. It seems by this date to have penetrated all classes of Chinese society as well. Thus during the initial efforts of the Japanese to emulate the Chinese state and adopt its culture, they must have learned that an essential element of Buddhism was filial piety (see Ch'en 1964: 179; Duyvendak 1926: 44).

In the bon festival as it reached Japan there was already a mélange of Central Asian Buddhist, Hindu, Taoist, and Confucian elements, to which the Japanese were to add many indigenous beliefs and practices. It may well be, as many scholars have argued, that the idea of venerating the ancestors had long been established among the Japanese, and that they seized upon memorialism and certain related sutras and rituals and early began to build chapels to the memory of their ascendants where Buddhist priests offered prayers on their behalf (Takeda 1961: 143–47). What the Japanese never did—as the Chinese subsequently were to do—was to divorce the ancestral cult from Buddhism entirely.

I have up to this point ignored a basic disagreement among Japanese scholars over the extent to which bon is an imported ceremony or is indigenous (Yanagita 1970: 55–85). Central to the argument is the question of the relationship between the rites of the New Year and those of midsummer. The position of Yanagita and his adherents is that both were originally spirit festivals (*tama-matsuri*) for the ancestors, and that they existed long before Buddhism entered Japan (Bownas 1963: 39). According to this view, these ancient Japanese festivals have been mistakenly interpreted in recent times. The rites of the New Year are today usually said to represent a very old folk (Shinto) tradition; bon is usually claimed to be an imported Buddhistic ceremony that has come to obscure almost completely the old Shinto spirit festival of midsummer. Once, the argument runs, they were counterpart festivals, exactly six months apart and both devoted to welcoming the spirits of the ancestors back to earth.

The folklorists and ethnologists have worked hard to accumulate evidence for this position. Let us take an example from what is now Gumma Prefecture (Tomaru 1967). In this region at the New Year a special domestic god shelf dedicated to the year-god (*toshi-gami*) is set up in each house. It is divided into two halves. On one side is the amulet of the god (*kami-fuda*), as we would expect. The other side is said by some to be a spirit shelf (*mitama-dana*), but many people have no explanation at all for why it is there. In old records of the area, Tomaru found references to a practice of setting up a spirit shelf opposite the shelf for the year-god, but again finds no reason stated. In his opinion, the spirits who came at the New Year were in fact conceived to be those of the ancestors, come back to earth to visit their homes just as they are thought to do at bon. Some people told him that they made identical offerings at the New Year to the Buddhist ancestral altar and to the altar for the year-god, a custom observed in Sone, one of the communities reported on in Chapter 5. We can only conclude, Tomaru suggests, that the New Year festival has remained essentially Shinto, whereas the midsummer spirit festival has become Buddhist, and that no one now remembers its pre-Buddhist meaning.

Analogous practices are reported from places in Chūbu and Tōhoku (Mogami 1959: 339–40), where at the New Year people make offerings to the altar and the god shelf alike and refer to both offerings as "New Year's spirit food" (*shōgatsu no mitama meshi*). In Yamagata Prefecture Mogami found homes in which there was a New Year spirit shelf very like the altar set out at bon for the ancestors. Yanagita and others see in these and many related practices clear evidence that long before the time of Buddhism there were ancestral spirit festivals in Japan in the course of which the spirits were welcomed back to their homes. They are undoubtedly right about the slow erosion of such observances by Buddhism, as witness Yoshida Kenkō's lament of the early fourteenth century: "The custom of paying homage to the dead, in the belief that they return that night [the last of the year], has lately disappeared from the capital, but I was deeply moved to discover that it was still performed in the East" (Keene 1967: 20–21).

There is another view, which asserts that Yanagita is quite wrong in his interpretation of the identity of the spirits who come at bon (M. Suzuki 1972). According to this view, Yanagita's contention that it was originally the spirits of ancestors who returned at the New Year and in midsummer—and therefore a much later and alien notion that the wandering spirits also must be comforted during these ceremonies—is altogether wrong. To Suzuki, the midsummer spirit festival all over East Asia—bon in Japan, *p'u-tu* in Taiwan, *manghon-il* in Korea—was originally a ceremony for offering food to the wandering spirits in an effort to prevent misfortune and epidemics. The worship of ancestral spirits at the midsummer festival was a later introduction—of Confucianism in Korea and Buddhism in Japan. Suzuki claims that the version of the ceremonies he has reported from contemporary Taiwan is closer to earlier versions of the ceremony. Although its name p'u-tu derives from the word buddha, it remains a feast for the hungry ghosts, just as it once was everywhere.

Whatever its original meaning, and however much it may have been altered over the centuries, we do know something about the spread of the observance of bon in Japan. As we have seen, it was introduced into the imperial court in the early seventh century; but it probably was not until the close of the twelfth century that it became widespread among the people, by which time offerings were being made directly to the ancestors and not to the priests on their behalf. If this estimate is correct, then it would have been at about the beginning of the Kamakura period that the native spirit festival was displaced by the Buddhist bon (Ashikaga 1950: 221). The popularity of the bon festival has continued unabated, and we are fortunate in having some accounts of the festivities written by Europeans in Japan between the mid-sixteenth century and the suppression of Christianity a century later (see Cooper 1965: 358–60). The descriptive passages in their journals and letters would be difficult to distinguish from those of nineteenth- and twentieth-century writers.

Closely related to bon is the ceremony of *segaki-e* (discussed in greater detail in Chapters 2 and 4), in which sutras are read and offerings of food made on behalf of the spirits of the dead who have no living kinsman to care for them. Often performed at about the time of bon, it is of an entirely different origin, being based on a sutra (called in Japanese *ku-batsu enku darani kyō*) designed to help one avoid difficulties and disasters and enjoy a long life on earth. It is said that this ceremony was brought back to Japan from China by Kūkai, founder of the Shingon sect, in the early ninth century; but the earliest reference to the performance of segaki-e dates from the Ōei period (1394–1428) (see *Bukkyō dai jiten* 1960: 2907–12). By the end of the Kamakura period many sects of Buddhism had taken up the segaki-e, basing it on one or another of a number of sutras. In 1788, all temples are said to have performed the ceremony after the disastrous eruption of Mt. Asama. We find frequent references indicating that the ceremony was held after great fires, floods, volcanic eruptions, and earthquakes, for it was feared that many victims of such disasters might not receive the proper rites due the dead, either because of the wiping out of whole families or because of the general confusion and disorder in the aftermath of the event. Such spirits would then become wandering ghosts, presenting great dangers to the survivors. Today segaki-e is generally regarded as an integral part of bon, although in theory segaki-e is for the quieting of *oni* ("demons" —the *ki* of gaki) and bon is for the seven generations of ancestors (*Bukkyō dai jiten* 1960: 2907–12). The distinction is clearly lost on most Japanese today, who prepare two altars at bon, one for the ancestral spirits and one for the wandering ghosts. With the one, the benign spirits of the ancestors, the object of daily or periodic worship, are summoned back to the world of the living to participate for a short time in the festivities; with the other, wandering spirits, potentially harmful because they are homeless and unworshiped by their descendants, are fed and comforted in the hope that they will be pacified and not wreak vengeance on the innocent.

The Tokugawa Period

It is neither possible nor necessary to review here the long train of events and ideological developments leading to the restoration of imperial rule in 1868. Before moving to a consideration of that era, however, it is essential at least to outline significant developments of the Tokugawa period (1603–1868) that were to shape the character of both emperor worship and ancestor worship in the twentieth century. The first of these developments was the decision to expel the Europeans, suppress Christianity, and forbid the Japanese to travel abroad. Anti-Christian edicts were issued as early as 1612 and culminated in 1639 with the adoption of the formal seclusion policy (*sakoku*). As a means of ensuring that no converts to Christianity remained in the country, the government required every person to affiliate with a Buddhist temple. In 1640 a bureau was established within the Tokugawa central administration to supervise the registration of the population by Buddhist sect and temple, and in 1664 the lord of each domain was required to set up a similar bureau in his own territories. Registers were instituted in which both the civil authorities and the temple priests certified that none of the persons listed was Christian, and that each was a bona fide parishioner of the temple with which he claimed to be affiliated. These registers were renewed annually in some areas and at some periods, less frequently in others. Although they provide demographic data of extraordinary interest (Hayami & Uchida 1972; Nakane 1972; Smith 1972), for our purposes their importance lies in the fact that they represent a turning point in the fortunes of Buddhism and in the development of ancestor worship in Japan.

As we have seen, ancestor worship and Buddhism had been inextricably linked for a thousand years, but now for the first time, every household in Japan was required to establish formal ties with a Buddhist temple in order to prove conclusively that none of its members was a Christian. The Buddhist temple was chosen partly because it provided an administrative structure capable of handling the registration and supervision of the population. This political act was to have far-reaching consequences, for since that time "every person in Japan has had a connection with the Buddhist temple, and that connection has been chiefly through funeral services" (Nakamura 1964: 585). Funerals were not the limit of their involvement, of course; priests were also charged to check on the fidelity with which the parishioners observed bon, the equinoxes, and the ceremonies of the death-days of the ancestors (Takeda 1961: 187–88).

What may well be a contemporary echo of practices established in this period when people were suspected of being Christian is noted by Norbeck (1954: 153). The villagers of Takashima set up their bon altars outside the house, a custom said to date from the time when it was required that one give convincing evidence of being a faithful and practicing Buddhist. The effect of these anti-Christian edicts was generally to standardize and universalize practices for all classes and in all parts of the country so that the household everywhere became tied to the temple just as ancestor worship had become tied to Buddhism. For the parishioners the temple became primarily the place where the ancestors were worshiped, and the priest the chief officiant at ancestral rites. What had until then been more or less household-centered ancestral observances, requiring no priests at all, provided the raw material for a structured Buddhist formulation of practices requiring the services of temples and priests for their proper execution.

How speedily and completely this fusion occurred can be judged from an essay written in 1683, only some twenty years after the registration policy was established (Takeda 1965: 595). Its author was Tokugawa Mitsukuni (1628–1700), Lord of Mito.

> When they carry out a commemoration service for the dead, they place the mortuary tablet in a position superior to that of the image of Buddha itself and make much of it with incense, flowers and food offerings, entirely neglecting the image of the Buddha. No greater mistake can be committed. The primary meaning of a commemoration service for the dead is to acquire religious comfort for them by the merits through the offerings to the Buddha.

Mitsukuni laid the primary blame for this perversion of orthodoxy on the priests themselves, accusing them of selling elaborate posthumous names for large sums of money and promoting the donation of chapels, memorials, and lands to the temples. His efforts and the efforts of many others to prohibit these practices were largely futile, it would appear, for there are many records of temples built as places to worship the ancestors of the donors. Indeed, a wealthy household might achieve some independence of untoward priestly influence by constructing its own temple and retaining priests to serve at the pleasure of the family (Takeda 1961: 191). But for the most part people resorted to established temples, with the result that the performance of ancestral rites became the chief basis for the temples' economy (Takeda 1961: 193–94). It is not an exaggeration to say that Buddhism still exists in contemporary Japan largely because it has continued to play a central role in ancestral rites; certainly there is little evidence that any concept of living a good Buddhist life on a daily basis exists in Japan today (Chinnery 1971: 32).

In the early religious registers that I have collected from the Tokugawa period not all members of a given household necessarily belonged to the same temple or even to the same sect of Buddhism; only later did the household as a unit become the parishioner of a single temple. Thus it was Tokugawa administrative constraints that forged the link between household and temple (see Singer 1973: 86; Takeda 1961: 194), dissolving the older affiliation of individual and temple. The fortunes of Buddhism prospered, but its content was fundamentally altered as it accommodated itself to the overwhelming concern of the household for the observance of ancestral rites (Noguchi 1966: 17). Sectarian doctrine became of negligible importance as the priesthood turned to meet the demand for ancestral rites (see Tamamura 1963).

There is much evidence to suggest that the form of this new popular Buddhism was distinctly uncongenial to the orthodox. Indeed, the noted contemporary Buddhist scholar S. Watanabe (1950, 1968) has made the sardonic observation that Buddhism died out in Japan around 1600. This too harsh if understandable judgment refers to the Buddhism of the theologians, Buddhism in its early form. This is the Buddhism of the canon and of the commentaries, which are both largely unknown to lay believers because they have been translated only in recent times into Japanese. Perhaps in Watanabe's sense Mahayana Buddhism has died out everywhere.

In any event, the Japanese religious forms common today were firmly established by the close of the seventeenth century. In the domestic dwelling gods, buddhas, and ancestors alike were all commonly worshiped. On the god shelf was an amulet from the shrine at Ise, which meant that to some extent each household participated in the worship of the emperor's ancestress (Bellah 1957: 81). It was a small step for each household to come to feel that it too was in some degree descended from the gods. In fact, the idea was not new. The eighth-century *Kojiki* and *Nihon-shoki* were both devised to establish the primacy of the imperial house, but as Pelzel remarks (1970: 43), they do more:

The main political emphasis of the myths was to establish the biological tie between the ruler of heaven and the rulers of the earth, but the descent of noble Japanese families from other deities was also, within that context, accepted. By the beginning of recorded history, at the latest, very large segments—if indeed not all—of the Japanese people may well have been considered genealogically related to the gods, presumably through some form of adoption to the aristocratic lines if not biologically.

In the eighteenth and nineteenth centuries this conception was given new life in the writings of two groups of scholars—the *kokugakusha* (national studies scholars) and the ideologues of the Mito domain (see Harootunian 1970)—who devoted themselves to the recovery and renovation of what they considered to be the indigenous Japanese tradition. Both groups sought to rid Japanese culture of the heavy overlay of influences from the Asian mainland. In their commitment to the rejection of Buddhism, they ignored the considerable contribution it had made to the maintenance of the imperial institution itself. The Japanese originally had been attracted not only to the filial piety of Chinese Buddhism, but also to Indian texts identifying the king as the son of deities who extended their protection to him. Although the source of this latter theory is found in brahmanistic legal writings only cited by later Indian Buddhists to describe the state of society at a particular point in history (Nakamura 1967: 154), and although the theory has no place in Buddhism itself, the Japanese found it extremely attractive.

However useful such alien ideas might have proved, they were rejected by the nativist scholars, who took as their sources the two chronicles and the imperial poetry anthology, the *Manyōshū*, which also dates from the eighth century. As we have seen, Yoshida Kanetomo, the founder of primal Shinto, had already reversed the honji-suijaku theory in the fifteenth century, making the gods the archetypes of which the buddhas were the transient manifestations. But the Tokugawa scholars rejected Buddhism altogether. As a first step, Yamazaki Anzai (1618–82) forged an amalgam of Confucianism and Shinto called *suiga-shintō*, which centered on reverence for the gods and the ancestors. A little later, Arai Hakuseki (1657–1725), a scholar firmly grounded in the Neo-Confucian school of Chu Hsi, denounced both popular religious beliefs and Buddhism, arguing that since the gods had been worshiped since the dawn of history they should have clear primacy in the faith of the Japanese (Nakai 1965: 3). It was his intention to restore this purely indigenous worship of the gods, stripped of what he thought was the superstitious magic of an alien religion.

The great nativist scholar Motoori Norinaga (1730–1801), eager to eradicate Chinese conceptions that he felt had almost destroyed the native Japanese tradition, discovered in the eighth-century materials both an emperor of clearly divine descent and what he called "the true heart" of the Japanese people. Without making the link between loyalty to the emperor and filial piety ultimately forged by the Mito scholars, Norinaga nonetheless did turn his attention to the issue of filial piety. In two poems he phrased the matter of the identity of the ancestors in such a way as to connect the gods (kami), the household (*ie*), and filial piety (*kō*). These poems from his *Tamaboko Hyakushū* (1786) were memorized by schoolchildren well into the twentieth century (Muraoka 1964: 146):

Forget not the blessings	*Yoyo no oya wa*
Of your many forebears.	*mikage wasuruna*
Your many forebears are	*yoyo no oya wa*
The Kami of your clan	*ono ga ujikami*
The Kami of your house.	*ono ga ie no kami*
Your father and mother are	*Chichihaha wa*
The Kami of your home.	*waga ie no kami*
Regard them as your Kami	*waga kami to*
And serve them, oh children,	*kokoro tsukushite*
With heart-felt piety.	*itsuke hito no ko*

The vocabulary of the poems is that of the *Manyōshū*, innocent of any taint of Sinicisms or Confucian terminology. Filial piety is there, of course, for even the nativists could not escape the elements of Confucianism so firmly embedded by that time in Japanese morality, but it is connected to reverence for the gods of the uji and the household. No Buddhist sentiments are invoked. Norinaga was telling his countrymen that all that was pure and noble in the "true heart" of the Japanese had been there long before alien systems of thought entered the islands. In those early times, he claimed, parents and the household dead alike were gods; indeed, we shall see that much of what we know about Japanese "folk religion" seems to bear him out, and that the remote ancestors have been so conceived in many parts of the country into the twentieth century.

This early period also saw the formation of the idea of *kokutai*. This ancient concept, revived to form the heart of the nativist scholars' ideology, may be defined as "noumenon, an inner essence or mystical force residing in the Japanese nation" (Earl 1964: 236). A complex idea, it is based on the theory that Japan is a patriarchical state, all of whose people are related to one another and to the emperor, who is the supreme father. Therefore, "loyalty to him, or patriotism, becomes the highest form of Filial Piety" (Earl 1964: 237).

The Modern Period

The power of the nativist ideas developed during the Tokugawa era was formidable. For the traditionalist, the credulous, and the patriotic, these ideas were to become obvious, unexamined truths. From the Meiji Restoration until 1945, the idea of kokutai was central to Japanese political ideology.* Promoted by the government, it achieved a degree of success that can best be measured by the extraordinary tenacity—even fanaticism—displayed by the Japanese during the Pacific War, and by the scale of the disaster that overwhelmed the country in 1945. My purpose here is not to dwell on the historical and political implications of the ideology, but rather to show that ancestor worship in the decades following the Meiji Restoration cannot be understood without reference to it. Although it would be difficult to find many people who still subscribe to the tenets of kokutai (far less difficult to find millions born after 1940 or thereabouts who have never heard of it), evidence suggests that the concept retains a latent appeal.

As an ideology kokutai was spare to the point of almost incredible simplicity. Fukutake (1962: 36) felt that its sole ideological basis was the family system with its emphasis on obedience to parents and filial piety. "Magnified on a national scale, this sense of obligation to the family was expanded to include loyal service to the Emperor. Filial piety and loyalty to the Emperor thus were united into one inseparable entity." This was precisely the formulation promoted by the government beginning late in the Meiji period (1868–1912). The philosophy thus expressed was meant to be taken literally and to serve as a guide to behavior.

---

* So complete was the dominance of the kokutai ideology that even the Japanese Communist Party could not totally escape it. When two party leaders defected in 1933 they issued a memorandum (Beckmann 1971: 166) stating that it was not only possible but even natural to envisage a socialist revolution under the aegis of the imperial family: "The Japanese people have a sense of being a great kinship group, of which the imperial family is the head. . . . We should grasp the feeling of reverence for the imperial family, trace it to its origins, and have the same attitude as the people. With the slogan 'Overthrow the Emperor System' the Communist Party goes against the people and for this reason is alienated from them."

What is more, from the time of its promulgation in 1890, the Imperial Rescript on Education—read at least annually to the assembled student body of every school in the empire—reaffirmed for generations of Japanese subjects the essential character of their relationship to the imperial house. The debates of the scholars and ideologues of the Tokugawa period and the contending political views of the men of early Meiji were ultimately resolved in a formula of stunning simplicity. Just as every person owed filial loyalty to the head of his household, so every subject owed loyalty to the emperor, head (*kachō*) of the national household (*kokka*). All Japanese were his children (*seki-shi*). In this light the doctrine of the inseparability of loyalty (*chū*) and filial piety (kō) becomes obvious.

In this connection it is worth quoting a significant passage from a book entitled *Kokutai no Hongi* that was published in 1937. There were about two million copies of this book in print by the end of World War II, and portions of it had been adapted and incorporated into many school textbooks. The section on filial piety itself is straightforward, but the next is noteworthy. Entitled "Loyalty and Filial Piety as One," it contains these lines (R. K. Hall 1949a: 90):

> Since our ancestors rendered assistance to the spreading of Imperial enterprises by the successive Emperors, for us to show loyalty to the Emperor is in effect a manifestation of the manners and customs of our ancestors; and this is why we show filial piety to our forefathers. In our country there is no filial piety apart from loyalty, and filial piety has loyalty as its basis.

In retrospective discussions of such matters as these, there always remains the nagging question of whether anyone really believed that the emperor was divinely descended and that all his subjects were his children. It is a question that cannot be answered now, I think, and I doubt that it could have been answered easily even in the heyday of Japan's pre-1945 nationalism. This much can be said, though: some people were put to death and many more were imprisoned because they professed not to believe this ideology; tens of thousands more went to their deaths for all the world as though motivated by it. And it would certainly be difficult to find in the published record any voice of prominence in letters, the arts, politics, or the professions that was raised in unequivocal opposition to this idea.

This reflects what in the late Meiji period the government defined as "the Japanese tradition." By exploiting the potential inherent in universal compulsory education, the government saw to it that tradition, as it was being newly defined, would be taught to all elementary school pupils from 1903 to 1945. Furthermore, it was taught as truth, not as mythology (Jansen 1965: 82). The 1910 revision of the school texts of ethics contained the phrase *chūkō no taigi* (the great principle of loyalty and filial piety), and a large number of popular books on the ancient tradition as it was then perceived began to appear. Catching the mood of the late Meiji period perfectly, Haga Yaichi published his delineation of the essential qualities of the Japanese national character in the light of what was widely touted as Japan's unique history. Published in 1907, *Ten Lectures on Japanese Nationality* was already into its twenty-ninth edition in 1933. The first chapter discusses "Loyalty to the Emperor [and] Love of Country" (*chūkun aikoku*), and the second "Respect for Ancestors [and] Honor of the Family" (*sosen o tōtobi kamei o omonzu*) (Spae 1971: 61). All these matters are of more than purely antiquarian interest, for the sentiments embodied in works like Haga's were for several generations at the heart of the history and ethics curricula of Japanese compulsory education. Since no counterpart to the Church existed, the educational system itself was put to politico-religious use (Caiger 1968: 51).

At the beginning of the era, the Meiji oligarchs attempted to establish National Shinto as a state religion with a nationwide system of shrines and an official priesthood. This effort extended from 1868 to 1889 (see Creemers 1968; Hori & Toda 1956). An essential first step was to effect the separation of Shinto and Buddhism (*shinbutsu-bunri*), which required the fundamental alteration of even the imperial household's ancestral rites. This was accomplished as early as 1870, when the Buddhist memorial tablets and altar in the palace were replaced by their Shinto counterparts (Hori & Toda 1956: 60). The imperial ancestral shrine, which first had been erected in the Office for Shinto (*Jingikan*), was transferred to the palace grounds in 1872 (Creemers 1968: 121).

The new state religion enjoyed the status of a government ministry for a time, and priests—at first drawn only from Shinto, but later from Buddhism as well—were trained and dispatched throughout the country between 1869 and 1875 to propagate the new faith (Creemers 1968: 33–34). The government even decided to regulate funerals (Oguchi & Takagi 1956: 336). The confusion during this period must have been considerable, for not only was the government promoting Shinto funerals, which had been unknown up to that time, but it was also encouraging the persecution of Buddhism. There seems to have been understandable doubt about how funerals were to be conducted so as not to run into trouble with the authorities (Yanagida 1957: 292–93), and in some areas Confucian funeral rites were even introduced. By and large, the efforts to establish non-Buddhist funeral rites had little lasting effect, so great was the hold of Buddhist practice on the people. Consequently, the government soon turned to an alternative policy that was to prove successful to a degree that even its planners probably did not anticipate. This new policy was to result in an alteration of the focus of traditional religious practice by binding Buddhism to emperor worship through the domestic ancestral rites.

The heart of the emperor's Charter Oath of 1868 was the large claim that the indigenous form of government as exemplified by the reign of the first emperor, Jimmu, would be restored. Since there was not a shred of evidence about the form of that society, much less about the relationship between the legendary emperor and his subjects, imagination could run free. As is always the case with invented traditions, various groups found aspects of the Charter Oath unacceptable. A particularly thorny issue was the effort we have just discussed to establish national religion in the Shinto idiom. In fact, efforts were set in motion almost immediately to alter the direction in which the government was moving in the religious sphere.

Early in 1871, the Legislative Bureau (*Sain*) petitioned the throne to abolish the Shinto Ministry and establish a Ministry of Religion and Education. The favorable reply from the emperor contained the following remarkable passage (Hori & Toda 1956: 88): "We should not only allow the people to believe elements of every religion; we should encourage this. For instance, we should disseminate the teachings of Confucius from China and those of Buddha from India. To the extent that these religions do not violate the will of the Japanese gods, we should accept them without asking their nationality, master them, and put them to our own use." Between 1872 and 1877 the new ministry comprehended both Shinto and Buddhism, since it was the government's intention to make use of priests from both religions as Teachers of Religion and Morals, whose mission was to spread the new teachings of loyalty to the emperor and the state (Norbeck 1970: 50). Nevertheless, the emperor's statement by no means heralded the beginning of any new religious tolerance. Shinto was still at the heart of the plan for a state religion, and both Buddhism and Christianity were actively persecuted (Masutani & Undō 1956: 111–24). Finally, in 1881, the priests of the two great Jōdo-shin sects, East and West Honganji, petitioned the throne for a cessation of the government's efforts to control religion. Their memorial is important to our understanding of the subsequent development of ancestor worship, for among other courses of action they urged was the abolition of the national priesthood and the purging of "all traces of religion" from Shinto. This accomplished, the memorial continued, Shinto priests should be given complete responsibility for the worship of the ancestors (Hori & Toda 1956: 94).

Was this an effort on the part of the Jōdo-shin priests to clarify what they considered the true nature of Buddhism by divorcing it at last from mortuary practices, despite the immense loss of revenues that such a separation would entail? It seems to me that this must have been their motive. I have found no record of any popular reaction to the proposal, but if there was any it surely would have been negative. We do know that some Shinto leaders—in rare concord with the Buddhists, with whom they generally quarreled bitterly—approved the idea, for they must have seen that the advantage was theirs. If ancestor worship could be divorced from other religions, the Shintoists would find their way clear to link the people and the government through ancestral rites led by the emperor himself (*ibid*).

In some senses both sides lost. Buddhism was unable to divest itself of its funerary role, and Shinto did not become the state religion. Pressure on the government from at home and abroad to guarantee religious freedom was in large part effective: in 1882 an edict forbade further preaching in the national shrines and the holding of funerals there; in 1884 preaching was forbidden in all other Shinto shrines; and the 1889 Constitution finally granted qualified religious freedom to all Japanese.

The alternative to the establishment of a state religion was found in the educational system, where the government had virtually a free hand. Moving the entire issue from the domain of religion into that of education was a brilliant decision, for whereas attendance at shrines and temples was hard to control, attendance in the classroom was compulsory (Coville 1948: 18). What was to be the character of this educational system? This question provoked a many-sided debate that has been often incorrectly interpreted as a clash between only two opposing elements, the conservatives and the progressives. In fact, there were many shades of both in Meiji Japan. But if there were many opinions, the basic issue was simple. Was the aim of the educational system primarily to develop the individual or rather to give universal training in morals and ethics in order to produce a loyal and obedient population? The unequivocal answer was contained in the Imperial Rescript on Education of 1890, which set the heavily Confucian tone that dominated Japanese elementary education until the end of World War II. By the end of the 1870's, the Confucianists had already carried the day against the European-oriented reformers (see Passin 1965; Pittau 1967). During the following decade a blend of Confucian and Shinto concepts had been developed to serve as the philosophical basis for the restoration of the emperor as both the sovereign and the father of his people. The relationship between these two systems of thought was explained in an extraordinary formulation: "the Sun Goddess was peerless in virtue, but Confucianism was needed to restore and expound her teachings" (Shively 1959: 314). All private virtues were subsumed under the general public virtue of patriotic loyalty. The Imperial Rescript on Education became "the basic sacred text of the new religion of patriotism," and in 1891 the new education regulations defined the development of moral character as the central mission of primary schooling (Dore 1964: 190–91).

In April 1903, the Ministry of Education assumed complete responsibility for the compilation, production, and distribution of texts for the elementary schools. Before 1907, when only four years of education were compulsory, Japanese history was offered only in the fifth and sixth years. But after the extension of compulsory education to six years in 1907, all schoolchildren were automatically introduced to the subject. This history was the cornerstone of the government's effort to bring the imperial institution into a direct relationship with the Japanese people. The history texts of the time were supplemented by teachers' manuals until 1920, when the greatly expanded Third National Textbook proved comprehensive enough to obviate the need for interpretation by the teacher. Here is how the manual in use up to 1920 dealt with the issue of the relationship between the emperor and his subjects (Caiger 1968: 67–68):

> Amaterasu Ōmikami is not only the ancestor of the Imperial House, but also of all Japanese. If we ... seek our ancestry and parentage the greater part of us will prove to be descendants of the Imperial House. [Those who are not are descendants of later immigrants, but since they intermarried] there is no reason now why our common ancestor should not be Amaterasu Ōmikami. But since the Imperial House and the Emperor are in the direct line of descent, we subjects, who are branch families, descended in an indirect line, must give special veneration to the Imperial line and humbly tender our respect and affection. The connection between the Imperial House and its subjects is thus: one forms the main house and the others form the branch houses, so that from ancient times we have worshiped the founder of the Imperial House and the heavenly gods. Our relationship to this house is sincerely founded on repaying our debt of gratitude to our ancestors.

Thus we can see how the conservatives found a way of welding the imperial house to the people through the institution of ancestor worship, which they construed as but one of a number of ancient Japanese usages to be revived and pressed into the service of the state (see R. K. Hall 1949b).

It is at once apparent that much of this philosophy derived from the writings of the nativist scholars of the Tokugawa period; indeed, their influence can be seen in the developing theories of the state as well. Representative of those whose ideas prevailed in the debates over the political direction that Japan should take is Hozumi Yatsuka (1860–1912), chief architect of the ideology of the state-as-household. His thesis was both simple and direct: the state is the household writ large; the household is the state in microcosm; differing only in size, they are made one through the medium of ancestor worship (Hirai 1968: 42). Hozumi wrote popular works in addition to scholarly publications, the most influential of which probably was *Kokumin kyōiku: aikokushin* (*The People's Education: Patriotism*), first published in 1897 and in its sixth edition at his death some fifteen years later. In this book he stressed the vital place of ancestor worship in defining the unique character of the Japanese polity (Minear 1970: 73):

> The ancestor of my ancestors is the Sun Goddess. The Sun Goddess is the founder of our race, and the throne is the sacred house of our race. If father and mother are to be revered, how much more so the ancestors of the house;

and if the ancestors of the house are to be revered, how much more so the founder of the country! The position of the head of the house is that of the authority of the ancestors; the throne is the place of the Sun Goddess. Father and mother are ancestors living in the present; the emperor is the Sun Goddess living in the present. For the same reason one is filial to his parents and loyal to the throne; and the national teaching which connects these two is the worship of the ancestors.

Nonetheless, the government was not content to leave the matter entirely to public sentiment and took pains to define precisely the legal status of the household through rules concerning succession to its headship (*katoku-sōzoku*) and inheritance of its property (*isan-sōzoku*) (see Ishii 1958). The provision of the Civil Code of 1898 relevant to the former matter is Article 987: "Ownership of the genealogical record, articles of worship, and tombs is a special right pertaining to succession to a house" (Sebald 1934: 232). In his commentary on this code, Hozumi Nobushige (1912: 130–31) writes: "This important provision means that those things which are specified therein form the special objects of inheritance. They cannot be bequeathed away, nor can they be seized for debt." In subsequent articles bearing on the issue of succession, elaborate provisions are made to specify alternatives to the preferred pattern of succession by the first-born son. Hozumi says of these provisions: "It will be seen that the law takes every precaution against the contingency of a house becoming extinct; for with the extinction of the house, the worship of its ancestors would come to an end" (*ibid.*: 135–36). The household was conceived to be a corporate body, and its members were expected to sacrifice personal desires and accept all major decisions of the household head. The headship passed to one child, in principle the eldest son of the incumbent, to whom both authority and property were transferred.

The younger sons and the daughters had no rights to inherit the House property whatever. These inequalities of rights were also accompanied by inequalities of duties; the eldest son bore the heavy responsibility to support his parents, as well as his younger brothers and sisters. . . . Thus the eldest son, on becoming the new owner, was expected to direct the efforts and work of the others so that the House property would support all. (Y. Watanabe 1963: 369.)

The new Civil Code of 1947, which went into effect on January 1, 1948, provides in most respects for a very different kind of family structure. The household is no longer a legal entity and its head is stripped of his powers (Steiner 1950). The emphasis throughout is on individual rights, and the most important stipulation in this regard is the one providing for equal inheritance of property by all the children. Nevertheless, one important exception to the general accordance of equal status to all children remains. Article 897 reads in part: "The ownership of genealogical records, of utensils of religious rites, and of tombs and burial grounds is succeeded to the person who is, according to custom, to hold as a president the worship of the memory of the ancestors" (Ministry of Justice 1966: 521). Such a person may be designated by the previous head of the house, or he may be the person who by custom would have been the legal successor in the past.

The survival of ancestor worship in the new Civil Code outraged those who had hoped it would retain no remnant of Japan's "feudal past." On the other hand, the weakening of the household has provoked the concern of many others who wish to see it restored to its former importance. The 1954 draft revision of the Constitution prepared by the conservative Liberal Party went so far as to provide for the "restoration of the duty of filial piety of children towards parents" (Y. Watanabe 1963: 379), among other similar recommendations. No such revisions have actually been made in either the Constitution or the Civil Code. Economic considerations in particular have continued to dictate that equal inheritance of property, especially among farm families, is far less common than we might have supposed would be the case by now. As for the obligation to care for the ancestral tablets and graves, that responsibility commonly devolves on the first-born son (or the adopted husband of a daughter) of the former family head. I was often told "I have the memorial tablets here in my house because I am the first son," as though that were the most obvious answer in the world to my questioning why a man had tablets at all. These are the very people who would have had the tablets in the prewar period as well. At a more explicit level, the syncretic sects that the Japanese call the New Religions have continued to foster the household ideal and concepts of filial piety. Seichō-no-Ie will serve as an excellent example. Wimberley (1969: 48) cites preliminaries to the "heart purification ritual" of this sect:

> [Preliminary lectures stress] the proposition that an individual's life is derived from his household, which is the product of the ancestors. For example, on

one occasion the relationship between the individual and his family was expressed figuratively with the aid of the image of a tree. The roots represented the founding ancestors, the trunk those ancestors who carried on the founders' will and purposes, and the limbs represented the parents of the listeners who as "fruit" of the tree received its "sap" of life.

The Meiji government was also active in a very different area from those of the school curriculum and the legal status of the household. This activity involved the establishment of a national program of Shinto shrine mergers whose double aim was to strengthen local self-government and to link village shrine worship directly to the emperor (see Fridell 1973). In some respects this program was the most audacious of all the Meiji reforms aimed at redefining tradition. Like so many other aspects of Meiji policy, the shrine-merger program took a variety of forms from 1871 to about 1900. From the outset, however, the one clear principle that guided policy was that all shrines in the country should be placed in some kind of a national system in the service of the state. But as we have seen, the attempt to develop a state religion failed and the focus of reform shifted to administrative and political goals. From about 1900, but especially following the Russo-Japanese War, the government was forced to face up to a growing economic crisis and rising domestic unrest. To counter these problems, two programs were launched. The first was the famous Local Improvement Movement, set in motion with an Imperial Rescript on Thrift and Frugality (see Pyle 1973). The second, inaugurated less ostentatiously around 1906, attempted to consolidate local shrines with the ultimate aim of having only one in each village. (The "village," in contradistinction to the old hamlet settlement of an earlier period, was the administrative unit that had been created not long before by the Meiji government.) Armed with the slogan "Every Village a Family," officials attempted to gather into one shrine all the deities worshiped up to that time in the hamlets, neighborhoods, fields, and roadsides of the area now within the new village boundaries. The people were urged to honor the gods, now defined as the ancestors of the community, at these new consolidated shrines. In addition to the gods, appropriate objects of worship at the shrines were said to include the ancestors of one's own household, all superior men (such as landlords and public officials), and the emperor.

There can be no doubt that one of the major outcomes of this extraordinary program was the successful promotion of the idea that one's own ancestors were gods and should be revered as such (Fridell 1973: 63–64). The idea was not an innovation, of course, nor did the government entirely invent the notion that local shrine worship was to some degree linked with reverence for the emperor. Rather, this program represents a generally skillful exploitation of long-established popular religious practices like the Ise pilgrimage. In 1911, for example, the minister of education instructed schoolteachers to take their pupils to shrines. Ceremonies usually featured the performance of rites by public officials, and in a variety of other ways the linkage of the imperial house with household and community ancestor worship was repeatedly emphasized.

I have dwelt on these issues because I believe it is essential to understand the framework within which the meaning of ancestor worship was defined and redefined at the highest political level. A few additional comments are in order here before we turn to the beliefs and practices relating to the ancestors and the gods. I have been careful to emphasize the important role assigned to ancestor worship by the theorists who created the Japan of the men and women who in 1963 told me about their ancestors. The country in which they grew up and were educated was in a great many ways very different from the one in which our conversations occurred. It was in prewar Japan that most of them had learned to recognize the overwhelming importance of the household, the great debt they owed its ancestors, and by extension the requirement of loyalty to the emperor that transcended all other obligations. These were the Japanese who had been taught to believe that they were all children of the emperor, and therefore that they were all related, sharing in descent from the gods of remote antiquity. In their schools had been enshrined the portraits of the emperor and the empress, and on innumerable special occasions they had all stood in the schoolyard or auditorium to hear the Imperial Rescript on Education read aloud (see Keenleyside 1937: 176–77, for a description of this rite). In such a world, paying proper respect to the souls of the ancestral dead was assigned a very high priority, for it was at once the highest expression of filial piety and the highest form of loyalty.

Of course, it would make no sense to leave the matter here. Profound changes have occurred since the end of World War II with respect to the forms of public worship generally known as State Shinto, the position of the emperor, and the aims and content of education. One of the first acts of the Allied occupation forces was to terminate the links between the government and Shinto. On December 15, 1945, a directive was issued that prohibited the teaching of "Shinto" in the schools, the school-sponsored visits to "Shinto" places of worship, and the holding of "Shinto" rituals on school premises. The directive was entitled "Abolition of Governmental Sponsorship, Support, Perpetuation, Control, and Dissemination of State Shinto" (see Creemers 1968: 219–22, for the text). Shortly thereafter, on December 31, 1945, another directive was issued—"Suspension of Courses in Morals, Japanese History, and Geography" (see Passin 1965: 272–74, for the text). And on New Year's Day 1946, the emperor's traditional message contained a renunciation of his own divinity (see Creemers 1968: 223–27). The 1946 Constitution defined the emperor as the "symbol of the state." In February of the same year the government created a new term, Shrine Shinto, and officially recognized it as a religion on a par with other religions. The Association of Shinto Shrines, which included the former national shrines of State Shinto, was formed. Thus within a few months the machinery of State Shinto and the educational system's program of instructing all pupils in the virtues of loyalty and filial piety were dismantled. In 1948, a Diet Resolution declared the 1890 Imperial Rescript on Education to be invalid and ordered it withdrawn from all schools.

This is not the place to take up the continuing postwar efforts to reinstitute moral training courses in the schools—efforts that have been a political issue since at least 1950, when the minister of education advocated the revival of such courses at the elementary level. The issue of the status of the Ise shrine has not been finally resolved either. In 1965, Prime Minister Ikeda was asked to comment on the shrine's position and especially on the sacred mirror, which is kept there. The letter Ikeda wrote in reply was unequivocal in its definition of Ise as a national shrine, provoking the following exultant response from Ashitsu Uzuhiko, a leading Shinto spokesman (Iisaka 1972: 318):

> The Ikeda cabinet clearly indicated the government position: Ise Shrine is where the imperial ancestors are honored, and the relationship between the Emperor and the shrine extends infinitely through the ages of history down to the present day. And it confirmed the principles of *kokutai* that the Sacred

Mirror is the august mirror divinely bequeathed by the imperial ancestor to be transmitted together with the throne of the Emperor of Japan. The efforts of many years by those who revere the shrine have not been in vain and are now confirmed in this official statement.

Anachronistic as this sentiment would seem to most Japanese of my acquaintance, many of whom would be either infuriated or amused by its tone, it is by no means viewed in so negative a light by all. The New Religion Seichō-no-Ie, for example, which in 1970 claimed 2,500,000 adherents, holds that care of the ancestors is the most important ritual activity. It also teaches that the highest moral goal is the care of the ancestors and "by extension the Imperial line of successors to the headship of the family-state" (Wimberley 1972: 183). Vogel (1963: 88) found that in 1958–60, among the white-collar families he interviewed in Tokyo, the politicians were blamed rather than the emperor for the disaster of World War II. In part because the emperor was no longer so isolated and remote a figure, many of Vogel's respondents seemed to have come to feel a greater affection for him than they had felt before the war. I suggest that such attitudes may in fact represent an older tradition in Japanese society, one that antedates the first decades of the twentieth century. In the 1940's and 1950's it was my pleasure to know several old people who had been born at about the time of the Meiji Restoration. They often used the words *tenshi-sama* when referring to the emperor, and seldom spoke of him as *tennō* or *tennō-heika*. The difference in feeling is important, for tennō-heika, the term favored by the government, has implications of awesome distance from the world of ordinary men. Tenshi-sama, on the other hand, is a term of much greater intimacy, as was shown in a revealing reply made by a very old man to my question about his feeling for the emperor: "Well, it's like talking about a very dignified person—maybe the senior man in one's main house. Do you understand? He would be a relative, to be sure, but very distant and very dignified. But a relative for all that."

Two. *Spirits, Ghosts, and Gods*

THIS CHAPTER will focus on a number of questions about the world of the spirits as it impinges on the world of the living, and about how both relate to the gods. We shall be concerned to discover, first, along what dimensions distinctions are drawn when they seem to be intended and, second, in what ways such distinctions as are made seem to be reflected in conceptions of the origins of the spirits and in the behavior and attitudes shown toward them. I shall return repeatedly to the question of the relationship between the spirits and gods, on the one hand, and the specifically ancestral spirits, on the other. What the reader will find is a highly indeterminate universe where some humans—living and dead—become gods and others buddhas, where spirits of the living may prove to be as malevolent as spirits of the dead, and where the deification of ancestors is only slightly more common than the "ancestorization" of deities. There is a very rich lexicon having reference to the great variety of spirits of the living and of the dead as the Japanese conceive them. Some prominent works in this area include Eder 1956, 1957; Harada 1959; Herbert 1967; Hori 1951, 1953; Shibata 1959; Takeda & Takatori 1957.

Spirits of the Living and of the Newly Dead

Every living person has both a body and a soul (*ikimitama*) capable of detaching itself from the body. On the most mundane level, this belief is reflected in the custom sometimes observed on festive occasions of welcoming back to its home the spirit of an absent male household member (Ōshima 1959: 91). Sometimes offerings are made in the form of a meal shared with members of the family. Many acquaintances have told me that this was done in their families during World War II, especially at the New Year, for fathers and sons who were serving overseas. As we shall see, sharing a meal is a central part of the rites directed to the ancestral spirits as well.

Another form of the spirit of the living is the malevolent *ikiryō*, thought to be capable of doing great harm to enemies and rivals. Perhaps the classic appearance of this spirit in literature occurs in the Nō play *The Lady Aoi (Aoi no ue)*. Rokujō has been rejected by her lover Genji in favor of the Lady Aoi, who is subsequently stricken by a mysterious illness that resists all treatment. The cause of the malady is the living spirit of Rokujō, who, consumed by jealousy, appears at Aoi's bedside wearing a mask called *hannya*, a hideously transformed woman's face, horned and of fearsome aspect. The emphasis of both mask and demeanor is on inherent humanity rendered tragically less than human by uncontrolled emotion and desire. A ritual of exorcism performed by a Buddhist priest eventually drives the spirit from the victim's sickroom.

Evidence for belief in malevolent spirits of the living is not confined to historical and literary texts. Some extraordinary contemporary materials on possession by such spirits can be found in a report on a community in Shikoku where the victims were thought to be the targets of envy, resentment, and jealousy. Significantly, possessor and possessed there were never patrilineal kinsmen and only rarely members of the bilateral kindred (Yoshida 1967: 250–54). This was in many ways a curious community, not least because it had no Buddhist temple; but belief in vengeful spirits of the living is found among other groups in less remote spots. The sect popularly known as the Dancing Religion (*Tenshō-kōtai-jingū-kyō*), which incorporates much of Shinto doctrine, attributes to spirits of this kind sudden illnesses and undeserved misfortunes that strike its converts. These spirits are said to be generated by jealous persons, usually peers or associates of the victims (Lebra 1970: 50). The sect also attributes misfortune and disease to spirits of the dead—both ancestral and unrelated—and to spirits of animals as well (Kerner 1974).

The *shirei*, the spirit of a person who has recently died, is accorded special treatment by members of the household until it is thought to have moved from direct involvement with the world of the living to a more remote realm. The spirit of the newly dead remains something of a threat to the living, at least until the first bon following death. Then it is welcomed back to the house with special greetings and offerings that are usually placed on an altar separate from that for the ancestral spirits. Often referred to as a "new buddha" (*nī-botoke*) until sent away with all the other ancestors at the end of its first bon, the shirei retains some of the contamination of death that must be ritually cleansed.

When a member of the household dies, the immediate concern is to begin the process of removing his spirit from the realm of daily life and ultimately from the entire world of men. Often the rites designed to accomplish this process are simple and direct: the spirit of the dead is elevated out of human place and time as the dead person fades from memory. At length the shirei is said to become an ancestral spirit (*sorei*), a protector of the household and its members; still later it becomes a guardian of the community, and ultimately one of the myriad deities. We can get a sense of the means by which the spirit of the dead is made into an ancestral spirit from a case reported from the Izu Islands (Ushijima 1966). At intervals during the first hundred days after death the memorial tablet for the deceased is raised shelf by shelf in the domestic altar, until on the final day it is put with the ancestral tablets on the highest level. Each time the tablet is raised it is said that "the spirit of the dead becomes more purified" (*shirei ga kiyomatte*). On the last day the spirit is referred to as a "new ancestor" (*nī-senzo*) for the first time, and is said to have joined the "old ancestors" (*furu-senzo*) of the house.

Wandering Spirits

The wandering spirits, most commonly called *muen-botoke* (buddhas without attachment or affiliation) or *gaki* (hungry ghosts), are of more than one origin but share many attributes. It is believed that if a man dies in a state of jealousy, rage, resentment, or melancholy, his spirit will remain both possessed by the worldly passion in whose grip he died (Matsudaira 1963: 183) and condemned to wander the earth unless or until the living intervene. Other wandering spirits are thought to be the souls of those who are not worshiped by their descendants; they are engaged in an endless search for food and comfort. In theory, at least, the muen-botoke can be calmed, freed from its circle of endless torment, and sent at last to join the legion of remote and peaceful spirits of the dead.

Wandering spirits are widely believed to have the power to enter the body of the newly dead. To prevent this a bladed object—sword, dagger, knife, or sickle—is placed by the pillow or on the chest of the corpse. There is also a fear that the wandering spirit may first enter the body of a cat or dog in order to approach the corpse and enter it in turn; thus precautions must be taken against letting these animals come near the newly dead (Inoguchi 1959: 293–94).

The muen-botoke are very different from the shirei and bear a close resemblance to the malevolent spirits of the living. The chief difference between them is that the malevolent spirit of the living can be forced to return to its living body, whereas the wandering spirit, permanently deprived of its body, must be dealt with in other ways.

One means of preventing the wandering spirits from harming the living is to perform a *segaki-e* on their behalf. The word segaki means "to give to the hungry ghosts," but in the sense that one gives to a beggar or that a wealthy person of rank dispenses largess to the poor. Just as food used to be given to unfortunates at bon, so the miserable hungry ghosts or the wandering spirits are the recipients of the offerings at a segaki-e. This Buddhist ritual may be performed privately at an altar set up outside the dwelling under the eaves, or it may be held at a temple. If it is a group observance, a priest ordinarily conducts the ritual (Earhart 1970: 126–27). After the altar is set up at a selected spot, offerings and a basin filled with holy water are placed on it. The priest sits facing east, that is, away from the Western Paradise. While he recites the sutras it is thought that the wandering spirits gather around the altar. When the ritual is formally observed, the five *nyorai* (Tathagata) banners must be placed on the altar (one at each corner and one in the center), along with a tablet inscribed "Tablet for the Myriad Spirits of the Three Worlds" (*sangai banrei hi*).

In Nagasawa (discussed in Chapter 5) a segaki-e is held on August 5. The altar set up at the temple there is an elaborate version of the private household's special altar for bon itself. A sermon by the priest opens the ceremony, and everyone offers incense at the altar. At the conclusion each person receives a *tōba* (Sanskrit *stūpa*—a thin wooden slat bearing Buddhist inscriptions) to take home and keep beside the special household altar until the end of bon, when the stupa are carried out to the graves of the family and stacked there (Ooms 1967: 227–28). In Suye the segaki-e is believed to be a service for all the dead of the village, and some people bring a memorial tablet from home to have it included in the service. Here the worshipers take home the paper banners that decorate the temple altar and put them up in the fields to ward off insects—a practice clearly related to the placating of vengeful spirits that are thought to send plagues of insects when farmers neglect to care for them (Embree 1939: 281).

From other accounts it appears that the segaki-e ritual is often performed at night without lights or music, in sharp contrast to bon. The sutras are recited in an undertone so as not to frighten away the wandering spirits, who despite their potential for harm are nonetheless thought to be fearful and suspicious of the world of the living. Today the rite is usually held between the first and fifteenth days of the seventh month, but it may be scheduled to coincide with the anniversary of an accident or natural disaster. For those accidentally drowned there is a special *kawa-segaki-e* (river segaki rite), which is usually held at the spot where the accident occurred, and which is intended to calm the souls of the victims and to prevent their spirits from causing further drownings at the same place. Often a memorial stone is erected at the site and a periodic service held for the spirits of those who died there. Monuments of this kind abound in Japan, and I have even seen one in southern Brazil at a ferry crossing where a boat sank some years ago killing several Japanese settlers. Segaki-e ceremonies were also held by many temples for a number of years after World War II on the anniversaries of American bombing raids on Japanese cities. Where civilian casualties had been particularly high, many large temples held especially elaborate services. The practice has declined considerably with the passage of time, but in recent years a nationally televised memorial service has been held for all the war dead—both military and civilian—with the emperor and prime minister as chief officiants. It is held annually on August 15, by cruel coincidence the date on which Japan surrendered to the Allied Powers and the last day of bon.

Distinctions among the various kinds of wandering spirits are not sharply drawn, but it is possible to differentiate them to some degree. First, there are the spirits of those hapless persons who either have died without posterity or are neglected by their descendants. Their fate is undeserved no matter whether their lives were good or evil, for normally the evil are as honored in death as the good. For whatever reason, these are unhonored and therefore unsettled spirits. Neglected by members of their household, or without descendants to care for them, they roam endlessly in a pathetic and potentially dangerous search for comfort from the living. Unable to make any claim of kinship with the living, they can only make the claim of common humanity. The concern that one may suffer misfortune for failing to offer comfort to these spirits is exemplified in an account of the treatment of certain kinds of graves in Takane (discussed in Chapter 5). Old gravestones still dot the fields, and a man who buys land with one on it is expected to take responsibility for continuing to care for the spirits it represents. As a consequence, the owner of a field may be offering prayers at a gravestone, "the inscription on which he cannot read, of a person with whom he is relatively certain that he has no direct relationship" (K. Brown 1964: 118), in order to make certain that no wandering spirits are left unattended.

Second, there are those spirits who either have met an unanticipated and usually violent death or have died in some sense unfulfilled and are thus reluctant or unable to quit the world of the living. People tend to conceive of such spirits as far more dangerous than the neglected ones, since they combine resentment at their untimely death with anger at their condemnation to wander in search of human intervention to bring them peace.

In some areas and among some religious sects people believe that if one has behaved properly in all matters but nevertheless suffers misfortune, the cause must lie with a wandering spirit. The proper course in such cases is to seek out a medium to determine the nature of the problem, which usually proves to involve a person's wish left unfulfilled or act left uncompleted before death intervened. Should the cause of the spirit's attachment to the world be discovered, the medium will often recommend that the victim make an effort to settle the unfinished business or pacify the spirit with an elaborate memorial service and rich offerings of food. Very often these spirits are said to be suffering from the emotional state of *urami*—bitterness, ill will, enmity, spite, or malice (Maeda 1965: 61).

The fear of wandering spirits appears to be especially intense in fishing communities. When corpses are found floating at sea, they are brought back to the village for interment in a graveyard reserved for drowning victims. Called "floating buddhas" (*nagare-botoke*), their spirits are thought to be the messengers or servants of some major god. This represents a contemporary version of the ancient concept of vengeful gods (*goryō-shin, tatari-gami*), that is, spirits of disaster victims that are thought to be dangerous if uncared for but beneficent if deified and properly venerated. Indeed, these spirits are often appealed to in the expectation that they can increase the size of the catch. When the corpse is hauled out of the water, the fishermen speak to it, asking for assistance in return for having taken it up for burial. No such special treatment seems to be accorded those whose bodies have washed ashore or who have committed suicide by drowning, for only the spirits of those who have died at sea in an accident or a disaster have the powers of the vengeful gods (Ōtō 1963). In parts of western Japan victims of accidental drowning are called "floating Kannon" (Kannon is Kuan-yin, the Buddhist Goddess of Mercy). The only way to prevent their spirits from taking revenge on the villagers is to perform a segaki-e on their behalf (Ōshima 1959: 85). Ōshima also reports that in eastern Japan lighted lanterns are floated out to sea at bon, apparently to comfort the wandering spirits or to prevent those who have drowned from becoming *yūrei* (ghosts) and returning to haunt the negligent villagers.

Ghosts are among the most common of the spirits of the unsettled dead, and they are said to haunt their own graves, hover about the scene of their murder or suicide, or sometimes lead a victim to his death. Frequently depicted on the kabuki stage in the summer months in plays specifically designed before the advent of air conditioning to chill the audience, they are invariably both horrifying and pathetic, for the idea of a spirit of pure evil is rarely encountered in Japanese folklore and literature. Who are these ghosts that intervene so directly in the world of the living? The implication of their plight is that they are the spirits of victims of some cruel or callous act, or that some awful tragedy of life still plagues them beyond the grave. They usually appear to seek revenge or to call attention to their pitiful state; seldom laid finally to rest, they continue to haunt the place where they once lived or where they met death. The recent popularity of pilgrimages to the battlefields of the Pacific War can only be explained by the desire of relatives and comrades to comfort the spirits of those who were never properly buried. They are felt to be a pitiable lot, for they made the ultimate sacrifice and have been abandoned; until services are held for their spirits at the places where they died they can only wander about the battlefield seeking help.

The poignancy of the fate of these ghosts is stressed in countless Nō plays, many of which offer a specifically Buddhist scheme of salvation. The protagonist is often a sinner, "a sinner not because he has committed a crime against society, but because he has suffered from the limitations of humanity, because he was born a human being" (Ueda 1967: 70). In the play *Motomezuka* (*The Sought-for Grave*) (Keene 1970: 33–49), this theme is played out beside an ancient grave mound. (In the following quotations I have generally ignored the assignment of lines in the interest of sense.)

A group of traveling priests stops near a village and asks a maiden to show them to the Sought-for Grave. She does so, along the way telling them the story of Unai, the girl who is buried there. Long before, Unai had committed suicide and her two lovers had killed each other over her grave. As the maiden comes to the end of her appalling tale, it becomes clear that she is in fact the ghost of Unai (by the conventions of the Nō theater, she appears in the first half of the play as she was in life and assumes her demonic form in the second half). She vanishes into the grave, saying:

> Each stabbed his rival, and they died.
> For this also the guilt is mine.
> Please pray for me!

The priests reply:

> Here we spend this night, our voices
> Raised in prayer for the repose
> Of the lost maiden's soul.
> For a moment, short as the space
> Between the antlers of a stag,
> She emerged from the shadows
> Of the grass that hides her tomb.
> *Namu yūrei jō tōshōgaku*
> May you attain right understanding
> O restless spirit!

Shutsuri shōji tonshō bodai
May you escape the wheel of life and death,
And know sudden enlightenment!

The girl speaks from within the grave mound, revealing how deeply she still longs to return to this world, and a priest cries out when her ghost suddenly appears:

O painful sight!
But if you abandon this evil obsession,
You surely can escape eternal punishment.
Shuju shoaku gokuki chikushō
This world of manifold and diverse evils,
This earthly hell, these realms
Of hungry ghosts, of brutish monsters,
Shōrō byōshi kui zenshitsu ryōmetsu
The sufferings of life, old age, sickness, and death—
All these in the end shall be destroyed!
May you quickly find salvation!

She thanks the priest for his prayers on her behalf, but is abruptly plunged into torment when the ghosts of her two lovers appear:

I am helpless, lost!
In the Burning House [this world]
Against a roof pillar
She presses and clings fast.
But suddenly the pillar's length
Bursts into flame. Now she embraces
A column of fire.
Alas, I am burning, she cries,
It is unbearable!
Every limb is transformed
To white-hot flame and pitch-black smoke,
Then once again I rise up, whole.

She is restored, only to suffer repeated torment. At last she vanishes once more into the tomb, having found no salvation.

This role perfectly exemplifies the stricture of Zeami, author of many of the classic Nō plays, with regard to how ghosts must be conceived by the actor playing the part (Waley 1921: 47): "Here the outward form is that of a ghost: but within is the heart of a man. If ghosts are terrifying, they cease to be beautiful."

If it seems too hard a fate that the innocent and the wicked alike may become wandering spirits, it can be understood if we realize that fault is not the issue; the wandering spirits are those that, for whatever reason, have not been assisted by the living from the state of being newly dead through the regular ascent to the realm of the remote ancestral dead. In some cases the living have failed the dead, in others the dead are themselves responsible for their plight. For both the effect is the same; they are equally outside the normal order. Perhaps the merging of the two types resulted from the Buddha's teaching that of all the creatures subject to rebirth, that is, who have not escaped the cycle of reincarnation, only those reborn into the plane of the preta can benefit from the prayers and offerings of the living. The reason they are in that plane is not important; the point is that their suffering can be alleviated, at least in theory. But it is by no means clear whether in the Japanese popular view the wandering spirits can ever be finally removed from that state.

They can be fed and given temporary relief from their hunger, though. Boyer (1966–67: 44) reports on the feeding of the hungry ghosts during bon at a temple in Nīgata Prefecture. A separate altar is erected for them, just inside the entrance and facing the altar of the Buddha, and special offerings are placed on it. In her travels Boyer also observed many ways of feeding the hungry ghosts on occasions other than festival days, and in most temples she found that each monk takes a few grains of cooked rice from his own bowl and places them on a wooden tray before beginning to eat. The tray of rice is then offered to the hungry ghosts. At the Tōdaiji in Nara, as the monks leave the refectory they cast small balls of rice outside the hall, where it is thought the ghosts may be assembled.

One of the few extensive English-language accounts of ancestor worship in contemporary Japan reports that a very different view of the wandering spirits is held by some of the residents of Nagasawa (Ooms 1967: 251–54). Here the muen-botoke are not the wandering spirits of strangers, but rather the spirits of the dead children of the household, for whom memorial tablets may or may not be made. During a visit to one house, Ooms was shown two new boxes for memorial tablets containing two parallel rows of small slips of wood onto which posthumous names had been copied from a record book formerly kept in the altar. At the front of each box were two black lacquered slips of wood side by side, the first reading "Spirits of the Generations of the Ancestors of the House" (*ie senzo daidai rei*), and the second "Spirits of All the Wandering Dead (*muen issai no rei*). The first is the usual legend on collective ancestral tablets, but the second is surprising, for one does not expect to find tablets for wandering spirits in a household altar, since a spirit for which there is a tablet is by definition settled and can hardly be considered unattached or unaffiliated. What is startling is that all the tablets behind the second slip were tablets of children, and not one was more than two generations old. Ooms found the same distinction at some of the grave sites of village households. The main stone bore the family name and the names of those adults who died as full-fledged members of the household, whereas a smaller stone alongside bore only the names of children.

Ooms followed up his discoveries with some questions about the conception of muen-botoke implied by these practices. He was concerned to find out who the wandering spirits were and what the element *en* of muen meant. He knew that these were souls lacking a "connection," but a connection with what? The first category of responses was the standard, almost abstract reply that muen-botoke are the spirits of those who have died a violent death or who have not been properly cared for by their descendants. The second was that just as each house has its own ancestral tablets for its hotoke (the ancestral dead, commonly referred to as buddhas), so it has tablets for its own muen-botoke. The former are remembered throughout the year, the latter only at bon. The third category of responses was like the second, but more specific: muen-botoke are the spirits of all who have died a violent death and of all children. Some of the respondents in the third category said that a married person who died a violent death would not become a muen-botoke because he had *engumi* (the common word for marriage).

The clearest case in which the spirits of dead children have been treated as muen-botoke is that of a woman who had a statue of Jizō put up in the family's grave site. She did this after several years of sickness and death in the family, which she attributed to the malign influence of some wandering spirit. A photograph (Ooms 1967: facing 247) shows this statue, on whose side is inscribed the phrase *Sekiguchi ke muen issai no rei* (All the Wandering Spirits of the Sekiguchi House). The choice of Jizō to mark the graves of children is a common one, for children in particular are thought to require his compassionate assistance in cross-ing the river that bars their way to paradise.

But for our purposes, the most interesting aspect of the situation re-ported by Ooms is this: many people in the same community were as-tonished to learn that anyone could possibly imagine children's souls becoming wandering spirits. This kind of microvariation in belief and practice is very common in Japan, as the data presented in later chapters will show. Indeed, I found no hint of any such view in my own inter-views. For the people of Nagasawa who do hold this belief, however, these spirits are not conceived of as harmful hungry ghosts or even as pitiable wandering spirits. They too belong to the household, differing from other members only in that they did not follow out the normal course of human life (Ooms 1967: 254). They are the young and un-married, who have died without issue and can never become ancestors; they remain forever as they were in life (Ooms 1967: 283). The nearest analogue to this conception known to me is Yanagita's (1970: 94–95) distinction between two kinds of what he calls *muen-sama*: one is the familiar wandering spirit, and the other is a category of souls of rela-tives who died young. This category includes unmarried siblings of one's grandparents, beloved children of great-grandparents, and others who may be thought of as being on the fringes of veneration; but apparently this does not include one's own children, as is the case in Nagasawa.

Ancestral Spirits

When the Japanese speak of the individual or collective dead, they most commonly use the word hotoke (buddha). The source of this uniquely Japanese notion that all men become buddhas merely by dying is by no means clear. Certainly nothing in orthodox Buddhism suggests such a happy automatic fate, nor does the idea square with the concept of rebirth. Even the wandering spirits are a kind of hotoke. It may well be that the explanation lies in a fundamental misunderstanding of the idea of nirvana (Japanese *nehan*) dating from a very early period in Japanese history (Takeda 1961: 221–22).

In orthodox Buddhist theory, the four stages of this life are said to be conception, birth, death, and rebirth. If a person is not to be reborn, that is, if he has escaped the cycle of rebirth, the result will be known seven days after death. If he has not escaped he will be reborn by the

forty-ninth day after death (on the last of the seventh-day rites). Although the end of the forty-nine-day period of mourning is called *imi-
ake* (lifting of pollution), and is Shinto in all its connotations, it is
firmly based in Buddhist doctrine and is clearly an imported idea, for
the number seven is found almost nowhere else in Japanese ritual contexts. The basic Japanese misunderstanding of orthodox Buddhism,
then, concerns the concept of nirvana. It originally meant "to be blown
out," as the wind extinguishes the flame. When wisdom extinguishes
the fire of human desire, one becomes a buddha, but this means to become enlightened in life, not after death. To the Japanese, however, it
seemed that ordinary mortals could not attain nirvana in this life, as
the Buddha had, but might do so after death. Thus "becoming a buddha" *(hotoke ni naru)* came to describe the person's state after death.
To die was to become a buddha, and death came to be interpreted not
as something that extinguished the flame, but as something that allowed
continued existence after death as a buddha. This gave a new and appealing meaning to the concept of nirvana, and the Japanese began to
conceive of their ancestors as living in peace in the Pure Land or Western Paradise of the Amida Buddha.

The Japanese belief that paradise exists in opposition to hell is yet
another reinterpretation of a Buddhist doctrine—one that was probably
brought from China during the earliest period of borrowing. This is a
far remove from the Mahayana concept of the Pure Land as the dwelling place of the buddhas who have freed themselves from all suffering
and desire, from life and death. Hell in the orthodox view is only the
worst part of this world (Sanskrit *saṃsāra*) (Takeda 1965: 598). Nonetheless, it is difficult to find much evidence that the Japanese really think
of their ancestors as ever being in hell—or in paradise either, for that
matter. Perhaps it is that they simply have never been deeply concerned
about the worlds beyond this one, and that only this world and the society in which they live are "really real to them" (Kitagawa 1965: 330).

There is one purely Japanese variant on this general formulation of
the fate of the soul. Whereas most people become buddhas after death,
some become gods, and some become both buddhas and gods, depending entirely on the context in which they are venerated. "The Japanese
consider that no person should be worshiped as a Shinto god ... unless
he is particularly outstanding" (Oguchi & Takagi 1956: 345); for ordi-

nary men the easiest way to achieve this distinction is to die in war. Those killed in wars or considered to have died for their country become "national gods" (*ibid.*). As such they are worshiped not only as buddhas in their homes, where they are represented by memorial tablets in the Buddhist altar, but also as gods at the Yasukuni Shrine by the emperor himself. This shrine, erected in Tokyo in 1869, became the principal point of articulation of the emperor with the ancestor worship of the common people (see Ponsonby Fane 1963: 118–34). Yasukuni initially was dedicated to the spirits of those who had perished in the struggles leading to the Meiji Restoration. In 1875, it was designated a special national shrine for invoking the spirits of those who had died for the country (*shōkon-sha*). From that year on, many national and private shōkon-sha were established, all enshrining the spirits of those who had died in war. In most schoolyards a memorial stone inscribed shōkon was erected to remind youth of the patriotic dead and the nobility of their sacrifice. Major festivals, entirely Shinto in character, were held at the national shrines at the equinoxes. Thus the war dead became the object of widespread veneration, which linked the imperial house and the people. The middle days of the equinoctial festivals, which had formerly been Buddhist festival days, were appropriated by the Meiji government and made into national holidays called Festivals to the Imperial Ancestors (*kōrei-sai*). On these occasions the emperor worshiped his own ancestors in the palace; in the schools these days began with the reading of the Imperial Rescript on Education and obeisance to the emperor's portrait. In the concluding section of this chapter we shall find that some extraordinary people who were not war dead have been made into gods rather than buddhas. But these are all exceptional cases, and the vast majority of Japanese simply become buddhas when they die. In some senses, then, hotoke has come to mean simply the spirit of the dead, and to say that a man has become a buddha is to say only that he has died. The household altar quite commonly contains no representation of a buddha, but only the memorial tablets for the ancestral dead of the house. Heads of neolocal houses frequently told me that they had no tablets yet because no one had died there; the expression they used was almost invariably the same—theirs was a new house with no new buddhas (*shin-botoke*). Does this mean that the Japanese identify their dead with the Buddhas themselves, or, as Dore (1958: 457) suggests, do they distinguish between hotoke (buddhas) and senzo (ancestors) on the one hand, and Hotoke (Buddhas) on the other? In Dore's view, one's grandfather, father, and son may be conceived of as "close-relative hotoke"; more remote kin are senzo, or "ancestral hotoke"; the Hotoke are Amida, Kannon, Shaka, Dainichi, and so forth. Armed with this postulated distinction, Dore asked the people in Shitayama-chō in Tokyo whether they felt there was a real differentiation. Fifty-one percent said that hotoke and Hotoke are different, the former being more intimate or the latter having a higher rank in some unspecified hierarchy; forty percent said that there is no difference between the two; six percent apparently had no idea what to say; and three percent were scornful of the whole business. Again, as in the case of the muen-botoke of Nagasawa, sharp differences in opinions on basic issues turned up within the confines of a small neighborhood.

Yanagita (1970: 107–10) rejects the claim that in the context of ancestor veneration hotoke means buddha at all. In a somewhat tortured argument he attempts to show that the term originally was *hotoki*, a word referring to the vessel for food offerings made to the spirits of the dead. Pointing out that in Japanese the word buddha is generally rendered *butsu*, and the word bodhisattva *bosatsu*, he suggests that because the same ritual vessel (hotoki) was used in making offerings to the Buddhas as well as to the souls of the dead, both became known by the word for the vessel, later transformed into hotoke and now misconstrued as the word for buddha. How can we believe that the spirits of the dead are thought to obtain buddhahood automatically, he asks, when there is an annual ceremony designed to help them enter paradise (Yanagita 1970: 112)? He may well be right concerning the etymology of the word, but I can detect nothing in ordinary usage today that reflects anything but the serene assumption that the dead of the family are all buddhas. Indeed, this attitude seems to follow from the doctrines of popular Buddhism in Japan. After all, Hōnen (1133–1212), founder of the Jōdo sect, taught that a single sincere utterance of the mantra *namu amida butsu* was sufficient to secure the intercession of the Amida Buddha on behalf of one's soul and deliver it into paradise. Shinran (1173–1263), founder of the Jōdo-shin sect, went even further in denying the necessity of both ascetic practices and the recitation of the mantra. According to him, salvation was gained through faith alone; thus all men, whatever their deeds in life, could become buddhas through faith. There can surely be few doctrines so infinitely merciful, and few so lethal to the concept of sin and to requirements for its expiation.

In this connection the question of karma and the cycle of rebirth arises once again. I am firmly convinced that the Japanese never fully assimilated these central concepts of Buddhism. Ooms (1967: 261) says that in a collection of hymns sung by a prayer group in Nagasawa, "the only reference to the doctrine of rebirth is a negative one expressing disbelief in it." Embree (1939: 261) found no evidence that the villagers of Suye believed in rebirth forty years ago. The ancestral dead are immutably the ascendants of the house and its protectors. They are not really thought of as ever being reborn, I think, in part because they need not be. For one thing, the Amida Buddha or another savior is thought to have delivered their souls into paradise; for another, the ancestral spirits collectively are the tutelary gods who are annually summoned back to the house and who eternally receive offerings from its living members. Furthermore, the most important consideration in the doctrine of karma is surely that the actions of this life determine the character of the next. There are few things so unlikely to the Japanese as the suggestion that one's own ancestor might be suffering the torments of hell for the misdeeds of life. Yet the Japanese are not entirely unfamiliar with the notion that there may be some relationship between the quality of a man's life and his fate after death. However, the notion is usually abstractly held, or may be phrased in such a way as to suggest that other people's ancestors may pay for their misdeeds, but not one's own.

Let me make one final observation here concerning the relationship between the ancestral spirits and the wandering spirits. Although it is true that the spirits of those who die violent deaths—victims of accident or murder, or suicides—are usually said to belong to the category of muen-botoke, some spirits that ordinarily would be in that category take their regular place as buddhas in the family altar. The decisive issue is the status of the person in life. Senior ascendants such as grandparents and parents who meet an untoward end are accorded normal treatment by the household and are not conceived of as joining the wandering spirits and hungry ghosts. The issue seems to be conceptualized as shown in Table 1.

The deceased, then, are usually called hotoke, but the word used to

TABLE 1
Type of Death and Fate of Soul

Type of death	Status	Fate of soul
Normal	Young[a]	A buddha (or a wandering spirit)
Abnormal	Young	A wandering spirit
Normal	Adult, unmarried[a]	A buddha (or a wandering spirit)
Abnormal	Adult, unmarried	A wandering spirit
Normal	Adult, married	A buddha
Abnormal	Adult, married[a]	A buddha (or a wandering spirit)
Normal	Senior	A buddha
Abnormal	Senior	A buddha

[a] Responses suggest some variation in these categories.

refer to ancestors, forebears, or forefathers is senzo. Although one may become a buddha by the mere fact of death, the process of becoming an ancestor is more complex (see Eder 1956, 1957) and has a time dimension. In Nagasawa, for example, the dead person becomes an ancestor only after a certain period of time has elapsed: for some this means after the last memorial service for him is held; for others the reckoning of ancestors goes back from their grandfather; still others "say that they do not include in the category of ancestors people whom they have known personally." Two instances will suffice to clarify the point:

Household A   1 ▲ ═╤═ ○ 2
                  3 △ ═ ○ 4

Household A was founded by 1. He died three years before Ooms interviewed 3, who said "since we are only the second generation, the ancestors of this house are the ones of the [main house]." The deceased household head is obviously still in the category of Dore's close-relative hotoke and not yet an ancestor. The second case makes the point in another way:

Household B   1 ▲ ═╤═ ○ 2
                  3 △ ═ ○ 4

In Household B, 4 volunteered that "since this year we had the last memorial service for the founder of the house, we now have an ancestor." The first five children of this woman had all died very young.

When asked if she thought this might have been a punishment inflicted on the house by some ancestor, she replied that that could not be so because the house had no ancestors when the children died (Ooms 1967: 248–50). Although it would be foolhardy to represent this or any other view as one universally held, it is faithful to materials collected in my own interviews.

The ancestors proper are not the spirits of people one has known intimately. Are they then gods? I think that they are, but of a special kind. Unlike other gods and spirits, the ancestors are thought to maintain an abiding concern for the continuity and prosperity of their house, for in many senses they retain full membership in it after death (see Plath 1964: 312). There is, in the most general sense, a regular process by which the spirits of the newly dead are transformed over time. This process can be represented as follows:

shirei	spirits of the newly dead
nī-botoke	new buddhas
hotoke	buddhas
senzo	ancestors
kami	gods

Outside this regular progression are the souls of the wandering dead, which are unattached or unconnected to any place of veneration.

Gods

Among the most fearful spirits in the Japanese world of the supernatural are the vengeful gods (goryō-shin, tatari-gami). I shall be concerned in the following pages chiefly with those who are deified humans worshiped by the living in an effort to ward off their potential for immense harm. Vengeful gods have long been the object of cults, which flourished from the eighth to the twelfth centuries in particular. During that period, no fewer than three systems of counter-magic were devised as ways to avert the evils that the vengeful gods might visit on the living (Dorson 1963: 19; Hori 1959b: 148–49). Worship was believed to be a means of pacifying them (Yanagita 1970: 122–24), and it was thought that with proper care in the form of rites and offerings they might prove a source of great fortune and luck, for it was clear that they could exert powerful influences over the affairs of this world. Spirits of fallen warriors and of others whose deaths were violent, tragic, or unnatural were ideal candidates for the status of vengeful gods. Unlike the ordinary dead, they have never seemed to merge with the generalized spirits, but have retained their individual identities except in cases where their great antiquity has rendered them anonymous as a kind of tutelary deity (Ōshima 1959: 96–97).

Perhaps the most famous of all goryō-shin in Japanese history is the spirit of Sugawara Michizane, a ninth-century nobleman and statesman who died in exile and disgrace in 903, the victim of plotting by the Fujiwara family (Sansom 1958: 215–16):

> Soon after he died in banishment . . . the Great Audience Hall . . . of the Palace was struck by lightning, and week after week the capital city was drenched by rainstorms and shaken by thunderbolts. More disasters followed, notably the violent death of prominent men and the constant outbreak of fires. These and other misfortunes continued for so long and were of such magnitude and frequency that they could be ascribed only to the vengeful spirit of Michizane. He was therefore restored to the office and rank which he had held in his lifetime, and all official documents bearing upon his sentence of exile were destroyed. Still the calamities continued, and members of the Fujiwara family anxiously caused masses to be said in the hope of removing the curse. At length in 942 an oracle was said to have decreed that a shrine should be erected, where Michizane was to be worshipped as a deity. This is the Kitano Temmangu, a shrine which soon become popular and where he has been prayed to by many generations of worshippers as Tenjin, the Heavenly Deity, a title conferred upon him by a royal decree of 986, which led to his being regarded as the god of learning, and especially of calligraphy.

The Kitano Temman-gū remains immensely popular to this day (see Ponsonby Fane 1964: 194–220), and the Tenjin Festival held annually in July is one of Osaka's major public events. Petitioners at the shrine ask for good health, protection from misfortune, and success in their studies, for Tenjin-sama is the patron of calligraphers and scholars. Summer festivals are common at shrines to gods of such origins, who are thought to offer protection against illness and epidemics in particular, whereas festivals at shrines dedicated to agricultural deities usually occur in spring and fall.

The practice of deifying humans other than those who become fearsome vengeful gods has occurred throughout Japanese history. The Meiji government sponsored the construction of many shrines, each dedicated to either a loyal subject or a member of the imperial line. But most

interesting of all, shrines were constructed for seven emperors whose
only common characteristic was that each had been in some measure
deprived of his rightful imperial prerogatives during his lifetime (Varley 1971: 155). This step was surely meant to confirm these emperors as
links in the unbroken line of succession, however irregular their reigns
may have been; it also strongly implies the continuation of the ancient
tradition of deifying those whose spirits might harbor a desire for revenge on the living.

As for the worship of beneficent humans, an interesting case is that
of Hippocrates, whose worship was taken up in the eighteenth century
by the families of Japanese physicians who had abandoned Chinese
medicine in favor of Western. Nothing could be more natural than their
adoption of the founder of Western medicine as their professional ancestor (Takayanagi 1972: 352), and picture scrolls of Hippocrates
(known from 1799 on) served as the object of veneration in the New
Year ceremonies for the ancestral spirits of these families of hereditary
physicians.

Throughout the Tokugawa period and into the present we can find
many instances where persons of no exalted position and whose spirits
have proved neither violent nor harmful have been deified after death
(Miyata 1963). These people may be called by the generic term living
gods (*ikigami*); interestingly, they were often not particularly holy or
even religiously inclined in life. They usually have been deified for one
of two reasons: either they have made some contribution to society, or
they have promised to assist the living if they are worshiped after death.

To the first category, for example, belong men who devise or perfect
irrigation systems or ponds. After death, these men are frequently apotheosized as *mizu-gami* (water gods). A case can be cited of a reservoir
builder in Ishikawa Prefecture who was worshiped as a popular Kannon.
District magistrates in Tokugawa times were occasionally deified when
they ameliorated the lot of the peasants during their administrations.
Such magistrates were often deified as millennial *yonaoshi kami sama*
(world-improving gods). At this level of popular deification we find
many instances strongly reminiscent of the worship of the vengeful gods.
For example, after the execution of the leader of a peasant uprising,
several harvests on Awaji Island were ruined by an insect that came to
be known by the dead man's name, Saizō. The *saizō-mushi* (Saizō insect)

disappeared completely after a stone image of Jizō was erected and an annual memorial service established for Saizō's spirit, which is still worshiped in the area as an agricultural deity (Miyata 1963: 4). The belief that harmful insects are sent by vengeful gods to damage crops has been widespread in Japan for centuries (Hirayama 1963: 69).

In 1784 a disgruntled warrior named Sano Masakoto assassinated the son of Tanuma Okitsugu, a government minister widely hated for his inflationary economic policies. Less than a year after Sano's execution the price of rice had dropped by half. Townsmen of all classes, associating Sano's bloody deed with the bettering of economic conditions, declared him to be a world-improving deity (*yonaoshi daimyōjin*) and huge crowds came to his grave with flowers and incense (J. W. Hall 1955: 133–35; Miyata 1963: 7). The deification of Sano owed nothing to official policy, and the practice of commoners according the status of living god and daimyōjin to heroes both living and dead persisted well into the Meiji period. In 1884, for example, Itagaki Taisuke, head of a liberal political party, was discomfited by the sentiments toward him revealed by the banners carried by participants in the Chichibu peasant rebellions, which read "Popular Rights—Itagaki Taisuke—daimyōjin—yonaoshi" (Scheiner 1973: 584).

To the second category belong those who vow before dying to help others if they will worship them. We could cite many well-known examples, among them that of the wife of a feudal lord who suffered all her life from severe toothaches. As she lay dying she swore that she would cure toothaches of anyone who venerated her spirit, and consequently she became the object of a popular cult. In the collection of tales called *Mimibukuro*, there is a story about a stone tablet to which people prayed for relief from hemorrhoids. A brewer's clerk who died after seven years of affliction with this malady had promised to help fellow sufferers who prayed to his spirit. Apparently the prayers produced effective cures, for his fame spread. Miyata (1963: 6) says that there is a small chapel to his memory in Awaji. There are great numbers of such local gods who are not tutelary deities in the sense of protecting a territorial unit, but who instead offer help to sufferers from an enormous variety of maladies. I have gone with friends to a shrine near Kyoto dedicated to a god believed to be especially effective in relieving or curing respiratory disorders. Although difficult of access, it is always a fairly busy place. Lest it be thought that this is a shadowy survival from Japan's past, patronized by the aged or ignorant, let me note that my friends—whose daughter is an asthmatic—are both college graduates, have lived outside Japan for some years, and reject all institutionalized religion as nonsense.

Living Gods and the New Religions

There is another, much more important way in which living gods are a part of contemporary Japanese religious life: this involves what are called the New Religions, whose founders, and many of whose present heads, are themselves living gods. Among the educated it is fashionable to deride these sects and their teachings, and to scorn their often colorful founders and leaders. Yet to millions of Japanese the New Religions offer comfort and security of a kind other religions in Japan no longer provide.

One of the most famous of these living gods is the foundress of Tenri-kyō, a sect that claimed two million adherents in 1970. Her spirit is treated as though she were still alive, and crowds of the faithful pay their respects at her quarters behind the main altar room of the head-quarters shrine. Another famous living god is the recently deceased foundress of Tenshō-kōtai-jingū-kyō, a sect that claimed 325,000 adherents in 1970. She was known to her followers as Ō-gami-sama (Great Goddess) during her lifetime, and is worshiped as a deity today. The story of her religious experiences is a very complicated one, but in 1945 she received at last the following explanation of the nature of the deity that had possessed her body (Anon. 1954: 56): "The male God Kotai-Jin, who descended into Your body on November 27 last year, and the Female God Amaterasu Meokami who descended on August 11, have united as one God, making Your body a temple, and thus forming the 'Trinity'!"

Kawate Bunjirō, apotheosized as the founder of the sect Konkō-kyō, which claimed about 500,000 adherents in 1970, was born in what is now Okayama Prefecture in 1814. His history is bound up with the god Ushitora-no-Konjin, the metal deity of the northeast who guards the demon gate (*kimon*), which lies in that direction. Konjin has been worshiped in Japan at least since the Heian period, and it is worth noting that the great complex of temples on Mt. Hiei, northeast of the Heian capital Kyoto, was placed there in part to guard the city from the evils originating in that direction. In the construction of dwellings it has been the practice until recently to avoid locating unclean things, such as the toilet, in the southwest or northeast corners (see Norbeck 1954: 124–25). Konjin is a very dangerous deity, quick to take offense and to mete out punishment to those who incur his displeasure. Furthermore, he is thought to revolve about the universe, so that it is essential before setting out on a journey to determine in what quarter he is located. This can be done by consulting an almanac or, in very special circumstances, a diviner. Should it prove that Konjin is in the direction of a planned trip, the traveler might well take a more circuitous route or postpone the journey until the signs are more auspicious.

Kawate remodeled his home in 1850, and although he took every precaution to avoid offending Konjin, the event appears to have precipitated disaster. Smallpox broke out in the community; there were deaths in his own family and his cattle died. He assumed that he was being punished for some offense against Konjin, but he could think of nothing he had left undone while the rebuilding was being planned and carried out. In 1855, Kawate himself fell victim to a severe throat infection. The date is significant because he was forty-two years old, an age the Japanese consider the most dangerous in a man's life. Konjin was responsible, for this time he made himself known directly by possessing Kawate's brother-in-law and speaking through him. Kawate immediately prayed to Konjin for forgiveness, and he recovered from his illness. Three years later the god once again possessed the brother-in-law and this time demanded that Kawate construct a god shelf for him. Kawate did so, and while at his devotions there was himself possessed by Konjin. By the end of 1858 he had been recognized as a living god by his disciples. Konjin ordered him to change his name first to Bunji daimyōjin, and then in 1859 to Konshi daimyōjin. Kawate died in 1883 without founding an organization of any sort. In 1885 his immediate followers organized the sect called Konkō-kyō, and in 1900 it was officially recognized by the government (Schneider 1962: 67–79). The deity worshiped is naturally Konjin, but known as Tenchi-kane-no-kami (the Heaven-and-Earth-Connecting Deity); Kawate Bunjirō, the founder, is worshiped as Ikigami-Konkō-Daijin.

The foundress of the sect Ōmoto, Deguchi Nao, was also possessed by Konjin. The principal deity of this sect, which in 1970 claimed 143,000 adherents, is a god named Kunitoko-tachi-no-kami, identified in dual Shinto as the Yakushi-nyorai, the healing Buddha (Cooper 1965: 307). Ōmoto places heavy emphasis on curing rituals, and the foundress is regarded as a living god with unlimited power to help the faithful.

The tradition of living gods, and the founding of religious groups by them, is by no means restricted to simple popular cult groups, although this is often the impression given by those who disapprove of both the founders and the cults. A case in point involves Kurozumi Munetada, born in 1780 in what is now Okayama Prefecture. The Kurozumi were hereditary Shinto priests (Hepner 1935: 56) and, like the great Fujiwara house, had taken as their ancestors of origin the Nakatomi, who claimed descent from the god Ame-no-koyane-no-mikoto. At the age of nineteen Munetada expressed the hope of becoming a living god. Both of his parents died suddenly when he was thirty-two, and Munetada, grief-stricken and feeling that he too was about to die, made a vow (in the form of the last words [*yuigon*] by which the Japanese set much store) to devote himself to the curing of diseases "when I die and become a god" (Hepner 1935: 61). He recovered, and in 1814, while at his morning prayers to the sun, he suddenly felt a oneness with Amaterasu, the Sun Goddess. Before he died in 1850 he founded what is now called Kurozumi-kyō, a sect that claimed some 400,000 followers in 1970. His popularity was great, and he received posthumous recognition of a very high order: in 1856 he was awarded the title daimyōjin by the Head of the Department of Shinto Affairs in Kyoto; in 1862 he was enshrined as Munetada daimyōjin at Kaguraoka in Kyoto, a *choku-gan-sho* (place for offering imperial prayers); and in 1866 he was granted court rank by the emperor (Hepner 1935: 88).

These cases of the deification of harmful spirits and the recognition of living gods should make it clear that there is no sharp dividing line between the human and the divine in Japan. All beings may be thought of as gods or as potential gods, although it is generally the extraordinary who are apotheosized. Among the founders of the New Religions, some have been deified in life and others after death. Most have been men and women of lowly origin, and perhaps it has been their very humanness that has made them so appealing to their followers. Like the sufferers from toothaches and hemorrhoids, they have all led ordinary lives, have been beset by mundane troubles, and have understood the lot of the common man. Having suffered, all the sect founders are credited with the ability to help others transcend their suffering. With the passage of time, individual personalities have often faded from the memory of the living, yet memorial stones and places of worship remain throughout Japan dedicated to gods of unknown origin whose powers are widely believed in and who are worshiped by persons from all levels of society.

Where Do the Spirits of the Dead Reside?

It might seem simple enough to determine where the spirits of the dead are thought to go, but this is far from the case. Certainly those of the recently deceased are believed to hover nearby, loath to leave the body at first, then attached to the grave and the temporary memorial tablet, and at last attached to the permanent tablet. In some respects the tablet is treated as though the spirit inheres in it, as we shall see in Chapters 3 and 4. During our tablet census in Takane, when people lifted the tablets out of the altar and carried them into the daylight many said "My! The ancestors must be surprised!" But of course the spirits are also thought to be somewhere away from both house and grave, for they are called back to the house and sent away again at bon. In many areas they are called down from the mountain and sent back to the sea. There exists also the notion of a paradise into which the soul is conducted through the infinite mercy of the compassionate Buddha. Better yet, it may be that a person's soul goes to the afterworld in which he believed in life (Embree 1939: 262), so that the Jōdo-shin adherent's soul goes to Amida's paradise, the Zen adherent's to another paradise, and the Shintoist's to the village shrine. And there is a hell to which some souls are condemned to suffer the peculiar horrors of punishments made to fit the person's crime: the glutton gorges himself in a doomed effort to achieve satiety; the erotomaniac suffers in ways that would have appalled de Sade; the slanderer's tongue is ceaselessly cut to ribbons, restored, and lacerated again; on the shoulders of the backbiter there rides a demon that rends and tears at him in a hideously literal form of retribution.

There can be no doubt that one of the oldest and most widespread beliefs as to the final destination of the soul is that it resides in the mountains (Earhart 1970: 107; Hori 1963, 1966; Mogami 1959). All over the Japanese islands there are mountains and high plateaus that are believed to be the abode of spirits. One of the best known is Mt. Osore in Aomori Prefecture, a place where people go at bon and on other occasions to comfort the collectivity of spirits there, or to make special offerings to the newly dead. It is thought that the living and the dead can meet in such spots, often through the efforts of a medium.

Another of these places is Morinoyama in Yamagata Prefecture (see Tsuyuki 1967). There are several legends about the origin of the practice of offering comfort to the spirits of the dead on this mountain— a practice that has been known for at least two hundred years. One legend relates that a priest who was reciting sutras on Mt. Kimpō heard moaning sounds and a voice reciting sutras from the direction of Morinoyama. He headed there at once—toward the west—and found the wandering spirit of his own mother, whom he had thought to be in paradise. Horrified, he determined that a great segaki-e should be held on the mountain on the twenty-fourth day of the seventh month for the repose of both her spirit and all the other wandering spirits. (The parallels with the story of how food came to be offered on behalf of the wandering spirits are obvious.) A second legend has it that in the Kamakura period, after a great battle, the women and children of the slaughtered warriors fled to the mountain to pray for the souls of their dead. And still a third story relates that because in the Sengoku period (1467–1568) the plain below the mountain was frequently flooded, the spirits of the drowned, or alternatively the spirits of the survivors who died on the mountain, were the original objects of the offerings. In any event, the place is thought to be so filled with the spirits of the dead that it is too dangerous to be opened to visitors except at the great segaki rite, which in recent years has been held on August 22 and 23.

Morinoyama has three ridges, on which are located small chapels (*dō*), most of them connected with the Sōtō sect of Zen. Until World War II there was a priest at each chapel when the mountain was open, but by the 1960's there were few to be seen. Early on the morning of August 22 each year, people carry offerings of glutinous rice cake and rice mixed with red beans—foods that are prepared for auspicious festive occasions—to the mountain. From a priest at one of the chapels they purchase either a five-colored paper representing the nyorai or a piece of plain wood, asking him to write on it the posthumous name and date of death of the deceased who is to be the object of the offerings. The papers or wood pieces are then taken to the permanent memorial marker erected by each of the hamlets from which the pilgrims have come, and there the food is offered and incense is burned. In front of each chapel is a segaki altar where offerings are also made, and rice is scattered along the paths for the wandering spirits to eat. The area around the memorial marker is also littered with another kind of offering. Before coming to the mountain some people consult a medium to discover what task the spirit of the dead is engaged in, and they bring along an appropriate item to render the work less burdensome—brooms, cleaning rags, and so on.

The three ridges are thought to be the dwelling places of three different categories of spirits. On the lowest ridge is a chapel for the souls of children; on the middle ridge is one for the spirits of adults; on the third is a place called *fuji-baka* (wisteria grave), which is not a chapel but where it is said that one may comfort those who have died a "hard death" or committed suicide. The first two, which are chapels under the supervision of the Sōtō Zen temple, face east to Mt. Kimpō, and it is said that the souls prayed for at these two places eventually go there. But the wisteria grave is said to be a secondary burial spot for bones of the dead; it is under the supervision of the Jōdo-shin sect and faces west toward the Pure Land, the paradise where the spirits prayed for at the wisteria grave are believed eventually to go. There is reason to think that the beliefs about the souls of the third ridge represent a special way of quieting the spirits of those who have met abnormal deaths and of speeding their way out of the world of the living into paradise. Mt. Kimpō itself may have been a sacred place from pre-Buddhist times; at any rate, it has long been a stronghold of mediums and practitioners of *shugendō*, one of the medieval systems of esoteric magic practices specifically devoted to the handling of vengeful gods.

Although places like Morinoyama are rapidly losing their hold on the popular imagination, some evidence nonetheless exists in our interviews to show concern for the destination of the soul. Some people made it clear, for example, that they thought it a poor practice to make copies of a memorial tablet. The principal objection was usually made in some form such as this: "If there are two tablets, the spirit does not know where it belongs and might become confused, wandering between the two." However, most people saw no problem at all. Indeed, it is the custom in some areas for all sons or all children to receive a copy of their parents' tablets; in the Sōtō sect, it is customary to make two copies of each tablet, one for the domestic altar and one for the temple. Dore (1958: 458) was told that it was not uncommon in families of the warrior class for the wife to have her parents' tablets in the altar of the house into which she has married. Usually these would be copies, the original tablets being kept in her natal house.

Is the spirit fixed in one place, then, or does it wander? In general, it seems not only desirable but essential for the spirit to be properly settled somewhere. It may be in or near the house, the grave, the tablet, or the altar, or it may be in the mountains or out at sea; but wherever it is, is important for the living to know where to summon it from and where to dispatch it to as the occasion demands. It is the unsettled, wandering spirit that is threatening, and it is to the end of fixing the spirits— whether in a tablet, an altar, or a shrine—that many rituals are performed and offerings made (see Singer 1973: 50). For all the apparent ambiguities of the formulation, one of the chief concerns of the survivors is invariant: to see to it that no spirit is cut off from normal intercourse with the living members of his household. Perhaps the most common explanation offered by those who hold a tablet for a person who ordinarily would not be found in their altars is that "he had no other place to go," or that "there is no other place where he will be cared for."

This discussion will be continued in Chapter 6, but at this point I want to suggest that the importance of proper place extends to comprehend both the living and the spirits of the dead. The Japanese are uneasy in the presence of any suggestion of irregularity in human relationships, and they seek to avoid it in the world of the spirits as well. Nevertheless, there remains an intriguing ambiguity with respect to the destination of the spirit after death, an ambiguity that Plath (1964: 308) describes well: "The world beyond cannot be described in any but equivocal phrases. Spatially it is both here and there, temporally both then and now. The departed and ancestors always are close by; they can be contacted immediately at the household shelf, the graveyard, or elsewhere. Yet when they return 'there' after the midsummer reunion they are seen off as for a great journey. They are perpetually present. Yet they come to and go from periodic household foregatherings." Certainly few people I interviewed were at all concerned with what we would surely see as contradictions among the many beliefs and practices relating to the locus of the spirit of the deceased. After a man dies, his spirit lingers near his body and then near his house for seven days, or perhaps forty-nine days, until his memorial tablet is put up with those of the older ancestral dead; these ancestral dead are in the mountains and in paradise, where they are joined by the spirit of the newly dead only after its first bon following death; at bon the living go to the mountains or to the graveyard to meet the ancestral spirits and escort them back to the house; at the end of bon the living send the spirits back until the following year, usually by floating boats bearing lighted lanterns onto the river or out to sea. For all that, daily offerings are made to the tablets in the household altar; the tablets are among the first objects likely to be removed from a burning building; and one may converse with a given ancestor at any time simply by addressing his tablet or by going to his grave and speaking to his spirit there.

Then is the spirit in the tablet and elsewhere as well? Does its location change with ceremonial context? Is the spirit merely where it is said to be at any given time, or does the question involve the intensity of contact? Certainly the world of the spirits is more immanent at bon than at any other time of the year. Is it only that the spirits' presence is more deeply felt then? Or is it that they are always present individually in the tablets and collectively at bon? This is, after all, the occasion when the spirit of the newly dead is elevated to the realm of the collective spirits, with whom it returns at the end of the festival.

Are the tablets primarily objects that both stand for the spirits and constitute the means whereby they can be summoned? Ordinarily the altar doors are kept closed. When the living wish to communicate with the ancestors, a number of ritual steps are taken to activate the tablets. The altar doors are opened, and on formal occasions incense and candles are lighted, food is offered, and deference is made. Is it only then that the spirits are actually present? In that case it might be that the tablets are not so much sacred objects in which the spirit inheres but objects into which it may enter and through which it may be summoned. When the report, petition, or rite is completed, the offerings removed, and the doors closed with a final bow, are the spirits no longer in the tablets or the house? This surely cannot be the case, for if the ancestors are in the most general terms thought of as protectors, they are likely to be thought of as being nearby.

It is tempting to pursue this matter further, but the enterprise is very likely too mechanical, reflecting the typical failure of the foreigner to understand what is going on. There is a lovely passage in the novel *Bodaiju* (*The Buddha Tree*) by Niwa Fumio (1966: 136) that reveals something of the character of the relationship between the living and the dead. The priest Soshu from the Butsuoji goes to a farmhouse for the monthly services and finds no one at home but a small child.

> The offering had been left on the altar by the flower vase, for Soshu to take. It was wrapped in plain white paper, without the usual inscription. The Izutas had expected Soshu would come while they were at work in the fields; and for them work was a greater necessity than being present for the sutras. Their absence did not imply any lack of respect for the monthly service—it was merely a custom, which their ancestors, who knew the importance of work, would understand. After changing the flowers on the altar, they had gone to the fields that morning comforted by the knowledge that the priest from Butsuoji would come and read the sutras before the family shrine while they were away.

Soshu, all alone, conducts the service, takes up the offering, and as he leaves says "Thank you." "Looking back at the empty room, Soshu spoke softly—greeting not the living but the dead; the unseen presences that now watched the priest of Butsuoji leave their home."

Three. *Caring for the Dead*

The death of a person sets in motion a series of rites and ceremonies that culminates in the observance of a final memorial service, most commonly on the thirty-third or fiftieth anniversary of death. Between a person's last breath and the final prayers said on his behalf, his spirit is ritually and symbolically purified and elevated; it passes gradually from the stage of immediate association with the corpse, which is thought to be both dangerous and polluting, to the moment when it loses its individual identity and enters the realm of the generalized ancestral spirits, essentially purified and benign. Ooms has described this transformation (1967: 319):

> The ancestor cult creates order in the passing of time as experienced in the household. It gives order to the inevitable fact of death and by the same token orders life: everybody is destined to become an ancestor. The order is structured as a process where the stages leading to this final purpose of life are outlined (memorial services, steps on the path to ancestorhood). Everybody finds himself in due time on the appropriate stage. The shift from one stage to the next and the acquisition of this new status are not the result of individual endeavor or personal achievement of the subject himself. The outsiders have a certain power over him, because it is thanks to their loyalty that one can become an ancestor. But their power of intervention is limited; the order is fixed and only when the time is ripe will the change occur almost as the result of a natural growth.

An outstanding feature of the ceremonies for the dead is that from start to finish they are primarily the responsibility of the household and its members, for all of whom, regardless of sex and of age at death, these same devotions will be performed in some degree. Indeed, the longer the time since a person's death, the more likely that only household members will look after his spirit. Many people will attend the funeral; fewer will attend the rites of the forty-ninth day; and the number will dwindle over the years as the memorial services are marked. The priest, too, has less and less to do with rites for the deceased as time passes. It can be said without exaggeration that the household members alone, through their observance of the rites, prevent the ancestors from becoming wandering spirits (Ooms 1967: 257–58). Some rites involve all the members of the house, others only the household head and his wife; still others may be performed by any individual who wishes to approach the ancestors.

In this chapter I will set forth in the most general terms a paradigm of the interactive worlds of the living and the dead. For every observance, belief, and practice entered in this paradigm, Japanese folklorists and ethnologists provide a myriad of local variations. Nonetheless, all these variations conform to a general pattern that reflects (with rare exceptions) a commonality of attitude and belief throughout the country. (For a discussion of the countless regional variations in details of funeral, burial, and memorial customs see Anon. 1971; Gabriel 1938; Inoguchi 1959; and Norbeck 1954: 188–94.) Where the variants occasionally provide a striking illumination of a particular point, or where they appear to offer evidence for a contrary view, they will be discussed for the light they shed on the historical and social contexts of ancestor worship.

Even within the same small district, and sometimes within the same hamlet, different ways of dealing with these concerns have been developed. Although some of this variability can be attributed directly to sectarian Buddhist doctrine, by no means all of it derives from this source. In this connection a priest of the Nichiren sect told me that he had faced an unexpected dilemma while serving an immigrant Japanese population overseas. Like most priests, he had learned to conduct the orthodox funeral rites of his sect, but in arranging funerals with his parishioners he often found that local customs of the regions from which they came had to be accommodated. Early on he protested what he considered to be unorthodox practices, but he gave in as he became more experienced. "I had never dreamed that local customs could be so divergent. Yet here were people telling me that in their village such and such was always done this way or that. They even reminded me that their families had been adherents of Nichiren temples for generations, implying that they were right and I wrong. So now I usually go over the funeral procedures with some older person in the family so that no one will be upset."

The problems of the priest are further complicated by the rather minor role he plays in the funeral—a role that is usually confined to the recitation of sutras whose words no one can understand (Embree 1939: 217). The principal actors in the funeral rites are the household members, although the meaning of most of the rituals is unknown to them (Embree 1939: 262). It is they who light the incense, carry the memorial tablet in the procession, and gather up the bones and ashes after the cremation. All direct participants in the funeral ceremony are thereby exposed to pollution, whereas the priest, essentially a bystander, is not. Not only are household members central to the funeral rites, they are also the chief officiants at the household altar, where the memorial services are held. In some important senses, then, rites for the dead have never been exclusively the province of the temple and the priesthood (see Hirayama 1959: 45).

Whatever the details of custom, the general outline and intent of the practices are clear enough. During the first forty-nine days after death, steps are taken both to separate the spirit of the newly dead from its association with the corpse and to free it from its attachment to the world of the living. To achieve these ends the survivors undertake first to confuse the spirit. The coffin may be carried in a circle around the room of the house where it has rested and only then be borne outside for the funeral procession. The mourners may return from the grave by a route other than that taken by the procession. The path of the cortege may be swept clean in order to obliterate the footprints of the mourners and prevent the spirit from using them to find its way back home. The funeral service itself ends in the symbolic separation of the corpse or ashes and the spirit: a temporary memorial tablet representing the spirit is taken away from the cemetery and serves as the object of veneration during the first forty-nine days.

Now what are we to make of the apparent contradiction that after seeking to make certain that the spirit cannot follow the procession back from the grave, the tablet representing that spirit is carried back to the house from the funeral ceremony? I asked several people about this, and their replies may be grouped roughly into two categories. In the first category, the larger of the two, no contradiction is seen, nor any rationale offered; both things are done and that is all there is to it. The other set of replies also sees no contradiction, but would have it that the efforts to confuse the spirit aim at preventing its returning to the wrong house, which is why the table is carried back from the grave directly to the deceased's household. There the spirit will be sure to be in the place where all the proper observances will be held so that it can rest peacefully.

Whatever the case, a succession of rites is then performed whose chief aim is to transform the spirit of the dead (shirei) to the status of an ancestral spirit (sorei). The temporary tablet is first set on a low table in front of, but not within, the altar, and it is often accompanied by a photograph of the deceased, candles, an incense burner, and a bell or gong. On the forty-ninth day in most instances, but in some cases as late as on the third anniversary of death (*Minzokugaku kenkyū sho* 1952b: 39), the temporary tablet is disposed of and the photograph put away. A permanent tablet, inscribed with the deceased's posthumous name, is placed with the others already in the altar, to be separated from them only once when it is singled out for special treatment at the first bon. On that occasion the tablet will be placed on its own altar in the main room of the house and will be the object of far more elaborate offerings than are made to the other tablets. It is obvious that the special bon altar for the newly dead is constructed "to keep the observance for purified souls of distant ancestors from contamination with mourning for the newly dead" (Yanagita 1970: 116–17). In many areas special boats of straw or paper are made to send off these new buddhas at the end of their first bon. The boats have sails bearing the words "paradise boat" (*gokuraku-maru, jōdo-maru*), and sometimes they contain a small altar bearing the mantric inscription *namu amida butsu*, the invocation to the Amida Buddha on behalf of the souls of the dead (Hashimoto 1962: 19). With the conclusion of the rites of the first bon, the spirit is thought to have begun the long process of becoming an ancestral spirit. Over the years, on occasions marked by successive memorial rites, the dead person becomes more and more remote and fades from the memories of family members. At length, the final services are held for the individual ancestral spirit, which thereupon passes from the ranks of the household dead into a larger collectivity.

All of the preceding materials deal with Buddhist households, for only a very small minority of households in Japan profess a family religion exclusively Shinto in character. It is generally assumed and often claimed by Shintoists that their domestic rites represent the preservation of ancient tradition unsullied by the centuries of Buddhist influence on Japanese religious life. In fact, the practices of the majority of them are unlikely to go back any further than the middle of the seventeenth century, and most of these families have been Shintoists only since the Meiji Restoration.

Their origins reflect a variety of circumstances (see Dore 1958: 458). Some are the houses of Shinto priests. Others are households native to such old fiefs as Aizu (now Miyagi Prefecture), Mito (now Ibaragi Prefecture), and Bizen (now Okayama Prefecture), where the influence of the nativist scholars was sufficiently strong to cause the domain lords to order households to be registered at shrines rather than at temples after the promulgation of the anti-Christian edicts of the Tokugawa period. Many of the households in these areas have remained Shinto since that time. Still other Shinto households are found among those native to provinces where the feudal lords (who for a short time after the Meiji Restoration were made governors of the newly created prefectures), in their initial enthusiasm for the Shinto revival, ordered the entire population to adopt Shinto rites. Many such households subsequently reverted to their former Buddhist affiliations, but some did not. There are households scattered throughout the country whose heads were persuaded by the new official ideology of the early Meiji period to abandon their temples in favor of shrine affiliation. In an entirely different category, there are some communities, such as that reported by Yoshida (1967), in which there has never been a Buddhist temple. And lastly, there are millions of households that belong to one or another of such predominantly Shinto-oriented New Religions as Tenri-kyō, Ōmoto, and Kurozumi-kyō.

There can be little doubt that the Shinto funeral service is late-nineteenth-century in origin. Writing at that time, Chamberlain (1898:

178–79) observed that only recently had the Shintoists been allowed to bury their own dead; up to then even Shinto priests had been given Buddhist funerals. In fact it is not really necessary for a Shinto priest to be present at a funeral, for the chief mourner among the kinsmen serves as chief officiant at the rites.

Most Japanese feel rather strongly that a Shinto priest has no place in any context touching on death, and many of the people we talked to about these matters find the whole notion of Shinto funeral rites a contradiction in terms. Nevertheless, the Shintoists have their own style of memorial tablet called *mitama-shiro* (spirit substitute), which is made of unlacquered wood with the posthumous name written on it in india ink. These tablets are kept on a spirit shelf (*mitama-dana*) or in a spirit house (*mitama-ya*), which is shaped rather like a miniature shrine or god shelf and is also made of untreated wood. The equivalent of the Buddhist forty-nine days of mourning is a period of five tenth-day rites culminating on the fiftieth day after death (see Dore 1958: 457). And of course, according to Shinto the dead person's spirit becomes a god immediately and never a buddha. At the memorial services the tablet is placed in the front of the altar at a slightly lower level than the other tablets and is venerated there (Yanagita 1970: 97–98). Yanagita thinks that all of these practices, like the funerals, are quite recent in origin; it is clear that for the most part the Shinto rites are modeled after the Buddhist ones (see Lay 1891; Reitz 1939).

Graves

The only kind of grave most Japanese today are familiar with is the type marked by a stone bearing the family name and having a niche in the back for depositing the small urns containing each person's ashes. The names of the persons are usually inscribed on the side or back of the stone. During the past century the custom of erecting a separate stone for each individual has gained some popularity, but it is still far from the rule. The family grave, then, is where visits are made and where prayers are said for the soul, and the grave is cleaned at the equinoxes and at bon. In short, the place of interment is also the place of ritual. Ordinarily one offers flowers and incense and pours water over the stone. This last gesture of purification has lost its meaning for most people, as has so much else in the funeral rites. Osaragi Jirō opens his novel *Tabiji* (*The Journey*) with a scene at a cemetery where a young woman is visiting the grave of her cousin, who was killed in World War II (1960: 6): "She filled the flower vase with water, and what was left she poured over the gravestone. She wasn't quite sure why she did so, but vaguely she remembered that it was customary when visiting a grave to sprinkle it with water."

The ritual grave site and the place of interment have not always been identical, nor have the implications of ritual always been so dimly appreciated. The folklorists have taken a particular interest in what may for convenience be called the double-grave system (*ryō-bosei*). Concentrated especially in the Kinki region, according to Mogami (1959, 1963), and in Kantō and Chūgoku, according to Hori (1959a: 405), the double grave is of great interest, highlighting as it does many central concepts and attitudes bearing on death and the spirits of the dead. I am concerned here not with the debate about the antiquity of the practice, but with the larger implications of this system for our understanding of ideas of pollution and purification in funeral rites. Mogami's surveys of these double-grave practices afford a useful starting point. There are two graves for a given individual. The corpse is actually interred in one, which is called by a variety of terms I shall translate as "burial grave." The other is marked only by a gravestone and is called the "ritual grave." The burial grave, usually located in some remote or isolated spot in the mountains, or along a steep river bank, often has no markers at all and is sometimes completely untended. Only family members go there in some regions, and then only for the funeral. The ritual grave is marked by a single family stone, and is ordinarily either in a cemetery attached to a temple or in a small plot near the house. This is the grave visited by friends and acquaintances and by the family after their first and only visit to the burial grave. It is the ritual grave that is cleaned on ceremonial occasions.

Mogami identifies three types within the double-grave system. In the first, visits to the burial grave are limited to the funeral or to the first forty-nine days of mourning. No further visits are made there and all subsequent activities occur at the ritual grave. In the second, the burial grave is visited throughout the mourning period and at the equinoxes and bon. And in the third, the two grave sites are treated in exactly the same way and are called by a single term. In Mogami's opinion, this list of types represents a historical progression that indicates a deterioration of the practice. However this may be, there seems to me no question that the practice of cremation, which was not really widespread until recent times, has done much to alter the circumstances that led to the development of the double-grave system in the first place.

We do have accounts of how the system once operated (Satō 1964). A family named Yanō in Usa County, Oita Prefecture, in northern Kyushu, holds records dating back to the Kamakura period. Since that early time they have been affiliated in ritual roles with the Tsumagaki-sha, a subsidiary of the great Usa Hachiman shrine. Near their house are several large stone memorial tablets, some of them natural rocks, and a statue of the Buddhist deity Jizō. The stone tablets are called *ran-tōba*, a term used only by this family. They also apply the term to the memorial stones at the gate of the Sōtō Zen temple that until the nineteenth-century separation of Shinto and Buddhism was the shrine-temple (*jingū-ji*) of Usa Hachiman, the War God. The Yanō family stones bear dates from the early part of the seventeenth century. According to family tradition, until the middle of the Tokugawa period (about 1750) they had a burial grave in a remote place in the hills, but the exact spot is no longer known. The memorial stones, they say, are their ritual grave. Their ritual roles at the Shinto shrine prevented them from visiting the place where the corpses were actually buried because of the pollution, so they worshiped their ancestors at these memorial stones, which, lacking all taint of contact with the dead, were ritually pure. It was only at the ran-tōba, then, that this Shinto priestly family could pray to its ancestral dead without fear of offending the god they served.

This clear separation of ritual universes is carried even further in this area of Kyushu, where there are a great many temples with long-standing connections with the Usa Hachiman shrine and its subsidiaries. On the fiftieth anniversary of death, for example, it is said locally that "the buddha becomes a god" (*hotoke wa kami ni nari*), and the memorial tablet is taken from the altar and placed on the grave. Then a branch is cut from a living tree, and a flat area is cut on its surface. The post-humous name is written on the flat area in ink, and the branch is stuck upright in the earth with the green leaves still attached. It is called a living stupa (*iki-sotōba*), and it greatly resembles the Shinto device by which the gods descend to earth and return to heaven.

Takeda (1961: 102–5) also devotes considerable attention to the double-grave system and the distinction it implies between the spirits of the dead, on the one hand, and the ancestral spirits, on the other. In Fukui and Hyōgo prefectures family members stop visiting the burial grave soon after the funeral. The local term for the burial grave is *sute-baka* (*suteru* is the verb meaning to throw out, cast away, discard, or abandon). The ritual grave, the place where the spirits are venerated, often contains nothing but old and sometimes illegible memorial stones, yet it nonetheless seems to serve satisfactorily as a place of worship for all. The chief implication of the double-grave system here, Takeda finds, is that the deceased cannot be allowed to retain his individuality for long; and one effect of holding rites at the ritual grave is to merge the spirit of the recently deceased with those of the generalized ancestors. Thus Takeda suggests that the burial grave is the ceremonial ground for the spirits of the dead, the ritual grave the ceremonial ground for the spirits of the ancestors.

The separation of grave sites occasionally takes on idiosyncratic variations. An excellent example is the case of the great nativist scholar Motoori Norinaga. Norinaga's family were devout adherents of the Jōdo sect of Buddhism, and despite his own intense preoccupation with the native Shinto tradition it is clear from his diary that he punctiliously observed the ancestral rites on the third, seventh, thirteenth, seventeenth, twenty-third, thirty-third, thirty-seventh, and fiftieth anniversaries of death, and even on the hundredth, hundred-fiftieth, and two-hundredth anniversaries in the case of the remote ancestors. His own devotions were directed toward both the gods and the buddhas, as an entry in his diary for 1748 reveals. What is of chief interest to us is the testament he left setting forth in detail his wishes for his own funeral, burial, and memorial services (Matsumoto 1970: 167–76). It is an excellent example of many of the attitudes dealt with throughout this book. In reading the following summary of it, keep in mind that Norinaga is the most highly regarded of all the nativist scholars and is credited with a major role in the revival of the pure Japanese tradition.

His first request was that his funeral service be held at the family's Jōdo temple. The priest of that temple was to recite the sutras at the household altar in which Norinaga's tablet and that of his wife would be placed. (If she was still living, the characters for her name were to be filled in with red ink.) He had already written out the posthumous names to be used for both of them, and he requested that they also be carved on the gravestone in the temple cemetery. But his interment was actually to take place at a different Jōdo temple, one that his family had some connection with also, at a spot he had always loved for its beauty. He directed his followers to take his body there secretly at night to avoid any trouble with the authorities over this unorthodox plan. Thus he was to have two graves. The "proper" one, in accordance with the customary observances of Jōdo piety, would be located at his family's temple near the graves of his ancestors and would bear his real and posthumous names. It was here that he asked that the monthly grave visits be directed. But should any stranger ask after his grave, he was to be directed to the other temple. This second and clearly more personal grave would be marked by a stone bearing only the legend "Grave of Motoori Norinaga" and by a cherry tree. It was here that his annual deathday rites were to be performed.

Furthermore, he specified the details of the annual observance his friends and disciples were to carry out at his study, the Suzunoya. He asked that his self-portrait be hung and his desk set out. There should be flowers of the season and a lighted lamp, but no incense. A meal, including fish and sake, should be served to those gathered for the occasion, who were then to spend the evening composing poems. The memorial tablet to be set out at the Suzunoya for these occasions was not a Buddhist one but Norinaga's own cherry-wood *shaku*, a tablet carried by Shinto priests and the nobility during ceremonies and considered the vehicle for the descent of the gods. On this tablet was to be inscribed his posthumous name, *akitsuki hito mizu sakura ne no ushi* (a Japanese man, the root of a beautiful cherry tree). The name contains no Chinese or Buddhist words.

Memorial Tablets and Posthumous Names

The origin of memorial tablets (*ihai*) in Japan is uncertain. They take many forms, varying by period, region, and sect of Buddhism. Two possibilities for their origin are suggested by the compilers of the *Bukkyō dai jiten* (1960: 168–69): one is that they are Confucian, deriving from the wooden tablets on which the Chinese write the names and ranks of generations of ascendants (see Shioiri 1965: 588); the other, which seems far less likely, is that they may be related to the shaku, the flat tablet through which the Shinto gods descend from heaven. Let me note in passing that here we have in microcosm the inevitable polarization of interpretation between the "continentalists" and the "nativists"; their disagreement on the origins of almost all Japanese practices and beliefs is total.

Memorial tablets appear to date from the Kamakura period when Buddhist funerals were becoming common (see *Minzokugaku kenkyū sho* 1952b: 39). The redoubtable Dr. Kaempfer, who was surgeon to the Dutch East India Company in Japan from 1690 to 1692, reports on ancestor worship and offers two drawings of very elaborate tablets. Both the descriptions of the rites and the drawings are to be found, interestingly enough, in his chapter on Japanese Confucianism (Kaempfer 1906: II, 68–69):

> Admitting no Gods, they have no temples, no forms of worship. Thus far however they conform themselves to the general custom of the Country, in that they celebrate the memory of their deceased parents and relations, which is done by putting all sorts of victuals, raw and dressed, on a Biosju, as they call it, or table purposely made with this view, by burning candles before them, by bowing down to the ground as if they were yet alive, by monthly or anniversary dinners, whereto are invited the deceased's family and friends, who appear all in the best cloth, and wash and clean themselves by way of preparation for three days before, during which time they abstain from lying with their wives, and from all impure things, and by many other tokens of respect and gratitude.

Although I have seen no tablets of the type shown in Kaempfer's illustrations, there are many old ones in contemporary household altars very different from those generally in use today. The date of death indicated on the tablet is itself no clue to its real age, for tablets lost in fires or floods will often be remade. But I did see many from the nineteenth century and earlier, primarily in rural areas, that are three or four times the size of the standard tablets of today and made of unlacquered wood with the inscription in india ink rather than carved into the surface and filled with gold. Some of them are obviously handmade, and on many the writing is illegible from having been darkened with age and the smoke of incense.

Contemporary tablets usually take one of two forms, the more common being an upright wooden plaque lacquered all over in black or gold and standing on a flat base. The overall height ranges from four to six inches. They can be purchased either in shops that specialize in Buddhist paraphernalia or in temples. The alternative form, which appears to have been gaining favor over the past decades, is called *kuri-ihai*. These are thin strips of unlacquered wood that are held upright in an open-faced container shaped very much like a miniature altar and decorated in the same way. These strips can be stored in any order, and the one with the name of the individual whose deathday is being observed is moved to the front of the container where only it is visible. All the information appearing on an ordinary tablet can be written on this kind as well. The kuri-ihai are much favored by households with so many tablets that they can no longer accommodate them, by persons unwilling to bear the expense of having separate tablets made, and by households that have moved or lost their tablets and have taken the opportunity to consolidate their holdings. A recent and even less expensive variation provides a similar container, but in place of the strips of wood a small brocade-bound book, rather like the traditional Book of the Past (*kakochō*) that was kept in the altar and contained all the names of the deceased members of the family (Takenaka 1955b). These small books, like Catholic devotional calendars, come with printed entries showing the deathdays of many famous figures in Japanese Buddhism as well as of many historical personages.

The kakochō themselves come in different forms. The oldest one known dates from 1295, in the Kamakura period. They are doubtless of Chinese origin, but seem now to be found only in Japan. Some simply list the days and months of the year, making no reference to the year itself. These are found mostly in temples and serve as annual deathday guides: under the date, say November 3, will be listed the names of all parishioners whose deathday it is. Another form of the Book of the Past lists only the days of the month, but neither months nor years. Under the day, say the third, will be found all the names of those whose deathday it is; it is a monthly deathday guide. The kakochō enable the temples to keep records of deaths in parishioner families and help the priest to remind people of approaching anniversaries that ought to be observed by a memorial service. In some temples individual households maintain their own kakochō focusing on the family descent line, but in general the whole system has gradually fallen into disuse. I found almost no up-to-date Books of the Past in family altars, certainly, and most people were only dimly aware that they were kept by the temples.

To return to the tablets proper, for the funeral a temporary one is made of paper or unlacquered wood and carried in the procession behind the coffin of the deceased. In some parts of the country two such temporary tablets are made; one is left atop the grave, and the other is carried back to the house. Eventually both will be disposed of on the forty-ninth day of mourning and replaced by two permanent ones, one for the household altar and one for the temple. Isaac Titsingh (ca. 1740–1812) has left us a translation from a "Chinese book"—collected on one of his three trips to Japan between 1779 and 1784—that describes this practice. According to Titsingh, two tablets are made for the funeral and are carried in the procession. The coffin is buried, and the bier and one of the tablets are placed on the grave, to be removed on the forty-ninth day. The other tablet is set up in the house. It is the object of veneration by family members and of prayers offered by a priest every seventh day during the forty-nine-day period. Two tablets of lacquered wood are then made, one for the temple and one for the altar (Hildreth 1905: 439–41, citing *Illustrations of Japan*, London, 1822).

The census material discussed in Chapter 5 shows that not all deceased members of a household are represented by permanent tablets in the family altar. Permanent tablets are not always made for children and other minor members of the house when they die, and their temporary tablets are sometimes burned or set adrift on a body of water. Ordinarily the temporary tablet serves as the object of veneration during the mourning period. Although it is treated differently from place to place (Mogami 1959: 336), the practice in an area of the San'in district is unusual only for its literalness (S. Tanaka 1961: 37–38). Here the temporary tablet is initially sheathed in a white cloth, white being the color both of the garments in which the corpse is clothed and of purity. Every seventh day the sheath is raised slightly, revealing a bit more of the tablet each time. On the forty-ninth day the cloth is removed completely, and the temporary tablet is taken to the cemetery and buried.

In the Izu Islands, we may recall, the tablet is placed on successively higher shelves of the altar on the seventh, thirty-seventh, and seventy-seventh days, until on the hundredth day it is raised to the top shelf with the ancestors. With each upward step it is said that the spirit of the dead becomes more purified (Ushijima 1966: 173). At the hundredth day the most dangerous period is past; now a broom or a hat may be placed over the spot where the temporary tablet is buried to suggest departure, as one might try to speed on his way an unwelcome guest or a person who has stayed too long by setting a broom in the entryway of the house. As the last step, the permanent tablet for the person is placed on the shelf with those of the other ancestral dead, there to be venerated with them.

The posthumous name (*kaimyō*), written by a priest, is carved into the black lacquered surface of the more common of the two forms of tablets and is filled in with gold. If the tablet itself is gold, as is the case in some special instances, the writing appears in black. The names are of varying lengths, depending on many factors, not the least of which is the fee paid to the temple. More important, no doubt, are the many considerations that lead to the determination of the amount of money the family wishes to spend. Such considerations will ordinarily reflect the status, age, and sex of the deceased; thus the length of the posthumous name, the seniority of the title, and the cost will generally correlate with the person's status in the household at the time of his death. To illustrate the patterning of posthumous names, I have set out in Table 2 a schematized set from an altar of a Nichiren sect household. The patterning is clear enough. Although the length of the names and the ranking of the titles differ greatly from generation to generation, husbands and wives are often given titles of the same rank. Thus we have the matched pairs for male and female, respectively, representing lower and higher rank: *shinshi—shinnyo* and *koji—daishi*. Both sets may be raised in rank by prefixing the character *in*. Where there are discrepancies in ranking, there is some reason to believe that the spouse who dies very young will have a less elaborate posthumous name than the survivor who lives to a ripe old age. But even in this one altar the correlation is imperfect.

A few individual names I recorded are more elevated than any of those given in Table 2. The most exalted, all for very old men and women, were the following:

80-year-old male, Shingon sect: – – in – – – – koji rei i
83-year-old male, Jōdo sect: – – – – – – – – mon
76-year-old male, Shingon sect: – – in – – – – – koji
97-year-old female, Shingon sect: – – in – – – – daishi i

The shortest names invariably are for very young children and the stillborn. All of the names are Buddhist, of course, and they are individualized. For men they usually include one character from the per-

TABLE 2

Posthumous Names from Tablets in a Nichiren Altar

Relationship to household head	Age at death	Posthumous name	Relationship to household head	Age at death	Posthumous name
Fa fa fa fa fa	73	– – – – shinshi	Fa	84	– – in – – – – koji
Fa fa fa fa mo	?	– – – – shinnyo	Mo	74	– – in – – – – daishi
Fa fa fa fa	48	– – zen mon	Elder brother	42	– – in – – shinshi
Fa fa fa mo	?	– – shinnyo	Younger sister	25	– – in – – – – shinnyo
Fa fa fa	32	– – shinshi	Wife's younger		
Fa fa mo	64	– – in shinnyo	brother	36	– – in – – – – koji
Fa fa	47	– – in – – – – koji	Wife's elder		
Fa fa 1st wife	25	– – – – shinnyo	sister	19	– – in – – shinnyo
Fa mo	69	– – in – – – – daishi	Wife's younger		
Mo fa	45	– – in – – – – shinshi	sister	17	– – in – – – – shinnyo
Mo mo	62	– – in – – – – shinnyo	Daughter	3	– – – dōnyo
Wife's fa	74	– – in – – – – koji	Son	2	– – – dōshi
Wife's mo	69	– – in – – – – daishi			

NOTE: Each dash represents a character; the words romanized are the titles referred to in the text.

son's name in life. For women this practice is less common, especially in older tablets, for until recent times most women's names were written with the syllabary rather than with characters. For both sexes the names include the following elements: an indication of the general age-group to which the person belonged at death; often a stereotyped but occasionally highly personalized reference to qualities ("obedient wife," "beautiful woman"); some detail of life history ("died at a tragically early age"); and in some instances the manner of death ("killed in war," "died in a mountain-climbing accident"). The formerly common practice (now apparently abandoned) of including a character to indicate social status in life reaches its extreme in the addition to the posthumous name of a deceased untouchable (*eta-hinin*) of the character for animal or beast (*chikushō*) (J. Suzuki 1961: 13), for in death as in life the untouchables were reckoned to be nonhuman. Ordinarily the date of death is written on the face of the tablet beside the posthumous name; the reverse usually bears the person's name in life and age at death, and often includes an indication of his relationship to the head of the household. In rare instances I also found brief accounts of the person's life on the reverse, with some information on the circumstances of his death.

The origin of the custom of bestowing names on the dead is of more than passing interest, and the changes in the original conception throw considerable light on the fortunes of Buddhism in Japan. The term for the custom used in the Jōdo-shin sect is *hōmyō* (*hō* is the Law), which brings us near the heart of the matter, for this term originally referred to a lay title given in recognition of strict observance of the Buddha's Law. A man or woman who went to a temple or monastery to undertake a religious regimen received a certificate bearing a title reflecting the degree of the austerities practiced. Originally, then, these were not posthumous names at all. The pieces of paper on which they were written may well be the prototypes of the wooden memorial tablets, for the more durable material would bear witness for a longer time to the faith of the person who had received the original certificate (Hashimoto 1962: 12). The title koji, for example, was originally conferred on an earnest lay believer who in his daily life followed the teaching of the Buddha, diligently spreading it among his fellow men (Hashimoto 1962: 14).

But today, as has been the case for centuries, the posthumous name has lost its early meaning and can be purchased for everyone who dies. The greater the sum of money paid, the more exalted the title. For the ordinary Japanese, when a person dies he becomes a buddha and in the normal course of events receives a Buddhist posthumous name. The more elaborate that name, the greater the respect accorded the deceased and the easier his passage across the river that bars the way to paradise (Hirayama 1949: 231).

The tablets themselves take on a very special significance because they stand for the individual and collective dead of the house. How special they are is shown by the familiar formula encountered in press coverage of fires: "Flames swept through six dwellings in Ward X last night, completely leveling them. The spread of the fire was so rapid and the warning so short that the residents had time only to carry out the altar and tablets." During the incendiary raids on Japanese cities during World War II, it was commonly reported that householders were able to save only the memorial tablets as they fled their burning neighborhoods. In his account of the experiences of those burned out by the American raids on Tokyo in 1944–45, Toland (1970: 673) writes of the actions of one seventeen-year-old boy when the incendiary bombs began to fall around his house, which the other members of his family had already left. He ran to his room to pick up three schoolbooks he thought he might need for an examination the next day, and he also went to get the tablets from the altar. Finding that his mother had already taken them with her to the air-raid shelter, he picked up an image of the Buddha made of precious metals and buried it together with some other valuables in the yard before running from the spreading flames. It is worth noting that the ancestors had been taken to shelter by his mother; the statue of the Buddha is only one of many valuable objects left behind. The ancestors, after all, are members of the household and need help like anyone else. The Buddha presumably can take care of himself.

> It is a fact that the Japanese hold a deeply rooted, though somewhat vague, belief or feeling that the spirits of their ancestors and family dead actually live in the mortuary tablets; consequently to the Japanese, the mortuary tablets are the ancestors themselves and their beloved deceased. There is the reason why most Japanese cannot bear to part with the mortuary tablets, or allow them to be burned, and feel a terrible reproach, and an unbearable sense of loneliness when such things happen. (Hashimoto 1962: 10.)

The quotation cited above was taken from a short work by a Japanese Christian minister that is essentially a diatribe against the practice of, if not the sentiment behind, ancestor worship in his country.

Are we dealing here with customs that have largely died out? The evidence suggests that the importance of saving tablets from fire or other harm is very much a part of the postwar scene. Plath (1964: 314), citing a communication from Yoshida Teigo concerning a study of some hamlets in Saga Prefecture in Kyushu, says that in answer to the question "What would you take out of your house first in case of fire?" 71 percent of the households (42 of 59) named the ancestral altar. It is not clear whether all fifty-nine households actually had altars. In 1956 a survey was conducted in Toyohashi City (population about 60,000) that provides some very interesting data on the importance of the tablets (Kawakoshi 1957). From a sample of five hundred people, 425 usable replies were obtained. The purpose of the study was to investigate the degree to which people still subscribed to traditional norms of behavior relating to the household and the family. The survey contained fifty-two statements, including these: "The ancestral tablets should be more carefully kept than anything else in the house"; "The heir and his wife should live with his parents"; "Filial piety is the duty of children"; "It is only natural that a wife obey her husband." To each the respondent could reply on a five-point scale from "strongly agree" to "strongly oppose." Of the fifty-two items, the one concerning the ancestral tablets received the highest degree of support. However, the higher the level of education, irrespective of sex, the more negative the response to this statement and others like it. This is a point to which we will return later.

Even when faced with the doctrinal demands of Christianity, people may be unwilling to abandon the altar and god shelf completely. Morioka (1966: 190–92) cites the case of two rural Christian churches in the Meiji period. Converts in the two communities where these churches were established had either burned or stored their domestic altars in response to pressure from the missionaries. It appears that most altars were in fact stored away, for by 1925 the Christian faith of the villagers had either weakened or become diffuse, and some of the altars were back in use. In that year eleven houses in one of the two communities were surveyed. Although it is unfortunately not clear whether the households were entirely or only partially Christian, the results are of interest. Nine of the eleven had restored both domestic altars, and eight of these nine said that they observed ancestral rites and visited the ancestors' graves (Morioka 1966: 193). The important thing here is not the altar itself but the memorial tablets, for ancestor worship was anathema to early Christian missionaries.

The God Shelf and the Domestic Altar

In their present forms, both the Buddhist altar (*butsudan*) and the god shelf (*kamidana*) seem to be of recent origin. At an earlier time the sacred places within the house probably were temporary, set up for specific occasions. Hirayama (1959: 67) thinks that worship of the ancestors at bon formerly took place at a temporary spirit shelf (*mitama-dana, seirei-dana*) rather than at the butsudan, which was an altar for the worship of the Buddha. Similarly, he suggests, Shinto gods were not considered to inhabit one place only, but could be invoked anywhere at any time by simply setting up an altar and summoning them there.

The Shinto god shelf is made of untreated wood, its ritual vessels are of unglazed or white ceramic, and it may hold a mirror and amulets from various shrines; but there is no image of the deity, for this is alien to Shinto. Ordinarily the god shelf is placed high up on the wall, often above a doorway in the sitting room. The worshiper stands and invokes the gods by sharp handclaps. As the abode of the gods, the shelf is shielded from pollution and death, as we have seen.

In the view of some scholars the domestic god shelf was largely a creation of the late Tokugawa period. Others believe it to represent an aspect of the Meiji government's effort to establish State Shinto and link it directly to household religious observances. Whatever the case, it is often asserted that Shinto's popularity has declined sharply since Japan's defeat in World War II, which was viewed as an unmistakable sign that the gods had failed to protect the country. Not only State Shinto but also what is usually called popular or folk Shinto has suffered a marked decline since the war ended. In a community in Okayama Prefecture, according to Norbeck (1970: 59–60), over fifteen years:

> . . . the local shrine community has essentially ceased to exist as a functioning social group; beliefs and customs concerned with agriculture and fishing had greatly weakened or disappeared; customs relating to ideas of pollution had essentially vanished; community rites centering on the local tutelary god had become at best token events; home worship of Shinto deities had become limited principally to aged people; and many beliefs and customs had become amusing superstitions.

Nevertheless, several postwar studies show that a substantial number of households still have god shelves. It is not possible, on the basis of the materials presented, to say whether worship of the gods occurs with any regularity or not, or whether it is indeed only the old who are involved. Nor can it be argued that all god shelves are ignored or that all the ones remaining are simply survivals from the prewar period. The figures from some of these studies are given in Table 3.

Table 3 represents the results of studies on possession of both god shelves and Buddhist domestic altars. Looking first at the findings on god shelves, we can see that they are more likely to be found in rural rather than in urban households. But the last two figures suggest the need for caution in generalizing about alleged urban-rural differences. (Much the same caution is indicated with respect to the possession of Buddhist domestic altars, as the figures in the next column show.) The

TABLE 3

Summary of Selected Postwar Studies on Possession of
God Shelves and Domestic Altars

Source	Date of study	Pct. having god shelf	Pct. having altar	Place of residence
Dore 1958	1951	55%	80%	Shitayama-chō, Tokyo
Sano 1958	1955	50	63	Tokyo
Sano 1958	1955	80	74	Rural Hokkaido
Spae 1968	1957	71	78	Urban
Spae 1968	1966	40	60	Urban
Morioka 1970	1964–65	95	92	Rural Yamanashi
Morioka 1970	1964–65	61	69	Tokyo (blue-collar)
Morioka 1970	1964–65	43	45	Tokyo (white-collar)

contents of the god shelf seem not to have changed very much. Amulets, which can be obtained at all the great popular shrines and at many smaller ones, are kept on the shelf, as are miscellaneous other objects whose associations with shrines range from the specific to the highly tenuous. Amulets from the Ise shrine are very popular, but their rate of distribution is not keeping pace with the rate of increase of households in Japan. In 1955, Ise distributed 6,610,000 amulets. If we assume that each went to a single household, that would account for 38 percent of all households in Japan at the time. In 1965, although the number given out had risen to 6,780,000, that accounted for only 29 percent of all households (Morioka 1970: 151).

Let us now turn to the consideration of Buddhist domestic altars. These altars can be purchased in a great variety of styles, sizes, and degrees of elaborateness (see Takenaka 1955a: 1260–61). Some very large and old houses have an entire room given over to the ancestral altar, but such rooms, never common, are becoming increasingly rare. In them one whole wall is usually covered by an altar; one we encountered but were unable to record in detail contained scores of tablets and a large array of Buddhist images, scrolls, and other ritual objects. This particular room was altogether reminiscent of a private chapel and undoubtedly had served as such in an earlier day.

The altar found in most houses today is a standing cabinet whose double doors are usually opened only when some activity is being directed toward the memorial tablets within. Most altars have a small drawer at the bottom where children's report cards, first salary envelopes of family members, certificates and diplomas, and other important papers are kept. Cynics have said that this is why the altar is often the first thing to be carried from a burning building. My own view is that such things are kept in the altar's drawer precisely because it is the first item that will be taken out in case of fire. The largest altars are almost ceiling-high; the smallest can be set on an ordinary bookshelf. Their exteriors are commonly of a near-black wood, highly polished but usually unlacquered. The interiors are sometimes faced with gold leaf. In any household the kind of altar and its cost will depend on such a large number of considerations that it is difficult to generalize about them at all.

Like the gravestones, the altar often represents an expense the family could ill afford, and thus it is shown with pride, for a man is thereby indicating that he cares for his ancestors. It is often claimed that the size of the altar varies by sect, but I have found no evidence to support such a view. Suffice it to say that the affluent, devout household head will purchase at least as large and expensive an altar as his means permit, and more than likely one that is beyond them. Consequently, a household whose fortunes have declined or whose head is uninterested in religious matters (that is to say, unfilial) may sometimes still have an expensive altar to which little attention is directed. In many other instances, through a combination of piety and a desire to impress its neighbors, a household will install an expensive altar. Nevertheless, the trend is clearly toward the smaller, less elaborate varieties, particularly in the minuscule apartments that are a feature of contemporary Japanese urban life. The figures on possession of domestic altars in Table 3 are of considerable interest and make one or two points of importance for understanding materials presented later, in Chapter 5. Having an altar essentially means that one has memorial tablets. This is why altars are least common in city households, for urban areas have the heaviest concentration of neolocal conjugal families where no death has yet occurred. These families therefore literally have no ancestors of their own to worship. Lacking memorial tablets, they have no need for an altar. When they do buy one after the death of a family member, it is likely to be small—and for reasons other than limitations of space alone, since there is a feeling that to purchase a large altar capable of holding many tablets is to court disaster.

The history of the altar (see *Minzokugaku kenkyū sho* 1952a: 499–500) provides ample evidence to support the claim that there has been a gradual separation of ancestor worship from institutionalized Buddhism, and that the household has tended to take upon itself more and more of the functions associated with the ancestral rites (Takeda 1961: 198). Probably only main houses had altars at first, and the branch houses had to join in the ancestral rites held at the main house. The large altar-room of the sort referred to earlier clearly was used in such a way. It may even be that only the principal house in each agricultural hamlet had an altar, where itinerant priests annually offered up sutras and prayers for the dead (see Morioka 1970). Hirayama (1959: 46) shares this view and notes that in 1633 it was reported from the Province of Higo that only the big landowners had Buddhist chapels. He assumes —correctly, I think—that ceremonies were conducted for all in the main house and that branch houses possessed no altars of their own. This was in the period just prior to the requirement that all households register as parishioners of a temple. Evidence from a survey conducted after World War II in the Hokuriku and Tōhoku districts reveals that in the houses of the largest landowners there were large altars in separate rooms holding both memorial tablets and representations of the Buddha. By contrast, the houses of small and of branch families had only little altars (literally "box altars") containing tablets but no images. Major rituals were doubtless performed in the main houses, and domestic rites in the smaller ones (Hirayama 1959: 46).

In recent times, however, it has become the custom for every family that has had a member die to purchase an altar, have a tablet made, and secure the services of priests for the funeral as well as for the successive memorial services. But it is clear that the development and increasing use of small altars, of tablets of the kuri-ihai type, and of the small books for recording the names of the deceased have rendered the priest and the temple less and less necessary to the performance of ancestral rites.

The offerings made at the altar include cooked rice, water or tea (sake is offered only at the final ceremony for the individual dead in most areas), flowers, incense, and a variety of cooked foods of the kind ordinarily eaten by family members—usually but not invariably excluding fish and fowl. Meat should never form a part of the offerings. The

TABLE 4
*Comparison of Items Commonly Offered
at Altar and God Shelf*

Items	Altar	God shelf
Foods and beverages		
Cooked rice	yes	no
Glutinous rice cakes	no[a]	yes
Water	yes	yes
Tea	yes	no
Sake	no	yes
Vegetables	yes	no
Fruits	yes	no
Fish	yes	no
Fowl	yes	no
Meat	no	no
Ceremonial confections	yes	no
Other		
Flowers	yes	no
Incense	yes	no
Sakaki branches		

[a] But see the discussion below.

principal occasions on which fish and fowl are offered—in violation of the general principle that the buddhas abhor all but vegetarian foods—are the memorial services, when the dead person is offered something he was fond of in life. The daily offerings are usually made to the ancestors before the family eats, as befits their position as the senior members of the house.

At the god shelf offerings usually include cooked rice, glutinous rice cakes, some kinds of vegetables and fruits (on special occasions), water or sake, and branches of the evergreen *sakaki* tree. In Table 4 I have set out the items usually offered at the two domestic altars. In a sense, I think, offerings are made to the gods, but are shared with the ancestors. The gods are remote; the ancestral spirits are still reckoned to be members of the family. Yet on one occasion these ritual distinctions are abandoned. In many places, including the community of Sone (discussed later in this chapter and in Chapter 5), at the New Year but never at bon households make identical offerings of glutinous rice cakes and sakaki branches to both the god shelf and the ancestral altar. Among the communities in which I conducted interviews, Sone is the only one where Shinto worship holds clear ascendancy over Buddhist.

Memorial Services for the Individual

The funeral is only the first of a series of rites conducted on behalf of the spirit of the deceased. There follow the seven seventh-day ceremonies, which culminate on the forty-ninth day after death. In addition, there is another ceremony on the hundredth day. For women there are usually only five seventh-day ceremonies. Buddhist doctrine at some early date incorporated the idea that the spirit of the dead spends this period—49 or 35 days—in an intermediate existence preparatory to rebirth. Since men's cases are judged on the forty-ninth day (the thirty-fifth for women), prayers may be said up to that time in the hope of improving the person's chances of becoming a buddha (McCullough 1968: 234). Thus the final day of mourning marks a turning point in the fate of the soul, which may take some action on its own to settle accounts with the living. In the eighteenth-century puppet play *The Woman Killer and the Hell of Oil* (*Onnagoroshi abura jigoku*), Yohei murders Okichi. As yet undiscovered, Yohei comes to the final service for her. He arrives just after a rat has run across the rafters of the room where the mourners are gathered, dislodging a scrap of paper containing irrefutable evidence of Yohei's guilt. Okichi's husband exclaims "It gives us a clue to the murderer of Okichi. I'm sure that the rat knocked down the paper tonight, the thirty-fifth night of mourning, as a sign from the dead person. This too I owe to Buddha's mercy. Namu Amida Butsu" (Keene 1961: 469–70).

It would appear that in India the Buddhists took the concept of the special character of the forty-nine days after death from a brahmanic rite designed to assist the passage of the soul into the next world. It was believed that if a person's relatives failed to perform it, his soul would be condemned to ceaseless wandering, posing a threat to the living (Hori 1966: 6). The custom was not found in early Buddhism, of course, for it would make no sense in the context of early Buddhist doctrine (Kazama & Kino 1965: 592); however, it had long been a part of Buddhist practice by the time the religion was adopted by the Japanese.

In recent times the seven ceremonies of the initial mourning period (*chū-in*) have been very much abbreviated. Formerly it was the custom to visit the grave on each seventh day, taking flowers and incense and sometimes calling a priest to recite the sutras there. On the seventh and forty-ninth days in some areas a stupa was taken to the grave and left there. Ooms (1967: 277–78) reports an interesting variation on this practice that reveals something about the transition through which the spirit of the dead is thought to be passing during this period. On the day of the funeral, seven small stupa are set up near the grave; on every seventh day one of them is broken. In Nagasawa, the ideal pattern is to take a new stupa to the grave on the hundredth day after death, at every bon, and on the first, third, seventh, thirteenth, twenty-third, and thirty-third anniversaries of death. In theory the length of the stupa increases with each rite, but in Nagasawa they are all of equal length. The inscriptions put on the stupa by the priest do indicate the soul's change in status on each occasion, but almost no one in the village can read them. On the thirty-third anniversary of death some families purchase a more substantial square stupa, the last, and plant it at the grave site.

The abbreviation and attenuation of the mourning rites are nowhere more evident than in the case of those practices that confront directly the issues of pollution and taboo. Close relatives of the deceased used to be avoided by others, at least early in the mourning period, and there were many activities in which they were not allowed to participate owing to their contamination with death (see Norbeck 1952). Few of these restrictions are now observed, but vestiges do remain of many customs intended to avoid pollution, particularly at the funeral ceremony and during the seven days following. Although the funeral rites and paraphernalia are almost exclusively Buddhist in character, it should be noted that many beliefs and practices related to concerns with pollution and taboo are Shinto. Many of the customs and usages of the early period of mourning are rites of passage. Norbeck (1970: 108–9) says of these rites: "Shinto death observances were rites in the home in which the entire small community participated less intensely, proscriptions and prescriptions of behavior with manifest goals of preventing harm from the pollution inherent in death."

The degree to which these concerns remain varies enormously, but the rites are everywhere much reduced in scale. Yet in 1965–66 Ooms (1967: 231) found in Nagasawa many funeral practices that reveal a clear concern with the avoidance of death's pollution. Stones, rather than a hammer, are used to close the coffin lid and are then buried with the coffin. A fire is lit at the grave, and all mourners are given a packet of salt to throw over their shoulders as they reenter their homes on returning from the graveside. (Fire and salt, it should be remarked, are the classic purifying agents of Shinto ritual.) A bladed implement and coins are left near the corpse while the coffin is still in the house; the coffin is carried in a circle about the room so that the dead cannot easily find his way back to the house; and the straw sandals of the men who carry the coffin are left at the grave. Reversals of normal practices and of regular positioning of objects are still found: the corpse is bathed from a vessel in which hot water has been added to cold; the body is placed with the head to the north, a position in which one is never supposed to sleep; the folding screen, if there is one, is inverted; the corpse's kimono is lapped over to the left rather than to the right; and mourners wear footgear up onto the floor of the house.

There can be no doubt that many of these practices, and related ones, survive today largely in the form of popular superstitions. Some people will always put hot water into a container first and adjust the temperature by adding cold. Most foreigners do not notice that their hosts take some pains to see to it that their bedding is not laid out with the pillow to the north, even when quarters are very cramped. And the horror with which some people view foreigners who step up into the house with their shoes on does not derive exclusively from a concern for the cleanliness of the floor mats. As for the reversal of the kimono fold, the presentation of the cash portion of the dowry of a friend of mine in her twenties had to be completely rescheduled when her mother discovered that someone had inadvertently folded the packet's white paper wrapping in the reverse of the normal direction.

In many parts of Japan the soul of the dead is thought to wander about the house or to reside atop the roof for seven days after death. The belief is found in Nagasawa, and Ooms discovered that during that first week it is the custom there to hang some article of the deceased's clothing in a dark corner in the north of the house and to keep the garment wet by pouring water over it. This may be an unusual extension of the more common practice of pouring water over the gravestone itself, but it is hard to see why the garment should be hung in so dangerous a direction in terms of geomantic principles. In Nagasawa it is said that on the forty-ninth day the soul leaves the house for the grave at last. It will stay there unless invited back by the living (Ooms 1967: 232–33).

There are other, more mundane practices intended to release the soul from this world. Sugimoto writes in her book *A Daughter of the Samurai* (1925: 42) that during the period of mourning after her father's death efforts were made to take care of all his unfinished business, neglected duties, and unfulfilled obligations, so that his soul could go unhindered to paradise. Analogous efforts among the living are made to clear up outstanding business before New Year's Day, so that one may start the year unencumbered.

However people may now mark the occasion, they used to believe that at the end of the forty-nine days of mourning, given the proper care, the soul would leave the world of the living tranquilly and at peace. Ooms (1967: 280) notes a marked difference in the attitude toward the spirit of the dead before and after the forty-ninth day. At the ceremonies held up to that day there is marked uncertainty and uneasiness in the house, but at bon, even when it falls very soon after the lifting of the mourning period, all is warmth and joy.

The end of mourning is generally called imi-ake (lifting of pollution), and with it the living return to full status in the community. There remain to be performed three sets of rites after this, all directed to the individual spirit. One is what I shall call the annual deathday rite (*shō-tsuki-meinichi*), which marks the date of the person's death every year. The second is the monthly deathday rite (*mai-tsuki-meinichi*), which marks the date of death on a monthly basis (for example, if a person died on May 8, the eighth day of every month). These observances are generally modest in scale and usually are not held over a very long period: for instance, in Yasuhara (see Chapter 5) both are ordinarily dropped after a few years at most. In Sone some families told me that they observe the monthly deathdays for parents and for the newly deceased only until their first bon. Others said that they mark these rites only for about three years, but hold them for everyone. The third in the series of rites is the periodic anniversary rites, called *nenki* (*shūki* in the Jōdo-shin sect). Practices vary widely, but in general these rites are held on all or some of the following anniversaries of death: the first, third, seventh, thirteenth, seventeenth, twenty-third, twenty-seventh, thirty-third, fiftieth, and hundredth. (Jōdo-shin observes the first, third, seventh, thirteenth, seventeenth, twenty-fifth, thirty-third, and fiftieth.) It would appear that only the forty-ninth-day ceremony is a feature of Buddhism as it came from the continent, although it may be that the rites of the first and third anniversaries are Confucian in origin (Ch'en 1973: 54); all the rest have been added by the Japanese (Hirayama 1959: 48).

The periodic anniversary rites are more or less elaborate services, depending on the inclinations of the family and the status of the ancestor. Household members invite close kin who may have moved away or married out, and sometimes also ask neighbors, close friends, and business associates of the deceased (Smith 1956: 91). Usually a priest is called in to recite the sutras, and the occasion is marked by a festive meal shared by all those present, who are expected to bring incense money (*kōden*) as an offering. The scale of these services varies greatly by sect. In Yasuhara in 1952 the most costly Jōdo-shin rite required that eight to ten priests recite the Amida sutra one thousand times over a period of two nights and three days. The least costly, and most commonly requested, required that two or three priests recite sutras over one night and part of a day.

There is great variation throughout the country in the choice of year for the person's final memorial service, but the most favored are the thirty-third and fiftieth anniversaries of death. In Yasuhara in 1952 (Smith 1956: 90) most people reported that the thirty-third anniversary was the last to be observed, for the very practical reason that usually by that time another important household member would have died and his rites would have taken precedence. Generally called *tomurai-age*, but also known as *nenki-age* or *matsuri-jimai* (the end of ritual), these true "last rites" are the final individualized observances for the deceased. Many Japanese scholars are of the opinion that this is when the ancestral spirit finally joins the gods (see Takeda 1961: 104). Until the individual's tablet is disposed of there is some retention of personal identity; the tomurai-age marks the end of this identity, and in many parts of the country the stupa or memorial tablet is replaced by an evergreen branch planted on the grave. This practice is doubtless pre-Buddhist and suggests that originally both the gods and the ancestors were summoned by means of a living tree branch, the classic vehicle for the passage of spirits into and out of this world.

Whether or not such an explicit device is employed, there is abundant evidence of the widespread occurrence of practices that clearly mark the transition from buddha to god (Ikegami 1959a; Inoguchi 1959; Matsudaira 1963). Naoe (1963) cites a great many such cases, including at least one in which the tablet itself is transferred directly from the Buddhist altar to the shrine of the tutelary deity. In some places the posthumous name is planed from the face of the tablet, which is then placed on the god shelf. In others the tablet is cast into a stream or river and a pebble is picked up from the streambed and deposited within the shrine of the tutelary deity, with the explanation that "the buddha washes its body and becomes a god" (*hotoke sama ga karada o aratte kami sama ni nari*) (Ōshima 1959: 94).

Mogami (1959: 334–35) offers many examples of analogous practices: a tree branch is thrust into the earth with the explanation that the spirit ascends to heaven as a god through the leaves; the family assembles on the beach for a meal that includes sake, which is not usually offered on other memorial occasions, and then builds a fire in whose rising smoke the soul ascends to heaven as a god (*kami to natte*); the stupa at the grave is inverted and the buddha thereby becomes a god; the buddha becomes a god and sake is drunk, which it never is at the earlier services for the dead (Iwate Prefecture); a five-tiered stupa is made for the grave, and it is said that the buddha has become a god (Hyōgo Prefecture); the memorial tablet is placed in the shrine of the tutelary deity, at whose festival in the eleventh month all such ancestors are worshiped (Miyazaki Prefecture); a small pile of stones is placed at the corner of the grave, and it is said that the spirit becomes the messenger of the gods (*misaki*) (Okayama Prefecture); the soul is said to become a tutelary deity (*ji-gami ni naru*) and is worshiped collectively by the members of the community (Fukui Prefecture); the ancestral spirit is said to become a tutelary deity (*chi-no-kami-sama ni naru*) (Shizuoka Prefecture); a cedar branch is taken to the shrine and the words *sugi-mashita* (*sugi* being the word both for "cedar" and for "to be over," "to be past," "to have gone beyond") are spoken to indicate that the ancestral spirit has become a tutelary deity (Fukushima Prefecture); the memorial tablet is taken from the altar on the hundredth anniversary of death and placed under the eaves of the shrine of the tutelary deity and left there (Fukushima Prefecture). More examples would be redundant; the interested reader should also consult Yanagita (1970: 117–20).

In theory, at the last rites the person's memorial tablet will be removed from the ancestral altar and either disposed of in one of the ways discussed above or taken to the temple for a kind of perpetual care there. My data on tablets (presented in Chapter 5) strongly bear out Ooms's observation (1967: 276) that this actually seldom seems to happen, for I have recorded a great many very old tablets still in domestic altars. Nevertheless, it is true that by the last rites there are few if any living household members who actually remember the deceased. As a result, little attention is paid to the old tablets, except that they are automatically included when the collectivity of the ancestors is worshiped. Individual identity is lost, as is remarked upon in a sour little story by Sono Ayako entitled "The Environs of Seiganji Temple" (1966: 152). The scene is a temple in a working-class district of Tokyo at bon. Two people meet at a grave. He is a childless adopted husband, and she is the former mistress of the recently deceased president of the company for which he works:

> "Do you know who are in this grave?" she asked.
>
> "My wife's father and brothers; all our relatives, perhaps. I don't care about an heir to my family. Having children may be a good thing in itself, but of what use is it to be the heir of a house like mine?... No great property and no name."
>
> "Just think, for ten or twenty years after death, perhaps, one may be remembered, but after fifty or a hundred years, who will care to remember unless an entertaining attraction is added to the program?"

The "entertaining attraction" refers to the bon dance held at temples on the nights of the festival.

Memorial Services for the Collectivity of the Dead

There are still other observances directed not to the individual but to the collectivity of the spirits of the household dead. In many families an offering of flowers, incense, and food is made at the ancestral altar on a daily basis. Some households do this once in the morning (*mai-asa*) and once again in the evening (*mai-ban*). Others make the offerings only once a day, either before breakfast or before the evening meal. There are, in addition, four seasonal holidays when the collective dead are honored: the New Year (*shōgatsu*—January 1–3), bon (August 13–15), and the vernal and autumnal equinoxes (*higan*—March 18–24 and September 20–26). The only exception is the first bon after death (*hatsu-bon* or *nī-bon*), when the spirit of the newly dead is singled out for special attention (Matsudaira 1963: 190–91). It is the custom in many households to include the ancestors in the New Year festivities through offerings and the sharing of meals with them, but they are far less central to the occasion than at the equinoxes and at bon.

At the equinoxes members of the family visit and clean the grave, and they may also schedule a special memorial service for the dead to be held at the temple or in the home. A kind of sweet called *o-hagi* is widely prepared or purchased on these days; some of it is offered to the ancestors and the rest is eaten at the evening meal, for which some households also prepare a special dish or two (Dore 1958: 427–28; Ooms 1967: 240). At present the middle days of both equinoctial periods are official holidays, called respectively *shumbun-no-hi* (March 21) and *shūbun-no-hi* (September 23). In terms of the intensity of the relationship between the living and the ancestral dead these days stand somewhere between the daily observances and the ceremonies of bon.

In all the foregoing discussions of the history and meaning of bon, I have given no description of the occasion. What follows is a synthetic picture of bon with some comments on important variations. Today on August 13, 14, and 15 most places of business close and millions of Japanese drive out of the cities for the countryside. Now, I do not know what proportion of the population observes any aspect of bon during those three days, and I would be the last to argue that the roads are clogged with people hastening to pay their respects to the ancestors. I know of no reliable way to assess either changes in the nature of the people's participation in the festival or the degree of its decline. What I shall outline, though, is in very general terms what millions of Japanese still do at bon (see Durt 1971).

Bon is by far the most elaborate of the four seasonal rites directed to the collectivity of the ancestors. Some time before August 13, members of the family go to clean the grave. In some areas this is done at Tanabata (the Star Festival), the seventh day of the seventh month by the lunar calendar, which is also called *bon-hajime* (the start of bon) (Bownas 1963: 96; Chinnery 1971: 30; Embree 1939: 283). It is thought that the ancestors begin their long journey back to earth on that day. Ordinarily some flowers are left at the grave and incense is burned. Water is poured over the gravestone, and a path may be cleared for the use of the ancestors. In the house itself the altar and its tablets will be dusted and perhaps decorated with some newly purchased item—a candleholder, an incense burner, a flower vase, a bell. Lanterns, of a type peculiar to bon, are hung about the altar and sometimes at the entryway to the house compound. Just before bon the shops that specialize in Buddhist paraphernalia are well stocked and are filled with customers. A very contemporary note was struck by a shop on Kobe's Motomachi shopping street in 1972. The shop was bursting with lanterns, streamers, miniature boats, and other objects for the celebration, and across its facade hung a huge sign which read *yasuragi sēru* (Tranquillity Sale).

On the thirteenth the altar is opened and flowers, food, and incense are placed before the ancestral tablets. Alternatively, a special low table is set up and all the tablets are removed from the altar and placed on it, with similar offerings. Many people set up still another altar for the wandering spirits, usually somewhere outside the dwelling. Special lanterns are lighted, and by early evening it is hoped that the family members will all have gathered to welcome back the spirits of the dead, who are greeted very formally by the living, just as honored guests would be. On this night the household head lights a welcoming fire (*mukae-bi*) at the entrance to the house. It is intended to guide the spirits of the family's dead back to their home. In many households, members will have earlier taken to the grave small "horses" made of cucumber or eggplant and straw, which the souls of the dead are thought to ride from the great distance at which they reside.

The bon dance, formerly an essential part of the public communal celebrations, is now very much in eclipse. Formerly it was held on the first night (in some areas on all three nights) of the festival. On the thirteenth (and the fourteenth, if the parish is a large one) the Buddhist priest makes his rounds, offering a brief prayer at each house. He plays no essential role in the proceedings, however, and often is not even invited inside. On the fourteenth people usually visit the grave again and may go to the temple. In many parts of the country this second night is the first occasion on which the bon dance is performed—if it is performed at all. On the fifteenth, in the evening, the farewell or sending-off fire (*okuri-bi*) is prepared at the house's entrance to light the ancestors' way back to whatever their destination is conceived to be. Formal farewells are said, and expressions such as "Come back next year" are widely used. In many places the family members all go to the graveyard, the seashore, a river bank, or a mountain carrying lanterns, small boats, or stupas in order to see the spirits off (Anon. 1971; Beardsley et al. 1959: 455–56; Bernier 1970: 103–10; Embree 1939: 283–87; Ikegami 1959b; Norbeck 1954: 151–53; Sugimoto 1925: 73–81). A comparison between the many published accounts of bon and the festivities I have witnessed myself reveals many variations in detail. Here no welcome fire is lit; there boats are not sent off but burned instead. In one place the tablets are taken from the altar and put in the place of honor in the main room of the house, in the alcove that usually contains a scroll and flower arrangement; in another the bon altar is set up outside the house under the eaves. Sometimes the vegetable offerings are eaten; sometimes they are thrown into the river or the sea.

As I have noted above, the bon dance is everywhere in decline. It was once the prime public expression of the corporate community's veneration of the ancestral dead. The stand on which the musicians and singer performed was usually set up in a temple courtyard or in some other open public space such as the schoolyard and was ringed by a circle of dancers. In the cities the dancers came from the nearby streets, and in the rural areas from all the houses of each hamlet. But in the past several decades fewer and fewer people have been turning out for the dancing. Only the drummer survived the introduction of phonograph records and public-address systems; finally, even in the villages, neither corporate groups nor temple parishioners could muster the interest or the funds to hold the dance at all.

Ooms (1967: 226) says of Nagasawa that all public aspects of bon there have disappeared. Indeed, he finds that all the public cults of that community are now in serious trouble as a result of lack of interest and declining participation. Yet household ancestor worship remains strong among the adherents of both the traditional and the new religious groupings (Ooms 1967: 225). It may well be, as he suggests, that the increasingly private character of the ancestral rites has rendered them more and more immune to change. But in considering the causes for the decline in public performance of ritual and ceremony we must not overlook the role of government policy. In Chapter 1 we saw how after 1900 the Meiji government began to promote thrift and frugality through a program initiated by an Imperial Rescript and infused with heavily patriotic sentiments. One aspect of the Local Improvement

Movement, another Meiji program of the same period, was the merger of shrines, which caused many traditional festivals to disappear from hamlets whose tutelary gods had been removed to a central shrine elsewhere in the village (Pyle 1973). The frugality campaign (a sample slogan: *zeitaku wa teki da*—"luxury is the enemy") discouraged heavy expenditures for funerals and weddings (Embree 1939: 284). In Suye forty years ago the simplified celebration of bon was attributed by its ethnographer to "the economy movement which is interfering with so many of the established customs."

Let us turn once again to a discussion of the particular kind of spirit that receives special attention at bon—the shirei, the spirit of the newly dead. This is the spirit of any family member who has died since the last bon. Until it severs its ties with the world of the living and becomes an ancestral spirit at the end of its first bon, it is a source of potential harm. The shirei is welcomed back at bon in some areas with a poignant local greeting—"You must be very sad" (*o sabishū gozaimasu*)—indicating that the family understands how hard it is to cut the ties at last with those who remain behind (Maeda 1965: 50).

Bernier (1970: 103–9) offers a valuable account of the differential treatment of these spirits at bon in the coastal village of Sone in Mie Prefecture (this village is further discussed in Chapter 5). On August 12 a special altar is set up for each shirei in its former household. On it are placed offerings more elaborate than those made to the collectivity of the ancestors in the domestic altar. On August 13 members of the shirei's household bring offerings of flowers and food to the temple. On August 14 the whole community takes notice of the presence of the "new buddhas": a group composed of one member from every household in the village (with the usual exception of the Shinto priest and members of the Sōka Gakkai) goes in the evening to pray at every house where someone has died since the last bon. The Buddhist priest does not accompany this group. On August 15 all the ancestral spirits are sent away for another year; but the spirits of the newly dead remain behind until the sixteenth, when there is a ceremony called *shōrō-okuri* (sending off the spirits of the dead).

This ceremony is a community affair, unlike most of the other rites of bon. The villagers of Sone gather at the harbor, where the priest recites a prayer. A small, locally made boat for the spirits of the dead (*shōrō-bune*) is filled with some of the offerings from every special altar to them. Some money is placed in the boat as well. Then the little boat is placed on board a fishing craft, which sets out, with relatives of all the deceased aboard, for the point where the Japan Current swings away from the coast. The miniature spirit boat is set afloat there to make certain that it will not drift back into the bay, an untoward event that might result in serious misfortune for the entire community. On August 19, after the final bon dance is held, the villagers gather once again at the harbor. The paper lanterns of bon are hung on a wooden frame, to one side of which a fire rather like the sending-off fire of the fifteenth is lighted. The priest says a prayer, and all the lanterns are set afire by a relative of one of the new buddhas. When they are consumed, the ashes are gathered up and thrown into the bay. People say that the lanterns represent the dead, and it would appear that with this act the special indeterminate position of the souls of the newly dead comes to an end. Until that time they have been naturally no longer counted among the living, but then neither have they been counted among the ancestral spirits. The outstanding feature of the treatment of these souls is the involvement of the community at large. A very similar situation is reported for Suye in the 1930's (Embree 1939: 283). In addition, Matsudaira (1936: 105–6), citing some mid-nineteenth-century material from the Province of Mikawa (now Aichi Prefecture), reports that the group of village dancers at the temple yard at bon dedicates its first dance to the ancestral spirits and then goes to each dwelling where there are new buddhas and dances for each of them. Sometimes all the tablets of the newly dead are placed in the temple yard itself, and special dances are performed for them.

Why are the newly dead given special community-wide attention? Certainly they are considered to be dangerous, unlike the ancestral spirits. Their treatment has analogues in the long-noted tendency for each hamlet household to have some share in the life-cycle ceremonies of the individual members of every other household. Of immediate relevance here are the ceremonies of marriage and death, which typically involve a representative of every household directly.

In a sense, the August 19 ceremony at Sone's harbor is the last of the cycle of corporate acts directed to the individual as a member of the community. At his birth he was welcomed into it; at his first bon after death he is sent away from it by its living members. Thereafter the person's soul is left to the care of his own household, for at bon each household is thought to receive only the spirits of its own dead. It is not the dead of the hamlet, the village, or any other social grouping that are welcomed back and feasted; bon is ultimately a household affair. Like the three-day New Year holiday, it is, or was until very recently, an occasion for scattered family members to be together again under one roof with the spirits of the household dead. "For the Japanese family the *o-bon* is the highlight of the year. During these days, each house becomes its own temple so to speak: a temporary sacred place, the altar is built where 'the sacred' will stay during the time of *o-bon*. The members of the household themselves perform the rites." (Ooms 1967: 240.) Bon is a collective familial observance, where each closed corporate entity welcomes back into its bosom its own ancestral dead. Yanagita (1970: 93) writes of an old custom of setting up a special altar for the souls of near relatives and sons and daughters who had married out into other families. They were called *o-kyaku-botoke* (guest buddhas) and entertained with offerings of food. As Ooms suggests, the periodic merging of the two worlds strengthens the sense of continuity of the house and reassures the dead of the living's continuing concern for their well-being. Neither death nor time can weaken or destroy the unity of the members of the house.

Patterns of Worship

In the course of my 1963 study (reported on further in Chapter 5), I asked members of 595 households at which of the ceremonial occasions discussed in this chapter they made offerings or performed rites at the ancestral altar. Tables 5 to 9 give my findings, but they are difficult to understand without preliminary elaboration. As we have seen, there are eight occasions when the ancestors may be venerated, leaving aside those special occasions that are not periodic (sharing gifts received from visitors, reporting events of importance in the lives of household members, and the like). These regular occasions are listed in Table 5 in descending order of frequency of observance. In interviewing about

TABLE 5
Households Observing Various Rites
($N = 457$)

Observance of rites, in descending order of frequency	Households	
	Number	Percent
Festival of the Dead (bon)	287	62.8%
Daily morning rite (mai-asa)	282	61.7
Periodic anniversaries of death (nenki)	275	60.2
Monthly deathday (mai-tsuki-meinichi)	255	55.8
Equinoxes (higan)	243	53.2
Daily evening rite (mai-ban)	204	44.6
New Year (shōgatsu)	197	43.1
Annual deathday (shō-tsuki-meinichi)	191	41.8
"When we think of it"	57	12.5
"Never"	7	1.5

NOTE: 26 households did not answer, and 112 households had no tablets.

patterns of worship, I asked people only which rites they customarily observed or would observe, not which ones they had conducted in the preceding year (or other fixed period). This allowed me to include families that observe periodic anniversaries of death even though the most recent observance might have been held several years before.

Table 5 reports the replies of 457 households, out of 483 with tablets. The two most frequent occasions when the collectivity of ancestors is honored are bon and mai-asa, the daily morning offering of newly cooked food. Yet perhaps the most significant finding is that only about 63 percent say that they even observe bon, which is usually represented to be the prime annual ancestral rite.

Only seven households admitted having tablets that they paid no attention to at all. This fact may be important to our understanding of possible directions of change in ancestor worship, so we shall analyze these seven closely. Obviously, other households may also neglect their tablets but did not say so. Of the seven households, two held some tablets, of which none was for an ascendant; three held tablets for one ascending generation and could identify the people represented by the tablets; and two held tablets for from six to fourteen generations. One of these last two households could identify the people in only two ascending generations; the other could assign names and household roles to all. In short, the seven nonworshiping households are not differentiated from the households that do observe the ancestral rites, for they are not of one type and clearly do not represent a trend.

Table 6 reveals, however, that the simple listing of frequencies of observance does not tell the whole story. Here we find set forth the fourteen most common patterns of worship, i.e. those patterns of ceremonial observances reported by nine or more households. These fourteen patterns, I hasten to point out, account for only 216 (47.3 percent) of the 457 households with tablets that responded to the question. This means that the remaining 241 households—more than half the total—reported other patterns of worship, none of which was common to even nine households! This finding represents a degree of variability in what is usually called customary usage on a scale hitherto unsuspected for Japan. Taking the four most common patterns in Table 6, two major types emerge: 111 households reported observance of the daily morning rite and 87 of the 111 made the daily evening offering as well (in patterns 1, 2, and 4); another 54 households reported making the daily morning offerings in addition to observing the periodic anniversaries of death and the monthly deathday (patterns 5, 7, 10, 12, and 14). The totals at the bottom of Table 6 list the number of times a given rite occurs in the fourteen patterns, irrespective of pattern composition. Three of the eight rites occur in ten of the patterns—the periodic anniversaries of death, the monthly deathday, and the daily morning rite. The first and second of these are directed primarily to the individual ancestor. The third offers comfort to the collectivity of the household dead by including them in the family's morning meal.

Up to this point, the distinction between those ceremonies directed to the individual spirit and those directed to the collectivity of ancestors has not emerged clearly. The grouping in Table 7 attempts to clarify the picture. In two of the fourteen patterns in Table 7, there are no rites whatsoever for the individual ancestors (patterns 1 and 3); in six of the fourteen there are no seasonal rites (patterns 1, 3, 6, 8, 11, and 13); in four of the fourteen there are no daily offerings (patterns 6, 9, 11, and 13). But if we look at the overall distribution shown in Table 7, it is immediately apparent that in the first seven patterns in the list (2, 4, 5, 7, 14, 12, and 10) at least one observance of each kind (individual, seasonal, and daily) was reported. That is, these households held rites for individual ancestors and for the collectivity on both a seasonal and a daily basis. The next two patterns (9 and 8) involve only two of the three categories of occasions, one (9) omitting daily rites and the other (8) omitting seasonal ones. The final grouping of patterns (1, 3, 13, 6, and 11) involves only one of the three categories of occasions, patterns 1 and 3 omitting all but daily rites, patterns 13, 6, and 11 omitting all but individual rites.

Looked at another way, if a household does observe daily rites, it is likely to mark either at least one seasonal collective rite and at least one individual rite in addition (patterns 2, 4, 5, 7, 14, 12, and 10), or no others at all (patterns 1 and 3). The single exception is pattern 8. Households that observe only the monthly deathday among the individual rites (patterns 8 and 13) will also observe either no others at all (13) or one daily rite (8). In three patterns (13, 6, and 11) only individual rites are observed, and in two others (patterns 1 and 3) only daily rites are observed. Finally, there are three patterns (2, 5, and 9) in which all three individual and all three seasonal rites are observed, and four more (patterns 4, 7, 14, and 10) in which two or three individual and two or three seasonal rites are observed. Of all seven of the latter patterns, only pattern 9 lacks any daily offering. None of the fourteen patterns involves seasonal rites to the exclusion of all others.

The fourteen patterns by place of residence of the respondents are shown in Table 8. Four patterns are found only in urban places (5, 14, 10, and 9) and one (pattern 1) is also entirely urban except for two households in Yasuhara. Five patterns (4, 7, 12, 6, and 11) are found only in rural communities, but in a curious distribution: all are limited to Sone. Indeed, Sone shares only pattern 2 with any other places, all of which are urban. Three patterns (8, 1, and 13) are found only in rural Yasuhara, and one (pattern 3) is found in both Yasuhara and Takane but not in Sone. What shall we make of Sone, where five of the fourteen patterns are unique and only one other is shared? The diversity and exclusivity of pattern in Sone cannot be explained by diversity of Buddhist sect affiliation, for almost all the households belong to the Zen sect and are parishioners of the local temple. Consequently, this offers an occasion for a more general discussion of the meaning of patterns of worship. If we group the six patterns reported for Sone and refer back to Table 7, we find that four of the patterns (2, 4, 7, and 12) include

TABLE 6

The Fourteen Most Common Patterns of Worship: Occasions When Offerings Are Made to the Tablets

(N = 216)

Patterns and number of households reporting them	Periodic anniversaries of death	Annual deathday	Festival of the Dead	Equinoxes	New Year	Monthly deathday	Daily morning rite	Daily evening rite
1 (35)							x	x
2 (29)	x	x	x	x	x	x	x	x
3 (24)							x	
4 (23)	x	x	x	x	x	x	x	x
5 (16)	x	x	x		x	x	x	
6 (13)	x							
7 (11)	x		x	x	x	x	x	x
8 (11)						x	x	
9 (9)	x	x	x	x	x	x		
10 (9)	x	x	x	x		x	x	
11 (9)	x	x						
12 (9)	x				x	x	x	x
13 (9)						x		
14 (9)	x	x	x	x		x	x	x
TOTAL	10	6	7	6	6	10	10	6

TABLE 7

The Fourteen Most Common Patterns of Worship: The Individual and the Collectivity

(N = 216)

Patterns	Rites for the individual ancestor			Rites for the collectivity of the ancestors				
				Seasonal			Daily	
	Periodic anniversaries of death	Monthly deathday	Annual deathday	Festival of the Dead	Equinoxes	New Year	Morning rite	Evening rite
2	x	x	x	x	x	x	x	x
4	x	x		x		x	x	x
5	x	x	x	x	x	x	x	
7	x	x		x	x	x	x	
14	x	x	x	x	x		x	x
12	x	x		x	x	x	x	x
10	x	x	x	x	x		x	x
9	x	x	x	x	x	x		
8		x		x	x	x		
1							x	
3							x	x
13		x						
6	x							
11	x		x					

NOTE: In the first seven patterns, at least one of each of the three types of rites (individual, seasonal, daily) is observed; in the next two patterns only two of the three types are observed; and in the last five patterns only one type of rite is observed.

TABLE 8

The Fourteen Most Common Patterns of Worship: Breakdown by Place of Residence

$(N = 216)$

Patterns and number of households reporting them	Urban households						Rural households		
	Tokyo (46)	Osaka (37)	Kyoto (22)	Hanshin (6)	Nara (8)	Misc. (8)	Sone (72)	Yasuhara (14)	Takane (3)
2 (29)	3	4	7	3	1	4	7	–	–
4 (23)	–	–	–	–	–	–	23	–	–
5 (16)	10	3	–	–	2	1	–	–	–
7 (11)	–	–	1	–	–	–	11	–	–
14 (9)	–	7	1	–	1	–	–	–	–
12 (9)	–	–	–	–	–	–	9	–	–
10 (9)	5	3	1	–	–	–	–	–	–
9 (9)	2	4	1	2	–	–	–	7	–
8 (11)	1	1	2	–	–	–	–	–	–
1 (35)	11	11	5	–	3	3	–	2	–
3 (24)	12	2	3	1	–	–	–	3	3
13 (9)	2	2	2	–	1	–	–	2	–
6 (13)	–	–	–	–	–	–	13	–	–
11 (9)	–	–	–	–	–	–	9	–	–

both of the daily offerings as well as at least one individual and one seasonal rite; the other two Sone patterns (6 and 11) involve only individual rites.

This situation permits at least one unambiguous interpretation. We can assume that when offerings are made every morning and night it means that a household is still maintaining traditional patterns of ancestor worship, despite differences in other respects. We could then argue that those who omit the daily offering of food care about the ancestors so little that they do not even offer them daily nourishment. This would further lead us to suggest that the Sone households participating in patterns 2, 4, 7, and 12 are quite traditional in that they observe a fairly full range of ancestral rites. Those involved in patterns 6 and 11, who direct their attention solely to individual rites and neglect all others, might be taken to represent some kind of new household, unconcerned with the worship of the collectivity of the ancestral dead and emphasizing instead individual memorialism. But would we be making the right assumptions? I do not think it possible to isolate one set of factors that can explain the great variability in this one small community.

What considerations affect the decision to hold a rite? The number of such considerations is legion, but they obviously include the questions of whether the household is the main or branch house and whether in the latter case it is a recently created domestic unit. The decision may also depend on whether there is a household resident who takes it upon himself to make the offerings. A recent death might increase the likelihood of marking deathday rites, whereas on the other hand the household simply may not command the financial means necessary to pay for priests and special offerings. As a last example, chosen to show just how complex the matter really is, it may even be that the family has recently given up the traditional breakfast, one consequence of which may be the abandoning of the morning offering to the ancestors on the grounds that they will have no fondness for eggs, toast, and coffee. In an effort to see whether some or any of these factors might be operating to produce the patterning peculiar to Sone, I looked at the households reporting each of them. Yet not one of them, nor any combination for that matter, will satisfactorily explain the situation. Age of the household head, composition of the household, dates of death of senior ascendants, recency of death of senior or junior family members, economic level, numbers and kinds of memorial tablets—none of these factors correlates even marginally with the patterns of worship reported.

Were the occasions of worship in any way based on the holding of tablets, we might expect to find that the greater the number of generations represented by the tablets the more rites will be observed, at least on individual anniversaries of death and on deathdays. We might also assume that rites for nonascendants are fewer in number and less generally observed. But the figures in Table 9 show that this is not at all true, or true only in the most restricted sense. Under the column head "Number of ascendant generations" are three groups of houses: those having no ascendants' tablets, those having one to three generations of tablets, and those having four to fourteen generations. The table gives the percentage of households within each group that reports observing the different rites. There is a steep rise in the percentage of households observing anniversaries of death as we move from the first column to the third, but that progression holds for no other rite. Indeed the overall pattern of worship is puzzling in the extreme. From the viewpoint of the generational depth of the tablets, the findings are as follows. The group of households with four to fourteen generations of tablets is more likely to observe anniversaries of death, monthly deathdays, the New Year, and the rites of the morning and evening than are the other two groups, and is less likely to observe annual deathdays, bon, and the equinoxes. The group of households with one to three generations of tablets is more likely to observe annual deathdays, bon, and the equinoxes than are the other two groups, and is less likely to observe monthly deathdays, the New Year, and the morning and evening rites. The group of households with no ascendants' tablets is neither most nor least likely to observe any of the rites.

There remains an alternative explanation. Might it not be that patterns of worship are determined by the personal predilections of the responsible members of the household? We have seen a broad range of attitudes toward the ancestral spirits displayed. Some people say that they should be the object of constant prayer; some feel that they must be fed every day; some find no reason to be concerned for them at all.

TABLE 9

Rites Observed in Relation to
Number of Ascendant Generations in Altar

($N = 460$)

Occasion	None ($N = 61$)		1-3 ($N = 335$)		4-14 ($N = 64$)		Total	
	No.	Pct.	No.	Pct.	No.	Pct.	No.	Pct.
Periodic anniversaries of death								
Yes	28	45.9%	204	60.9%	43	67.2%	275	59.8%
No	33		131		21		185	
Monthly deathday								
Yes	33	54.1	181	54.0	41	64.1	255	55.4
No	28		154		23		205	
Annual deathday								
Yes	23	37.7	148	44.2	20	31.3	191	41.5
No	38		187		44		269	
Festival of the Dead								
Yes	37	60.7	218	65.1	32	50.0	287	62.4
No	24		117		32		173	
Equinoxes								
Yes	32	52.5	189	56.4	22	34.4	243	52.8
No	29		146		42		217	
New Year								
Yes	26	42.6	142	42.4	29	45.3	197	42.8
No	35		193		35		263	
Daily morning rite								
Yes	38	62.3	202	60.3	42	65.6	282	61.3
No	23		133		22		178	
Daily evening rite								
Yes	28	45.9	140	41.8	36	56.3	204	44.3
No	33		195		28		256	

Perhaps the ancestral rites are, above all, an area where individual preference is given free rein. With the weakening influence of institutionalized Buddhism, households no longer need to be so concerned as they once were with the formally prescribed occasions of worship. The household may now worship its ancestors in the ways it deems fitting and most efficacious. This may well represent the ultimate effect of the privatization of worship, for it is significant that no household reporting the most common patterns of worship apparently feels constrained to observe the seasonal, semipublic rites to the exclusion of all others. Of even greater significance is the willingness of so many household members to tell us when they worship the ancestors, totally without regard for the orthodox version of when the Japanese are said to perform these rites.

Our concern in this chapter has been with how the Japanese deal with the dead. Whatever the variations in practice, we have found evidence of beliefs strongly suggesting that death does not completely sever the ties between the deceased and the members of his household. A person can expect that in the normal course of things his spirit will continue to share in the life of his immediate kinsmen, at least until that distant time when he will be honored only as one of the remote ancestors.

Four. *Approaches to the Ancestors*

> Is *pietas* bound up exclusively with ancestor worship or does it reflect a
> general factor in the relations between successive generations that is only
> mobilized in a special degree and form in ancestor worship? ... A study of
> Japanese religious practices and values would be particularly rewarding
> from this angle, since they do not appear to have an ancestral cult but have
> practices that resemble ancestor worship.
> —*Fortes 1961: 188, 190*

IN THE PRECEDING chapter we have seen something of the ritual objects used in or connected with the worship of the ancestors and other
kinsmen, and we have also learned something of the occasions when
such worship occurs. But we have yet to consider the nature of the inter-
actions between the living and the dead members of the household. We
may recall that when any member of the household dies, no matter what
the quality of his relationships with others during his lifetime, no matter whether he was evil and outrageous or good and gentle, obsequies
are performed and a memorial tablet prepared. "It is recognized that
possibly there were some among the ancestors whose total contribution
to the welfare of the stem family would have to be counted as a minus
rather than a plus, but these ancestors are not sorted out and given any
less or different respect and attention. The mere fact that they were
predecessors is sufficient to command respect and attention from their
descendants of the family." (K. Brown 1964: 121.) This does not mean
that death wipes out memories of enmity and conflict. Indeed, veneration may reflect in part a concern that a slighted or neglected spirit of
the dead might return to harm the living.

How concerned are people that the ancestral rites be observed? In the
Iwate community of Takane (K. Brown 1964: 120), there is a strong
feeling that one should care for the ancestors through the proper observance of bon and the equinoxes, and through periodic offerings at
the altar. In Tokyo's Shitayama-chō (Dore 1958: 316), interviews with
78 people living in households where there was an altar turned up only

nine who reported that they never performed any acts of worship there. Significantly, eight of the nine were under twenty-five years of age, and only two were household heads. The significance lies in the fact that many people do not take part in ancestral rites until they become heads of families, unless they are first-born sons. Worship at the altar is primarily a family duty rather than an act of personal devotion. Only thirteen of Dore's 78 informants revealed any hostility toward acts of worship, and ten of these were under twenty-five; two of the thirteen said that they would hold no memorial services for their parents when they die. In Nagasawa (Ooms 1967: 297), no one gives any clear reason for holding the memorial rites, nor does anyone appear to offer principled objections to their observance. The results of my own research—a 1963 tablet census of 595 households in both rural and urban communities (discussed further in Chapter 5)—show that of the 457 households with any tablets at all that answered my question about occasions of worship, only 1.5 percent said that they never paid any attention to the ancestors.

Only one comprehensive sociological study of attitudes and practices relating to ancestor worship has been published in Japanese (Maeda 1965). It is obviously not possible to do justice to it here, but a summary of some of Maeda's findings will be helpful. His thesis is that the future of ancestor worship in Japan is very dim indeed, largely because of the decline of the household system itself. His data are drawn from studies conducted chiefly in the late 1950's of 21 rural communities throughout the country. One of Maeda's special concerns is the relationship between a person's age and his attitude toward ancestor worship. People in their twenties and thirties tend to evince little interest in ancestral rites, in part, they say, because they often have no memory of the people represented by the tablets, but also because they define the rites as properly the concern of the older household members (Maeda 1965: 181).

It would be a mistake to think that as a group the young are not religious, for many of these same young informants are quite active in religious organizations. Maeda concludes that ancestor worship is conceived of as a household duty and not a religious activity. Significantly, young people demonstrated about an equal degree of apathy toward both the community's tutelary deity and the ancestors (Maeda 1965: 185). But it is still rare for a household to ignore its ancestors altogether,

TABLE 10

*Age, Education, and Occupation of Those Offering
Daily Prayers at the Ancestral Altar*

Education and occupation	Age	
	20 to 39	Over 60
Education		
Minimum compulsory	24.6%	66.7%
More than minimum compulsory	17.4	56.7
Occupation		
Agriculture, fishing, and forestry	31.0	65.0
All others	16.6	55.0

SOURCE: Maeda (1965: 234–35).

and there is much evidence of a considerable difference between attitude and practice even among those who say they do not believe in the existence of ancestral spirits. The number of those who deny the existence of the spirits is much larger than the number who say they never pray at the altar. One of the few clear statements of disbelief was made by a young man quoted as saying "I participate only because I want to avoid criticism by the villagers. I don't believe in ancestor worship at all." Maeda says that such rational positions of dissent are often overwhelmed by emotions or circumstances that lead the unbeliever to offer prayers to the ancestors (1965: 188–89).

In a postscript, Maeda presents some tentative findings based on a later study (undertaken in 1964) that focuses particular attention on the factors of age, education, and occupation as they relate to attitudes toward ancestor worship. Table 10 gives the percentages of those who replied affirmatively to the question "Do you offer a daily prayer at the ancestral altar?" Although at both age levels those with more education are less apt to pray at the altar daily, the overall percentages for the over-sixty group are much higher than those for the younger group. The breakdown by occupation is obviously intended to isolate very roughly those households where the corporate principles are likely to be strongest, i.e. those engaged in agriculture, fishing, and forestry. The descent line and the inheritance of property are important considerations in such households; in them the percentage of young people who say they worship daily is almost double that in the other occupational group.

There has long been some dispute over the identity of the person

TABLE 11

*Persons Responsible for Care of Memorial
Tablets, by Household Type*

$(N = 460)$

Persons responsible	Head unmarried		Conjugal		Two- and three-generation stem		Total	
	No.	Pct.	No.	Pct.	No.	Pct.	No.	Pct.
Head (male)	3	42.9%	28	8.8%	8	5.9%	39	8.5%
Head (female)	2	28.5	31	9.8	7	5.2	40	8.7
Wife	—	—	154	48.4	22	16.3	176	38.3
Mother	—	—	3	0.9	42	31.1	45[a]	9.8
Head and wife	—	—	38	12.0	3	2.2	41	8.9
Male head and mother	1	14.3	—	—	2	1.5	3	0.7
Female head and mother	1	14.3	—	—	1	0.8	2	0.4
Wife and mother	—	—	1	0.3	10	7.4	11	2.3
Not fixed	—	—	44	13.8	15	11.1	59[b]	12.8
Other	—	—	19	6.0	25	18.5	44	9.6
TOTAL	7	100.0%	318	100.0%	135	100.0%	460	100.0%

[a] Includes two households with female heads.
[b] Includes five households with female heads.

accorded primary responsibility for caring for the memorial tablets, i.e. for offering them food and drink, flowers, and incense (Morioka 1968: 42). It has generally been argued that it is usually the women of the house who assume this task, but my data offer only limited support to this position (see Table 11). I obtained 460 responses to the question "Who has primary responsibility for taking care of the ancestral tablets in your house?" Wives or mothers of the household head are reported to be responsible in almost exactly half of the households (232); the wife of the household head in 176 cases (75.9 percent); the mother of the household head in 45 cases (19.4 percent); and the wife and the mother together in 11 cases (4.7 percent). In an additional 44 cases (about 10 percent of the total) a woman is said to hold joint responsibility with the male household head. In still another 44 cases a woman other than the wife or mother of the household head—usually a grandmother, a daughter, or a son's wife—is reported to be responsible. Thus more than two-thirds of my 460 responses show a woman figuring in the care of the memorial tablets.

However, women share the responsibility with males in a particular way. It may well be that, on the one hand, responsibility for the care of the tablets is conceived as belonging to the head of the household, who plays a central role in the formal memorial services (at least this was formerly the legal requirement), whereas on the other hand, the purely domestic activity of offering food and drink on a daily basis is conceived as the woman's duty. But even this distinction does not hold universally, as the following personal communication from Etsuko Ohnuki-Tierney reveals: "The practice at my home . . . was that it was the responsibility of my parents. Now that I look back, I am rather intrigued that my father, who never participated in food preparation and did not even dream of doing so, voluntarily served the offering of meals at the family altar whenever he was around and mother had not done so. Sometimes either one of them would tell one of us children to do it."

In this connection, Morioka (1968: 41–42) has some extremely perceptive comments on the observance of bon in the hamlet of Niike in Okayama Prefecture in the late 1950's. He found that the most popular activity was the visit to the graves of the ancestors, which almost everyone participated in. The next most popular was the sending off of the souls—here called *hotoke-okuri* (sending off of the buddhas)—at the stream that flows through the community. The only three households not participating were recently established, and had no one to send off. Morioka discovered that "the old people with the assistance of women and children assume the main responsibility for household religious events which are organized around the ancestor festival as the core ritual. It follows from this that the task of socializing the younger generation into these household rituals is mainly done by old people." He thinks that when the old people are gone, the young will maintain only such essential rituals as visits to the graves and the sending off of the ancestors. In the absence of the grandparental generation, "a young household head will begin to be involved deeply in religious events in the family. However, the total volume of participation of the household in this stage of family cycle will decrease if compared with the stage when the old were still alive." (*Ibid.*)

Who teaches the children of the family to venerate the ancestors? An answer to this momentous question would tell us a great deal about the future of ancestor worship in Japan. However, an answer is not easily come by. The conventional wisdom among Japanese who have given the matter any thought may be easily summed up: if there is a grandmother in the house, her grandchildren will learn from her; but if there are no old people at all, then the children are likely to know nothing about the ancestors. It is not hard to see why this view is so commonly held. Since grandmothers have more free time than do their busy daughters-in-law, they can be assigned relatively light household tasks. In recent times, these tasks have increasingly included baby-sitting as husbands and wives alike have taken jobs. The traditional role of the grandmother has always embraced looking after the children, and grandmothers are thought "naturally" to take more interest in religious and ritual affairs. Therefore, they are the logical choice to teach the children about the ancestors. But there is more to it than that. Since women have longer life expectancies than men in Japan, the grandmother, where there is one, is usually the oldest household member. Such an elderly woman is, above all, the closest link with the ancestors. She more than anyone else in the family *knew* the people whose memorial tablets are in the altar. Those tablets represent her husband and his parents, perhaps some of her own children, and sometimes even members of the household in which she was born. She will in due course join them, and so she does what she can to see to it that the surviving family members will remember her as she remembers and cares for those who have died before her.

But in Japan today most families are bereft of grandparents. Do they then neglect to teach the children to venerate the ancestors? And if not, who takes the responsibility for instructing the children in this family duty? The best study I know of that attempts to answer these questions was conducted by Morioka in 1964–65 (Morioka 1972). Since I am not one who believes that Japanese society undergoes cataclysmic change every decade, I suggest that it is entirely appropriate to deal with his data as though they were contemporary. The number of families surveyed was 295, each with a first son or first daughter in the fifth or sixth grade of primary school. Ninety-two were rural households in an agricultural community in Yamanashi Prefecture; 103 lived in areas of small commercial and industrial enterprises in Tokyo; 100 lived in residential areas of Tokyo. The percentages of households having domestic altars were 92.3, 68.9, and 43.0, respectively (see also Table 14, page 160).

The children, all about ten or eleven years old, were asked if they were ever told to worship at the altar (the verb used is *ogamu*, which has the broad meaning "to worship, to venerate, to pay respect to, to pray to, to bow before"). In the rural households, 65 percent said yes; in the commercial, blue-collar areas of Tokyo 51 percent said yes; and in the Tokyo residential districts 71 percent said yes. This last figure is a real surprise; although these white-collar families have the fewest altars, they have the highest rate of telling their children to venerate them. And we should not forget that it is in this very kind of family that grandmothers are least commonly found. Now, place of residence is at best a shaky guide to the prediction of religious behavior. Because it is often said that in agricultural households we will find contemporary residues of the most traditional behavior, the obvious question is whether reclassifying households by occupation of the household head will provide a more sensitive index of the situation. The reclassification yields, in fact, about the same results. For agricultural households the figure is 64 percent; for commercial ones 57 percent; for white-collar families 72 percent. There remains the possibility that family composition is an important consideration in determining domestic religious behavior. Indeed, there is a difference, if a not terribly striking one, between nuclear families (both parents and children only) and extended families (both parents, children, and at least one grandparent). The respective proportions are 55 percent and 66 percent, and this spread is increased if we distinguish between "created" and "succeeded" families—49 percent and 65 percent, respectively. That is, children in succeeded families are apparently much more likely to be told to venerate the ancestors than those in created or neolocal families. And lastly, about 60 percent of both girls and boys say that they are told to go to the altar, suggesting that it does play a role in the daily life of household members of whatever type. (Although there is no difference by sex for venerating the altar, there is for the god shelf, at which 56 percent of the boys and only 46 percent of the girls say they are told to worship.)

The genuine surprise in all the foregoing is this: that in the rural districts and the Tokyo commercial district, where the proportion of households with altars is high, the rate of telling children to venerate them is low; whereas in the Tokyo residential area, where the proportion of altars is low, the rate of telling the children to venerate them is the highest rate of all. Why? If we knew the answer to that question, we would know what the future holds; for although these must be considered highly tentative findings, the wholly unexpected characteristic of the households in the Tokyo residential area—largely nuclear families with less than twenty years in their present houses, and whose heads are employed in white-collar jobs—deserves close attention. Put the other way, in the rural and commercial areas the proportion of households with altars is much higher than the proportion of children being told to venerate them.

Why should this be? Morioka suggests the possibility that the training of children (he uses the word *shitsuke*) is more strict in the white-collar families than in the others. It is possible, then, that in teaching their children "proper" behavior these white-collar parents simply include the paying of respect to the ancestral altar. Children in neighborhoods such as these also have very little contact with religion outside the home, for there are seldom any public ceremonies or rituals for which they would go to or be taken to either a shrine or a temple. But children in rural areas, and to a somewhat lesser extent in the commercial districts of Tokyo, do encounter other kinds of religious contexts—festivals at the shrine of the tutelary deity of the hamlet, village, neighborhood, or ward, and temple activities of various kinds. They may simply not have to be told so often to pray at the domestic altar because it is a natural act in the course of the daily routine in their households. To these tentative suggestions of Morioka I would add one of my own. It may be that fewer nuclear families in the Tokyo residential area just casually keep an altar, and that those who have altars are the committed, who teach their children to venerate them.

The children were also asked which members of the family saw to it that they worshiped at the altar. In the rural community it was overwhelmingly the grandmother and the mother; in the Tokyo commercial district, the father, the mother, and the grandmother; in the Tokyo residential areas, the father and the mother. Only in the rural area and in the extended families is the role of the grandparents in this particular aspect of child training more important than that of the parents. Is this because where a grandparent is present the overall training of children is generally his or her responsibility? If this were the case, then we could make nothing of the grandmother's key role in the single aspect of teaching children to venerate the ancestral altar. But this is not the case at

1. Gate of the Kōanji, a Buddhist temple in Tokyo. In the foreground are several gravestones and stupas.

2. Graves along the coast near Cape Muroto (Kōchi Prefecture). The natural rocks are gravestones. A new grave is covered with a small roof.

3. Priests gathered for the final funeral prayers in the deceased's house. At left is the *butsudan*, filled with offerings of food. In the alcove (center) is the coffin, of untreated wood bound with straw rope.

4. Procession to the place where the "farewell rite" will be held. The coffin is in the palanquin. The woman in formal dress behind the rear palanquin-bearer carries the cloth-covered memorial tablet.

5. The "farewell rite." The coffin (still in the palanquin) is at right. Paper umbrellas mark the locations of priests.

6. A relative lights incense and prays at the palanquin containing the coffin. Note the temporary tablet, from which the sheath has been removed, on the larger of the two small tables.

7. A living stupa marking the 50th anniversary of death.

8. New grave. Seven miniature stupas, one to be broken each week during the mourning period, are framed by flower offerings.

9. New grave. Temporary tablet partially covered, and two trays of offerings.

10. New stupas, all for the same person, at a grave during the funeral.

11. Ancestral altar, with memorial tablets on the top shelf. Scrolls of the Amida Buddha are on the wall.

12. *Butsudan* of the same household as 11. The memorial tablet at the left is for "the spirits of those who have died for their country."

13. Priest at a *butsudan*. The boxes, still in their store wrapping paper, contain gifts of food. A bottle of soda stands beside a cucumber horse.

14. A gravestone in the form of an old *ihai*.

15. Special altar for the first *bon* of the deceased. The temporary tablet bears a posthumous name ending in the title *daishi*.

16. Main ancestral altar at *bon*. It bears several memorial tablets and offerings of fruits and tea. The posthumous name on the central tablet also ends with *daishi*.

17. Feast at *bon* in front of the altars shown above.

18. *Ihai* room in a Zen sect temple. Each *ihai* is dedicated by a separate parish family.

19. Three *ihai* in the old style from a Jōdo sect temple.

20. Three modern *ihai* from the Takeda family household altar.

21. Receiving stupas at the end of the *segaki* rite. Note the *nyorai* banners over the *segaki* altar.

all, as it turns out. The children in all three areas, when asked who was responsible for their overall training, seldom mentioned grandparents —everywhere it was the mother who figured most prominently. It is true, then, that grandmothers have a great deal to do with teaching the children to worship the ancestors; it is not true that families with an altar but no grandparents neglect the ancestors.

Caring for the Ancestors

We know that many people pray at the altar daily or on special memorial occasions, but we have yet to ask why they do so. We have noted that the spirits of the ancestors are wholly dependent on the living for comfort and lack any capacity to improve their own lot after death. One of the major reasons for holding observances at the altar is to extend to them the care they are thought to require. It is also generally believed that should they be neglected they may manifest their sorrow and anger in a way potentially dangerous to the living. We have seen that a common theme of ghost stories is the appearance of a spirit whose sorrowful mien or menacing attitude provides a stimulus for the living to perform some act designed to quiet it. Such acts may include making a more elaborate memorial tablet, holding more complete memorial services, offering up special prayers for the soul, or simply making more regular offerings of food. All are intended to make up for the neglect or ill-treatment of the spirit.

Yet another spur to ancestral rites is the assumption that success and prosperity flow in part from the beneficent protection of the ancestral dead. Not that most people anticipate any kind of direct intervention on the part of the ancestors, for the Japanese believe that the actions and initiatives of the living determine the outcome of efforts to improve one's lot in this world. The ancestors are rather felt to enjoy a generally passive existence, overseeing the actions of the living in the manner of tutelary deities (Asakawa 1903: 35–36). Thus, the living bear a heavy burden with respect to the household dead. The spirits of the ancestors are felt to be overjoyed at any positive achievement by a descendant, and are indeed given some of the credit for success, but the full onus of failure falls on the living alone. Much the same attitude is reflected in the ritual reporting to the gods in Shinto (Mason 1935).

Although it is usually the wandering spirits and vengeful gods, as well as the spirits of the recently dead, who are thought to be potentially harmful, it would appear nonetheless that even the spirits of the ancestral dead are not always felt to be benign, for we do have reports of harm or troubles visited on people by their direct lineal ascendants. Bernier (1970: 110) says that the people of Sone believe that the spirits of the dead harm only members of their own households. Few Japanese with whom I have discussed this possibility entertain it seriously (see also Ooms 1967: 300), but when pressed they have suggested hypothetical instances. One man said "All right, suppose that a man whose father left him a good house and fields begins to neglect his work. He may get caught up in Mah-Jongg or something like that. Eventually he might be ruined and might have to sell all the property assembled over the years by his ancestors. In such a case the father's spirit might try to warn his son, or might even punish him. He might fall ill or be hurt in an accident, or his animals or children might turn sickly. That would be the way the father's spirit would take revenge on his son, although he would probably first try to give him a warning that he ought to change his ways. [Long pause.] But I have never heard of a case like that." This informant may never have heard of such a case, but he was certainly at no loss for a graphic example.

However strongly most people feel that they have nothing to fear from their own ancestors, some have a very different view. The sect Tenshō-kōtai-jingū-kyō, one of the New Religions, is an example (Kerner 1974; Lebra 1974). The teachings of the foundress are unequivocal in attributing to the karmic link (*innen*) between ancestor and descendant the chief cause of human suffering and misfortune. Converts are admonished both to sever their ties with family members who do not join the sect and, as one step in the cutting of the bonds of karma, to destroy the ancestral altar and the god shelf. Once the bonds are broken the sect member may hope for a healthy and happy life. In reckoning ancestral status no distinctions are drawn among lineal, collateral, or cognatic kin, or between spirits of the newly dead and those of remote ancestors; all are equally malevolent (Kerner 1974).

But this sect is relatively small, and I think it fair to say that to the extent that most Japanese attribute misfortune and illness to the ancestors at all, it will be said that the cause lies in the neglect of the collectivity of the ancestors rather than in the malign disposition of any single forebear. Yoshida (1967) does report some cases of direct individual retribution, to be sure, but it is my impression that a series of misfortunes is usually thought to result from poor orientation of the house (not the grave, as in China). In such a case a geomancer will be called in to find out if alterations are required to put an end to some unsuspected offense to a god such as Konjin. The ancestors seldom figure in such diagnoses. If the family should consult a medium instead, it is my impression, shared by Plath (1964: 310), that the cause of trouble is likely to be identified as the spirit of a specific person. Whether this identification results from the fact that mediums deal largely at this personal level, I do not know. Ordinarily the medium will find that some spirit not generally given to hostile or aggressive acts has become angry or bitter. This particular spirit may have been consciously or unconsciously omitted from the rites or may have been given too little attention; or some event in the world of the living may have precipitated its outburst. The remedy is usually to make amends in some way specified by the spirit through the medium. The most common lay explanation for a spirit's anger is that the ancestral rites in general have been neglected. The collectivity of the ancestors may well give some sign that is unmistakably a warning and a punishment—perhaps a succession of deaths or the death of a young family member. Special memorial services for the ancestral spirits may then be held, or the scale of regular observances may be increased.

On some occasions the dead do reach out directly to intervene in the world of the living. The following story was told to me in 1951, when I was living in Yasuhara in Kagawa Prefecture. During World War II, at the time of severe food shortages, a man from a nearby hamlet told an aged female relative that she might as well die if she could no longer work and earn her own keep. Not long afterward she hanged herself. The event shocked the villagers, and the man was widely censured. It was with obvious satisfaction that I was told how her spirit had taken revenge on him. One dark night, while he was walking along a path on his way to a Buddhist prayer meeting, the lantern he was carrying went out. As he stopped to see what was wrong with it, the ghost of the old woman rose up on the path beside him. He ran into a nearby house, all disheveled and in a state of shock. It was several days before he regained the ability to speak. People said that it was no more than he deserved, and they expressed pity for the woman who had been driven to take her own life.

The idea of being haunted is a staple of Japanese fiction and folklore. Akutagawa (1957: 131) has written a short story similar to the episode related above in which an old woman, furious at being told that if she cannot work she might as well die, screams at her tormentor, "I'll die and haunt you for life!" However, the apparition in the case from Yasuhara was reacting to an event that had occurred while she was still alive. Her ghost appeared to the proximate cause of her death, her tormentor, not to someone who had failed to care for her spirit after death. Indeed, it is the common view that ghosts strike out most often at those who angered them in life, for they remain possessed by the emotions that they felt in life. I asked several people in Yasuhara if they believed that neglect of ancestral rites alone could precipitate a malevolent act by a spirit of someone long dead. They denied the possibility. In their view, the neglect of proper observances was far more likely to produce general misfortune or malaise; in addition, all the ancestors would be involved, both as victims of the neglect and as perpetrators of the revenge. At the very least, the ancestral generations might fail to provide assistance in preventing the decline of a household's fortunes. In a failing house the ancestral rites may well be neglected; thus everything conspires against it. Neglected or abandoned entirely, the ancestors can no longer exercise a tutelary function; this deprives their descendants of the sustaining presence and the abiding concern that they might otherwise have provided.

Like many of the New Religions, Reiyūkai-kyōdan, founded in 1930, strongly supports the worship of the ancestors. By 1970 this sect claimed more than four million adherents.

> Reiyūkai teachings represent a fusion of two primary ideas: the virtue of the Lotus Sutra and the importance of ancestor worship. It holds that the spirit of the individual is indissolubly connected with the spirits filling the universe in all three stages of being that are set forth in Buddhist doctrine. The service of offering food, drink and worship to the ancestral spirits is consequently a service to all spirits, Buddhas and *kami*. Conversely, neglect of the ancestral spirits ... is the cause of all misfortune. In order to avoid adversity people are advised to gather together as many of their ancestors' mortuary tablets as possible and serve the spirits they represent with reverence. (Agency for Cultural Affairs 1972: 209.)

Similar sentiments are expressed in a publication of the lay Buddhist organization called Risshō-kōsei-kai, which was founded in 1938 and which claimed about five million adherents in 1970 (Anon. 1966: 132):

It is natural for man to thank his parents and perform filial duties wholeheartedly. There is no difference between filial piety and ancestor worship. It is originally an act of expressing thanks, in which a grateful mind is extended from parents to grand-parents, from grand-parents to great-grand-parents, and so on, infinitely to the most remote ancestors.

This grateful mind, extended chronologically, may also be directed to every object in one's surroundings as a true development of the Bodhisattva Way. If it is universally practiced, the world will never fail to be a peaceful and cheerful community. This is the real significance of ancestor worship.

Since the ancestors are not expected to intervene directly to affect the outcome of actions taken by the living, prayers said to them are usually of an extremely general character. A common word in these simple prayers is *mamoru* ("to watch over," "to take care of," "to look after"). This word points up the reciprocal nature of the relationship between the living and the dead, for just as the ancestors are asked to look after the household, so one of the chief duties of the living is to look after the spirits of the dead. There is, nonetheless, a difference in degree. The dependency of the ancestors on their descendants is total, and it is generally believed that only through the ministrations of the members of his own household can the spirit of the dead at last find peace. One of the ways the living may bring unhappiness to the dead is shown in a scene from an early-eighteenth-century puppet play, *The Drum of the Waves of Horikawa (Horikawa Nami no Tsuzumi)*. Ofuji, distressed by the misbehavior of her sister Otane, reminds her of their mother's last words, which were an injunction to Ofuji to watch after Otane as though she were her mother. Ofuji cries out "These were her last words. Every day, morning and night, I repeat those last injunctions before her memorial tablet, just as if they were some holy writing. Have you forgotten them so soon? To think that you could wish to bring grief to your sister in this world and suffering on Mother's dead body in the world of the hereafter!" (Keene 1961: 77.)

It is entirely correct, I think, to say that offerings and prayers are made directly to the ancestors, not to the Buddha, and certainly not to the priests on the ancestors' behalf. In all fairness to the actual teachings of sects such as Jōdo-shin, which is the largest in Japan, it should be pointed out that its founder specifically denied that human beings could assist the souls of the departed. The purpose of all services for the dead, he taught, is to express gratitude to the Amida Buddha, who alone can deliver the soul into paradise. It follows that the true purpose of the funeral and memorial services is neither to pray for the happiness of the deceased nor to offer consolation to his spirit. Rather, services are conducted for the sake of the bereaved (Hanayama 1969: 38–39). However, in my interviews with families belonging to the Jōdo-shin sect I found only marginal appreciation of this point.

We have not yet done with the implications of the reciprocal character of the relationship between the living and the dead. If the spirits of the dead are felt to be benign overseers, and yet if death has deprived them of all further capacity to affect their own fate and the living are thought able to help them, then it follows that prayers are offered *for* the dead on some occasions and *to* them on others. The distinction between *sosen-kuyō*, where they are prayed for, and *sosen-sūhai*, where they are prayed to, is a very real one, as I shall attempt to show.

In memorializing all the deceased of the household, the survivors do not lose sight of the primacy in death of those who in life were chiefly responsible for maintaining the continuity of the house—especially the members of the direct ascent line of progenitors, with particular emphasis on the most recently dead. For those direct ascendants who have lived with the survivors will most obviously appreciate and be gratified by the successes and accomplishments of the living members of the family. The more remote ascendants, less and less strongly linked to this world, exercise their tutelary powers with a calm detachment. The other memorialized household members are in death roughly of the same relative importance to the affairs of the domestic unit as they were in life. Thus it is not simply that on some occasions the ancestors are prayed for and on others prayed to; the major ancestors are more often prayed to, the minor ones more often prayed for. After all, because the latter have contributed little to the house, little can be asked of them. A man's young son requires in death what he required in life—support and comfort—but a man's father requires not only these, but continued deferential respect as well.

Those who exercised most authority and bore most responsibility in the affairs of the house in life receive proportionally more honor in death. It is for them that the richest tablets and the lengthiest posthumous names are purchased; it is for them that the deathdays are most carefully marked over the longest period. It is unlikely that most households would observe all the anniversary rites for an uncle of the present head who died unmarried. For one thing, if he died very young, his tablet was probably placed in the altar by the present head's grandfather, to whom the child was a son whose life had been cut short. However, the likelihood is very great that the anniversary rites for the head's father will be observed. In theory, all other spirits are venerated as a collectivity during the rites of an important ancestor's memorial service. Dore's view (1958: 144), though, is that with the exception of bon the rites are held for those who live in the memories of family members, rather than for all the spirits. In Nagasawa, most households have many kinsmen "on the fringes of veneration" for whom regular tablets are never made. The temporary paper tablet is sometimes kept for years, or it may soon be burned in the year-god (toshi-gami) fire of the Little New Year (ko-shōgatsu), or in the sending-off fire of bon. These "marginal ancestors" figure largely in Chapters 5 and 6.

The deceased are not equal in death, although the ordering of the tablets on the altar shelves seldom reflects the inequalities. Instead, the inequalities are embodied in the tablets themselves and are based on age, sex, status in the household, and position in society. The following relevant exchange occurs in the 1915 novel *Michikusa* (*Grass on the Wayside*), by Natsume Sōseki (1969: 109):

> She bored Kenzō even more when she talked about her dead child. He had never seen the baby, alive or dead. "Let's see, what was his name?"
>
> "Sakutarō, it was," she said, and pointed at the small buddhist shrine on the wall.
>
> It seemed not only appropriately gloomy inside but quite dusty. From where he sat, it was impossible to make out the posthumous names engraved in gold on the black memorial tablets. But he was not going to get up to find out. "I suppose the small one is his."
>
> "That's right. We decided that the normal size wouldn't be quite right for a baby."

But it would be a mistake to lose sight of the degree to which affection and sentiment, as well as status and related considerations, bind the living and the dead. Dore (1958: 144) believes that household-linked considerations are heavily outweighed by idiosyncratic and personal associations in determining the nature of the relationships between living and dead household members. My interviews abound with material that bears out this view. One woman told me of the tablet for her two-year-old daughter, who had died seventeen years before, "I have it because I want to keep her near at hand (*temoto ni oite oki tai*). A man in his fifties, holding the tablet of his eldest daughter, who had died at the age of four during World War II, said "I have learned about Buddhism so that I could insure my daughter's tranquillity." And a male household head told us that he had taken almost no interest in the care of the tablets until the death of his twenty-two-year-old son some six months before. "My wife always made the morning offerings before, but now we both take care of his spirit. I lead the observance of his monthly deathday."

But relationships between the living and the dead cool with the passage of time and with changes in the status of the survivor. Tanizaki Jun'ichirō has written a short story that touches on this very human theme (1963: 95–159). The narrator recalls how after his mother died when he was still a child, "Father always spent an hour morning and evening reading aloud from the sutras before the memorial tablet. As soon as I thought he was going to stop I would steal up to the altar and sit beside him for the few remaining minutes, running my little string of prayer beads through my fingers. But sometimes he led me there by the hand, saying, 'Come to pray for your mother'; and I had to sit still beside him for the whole hour" (p. 110). His father decides that it would be appropriate for him to remarry after the second anniversary of his wife's death. "After that, Father stopped taking me in to sit beside him during the morning and evening worship at the memorial tablet. The time he spent reading the sutras gradually became shorter" (p. 116).

Nor can the role of guilt and its expiation be overlooked in this context, for where shall we find the child who in his heart of hearts believes that he did everything possible for his parents while they lived? Still, I have the strong impression that guilt is less a determinant of the relationship between the living and the dead than affection and respect are. In Chapter 6 I shall deal with the great variety of tablets that have been made as an expression of personal intimacy; here let me report a relevant account for which I am indebted to Keith Brown:

I went to a New Year's party at the house of a farmer-salaryman's family near Mizusawa. All the usual dōzoku people were there, in addition to various other people born in the house who had moved out as well as people born in other houses who had moved in. One elderly woman who had married out of the house many years earlier was waxing nostalgic about how good it was to be back in the house where she had been born. I asked her why she felt that way, since all her siblings were gone and the building itself was brand new. She turned to the butsudan and said it was because of all the people in there, especially her father. Then she turned to another wall of the room and began pointing out photographs of the ancestors, explaining to me which of them had tablets in the butsudan. She obviously felt warm and close to the altar and to the tablets it contained.

This attitude of intimacy and warmth, which I have often observed as well, needs to be discussed more fully. Although the Japanese do fulfill duties and obligations, they are not automatons locked into an esoteric world of rigid codes of behavior (see Benedict 1946 for the best-known discussion of these matters). There are in Japan, as elsewhere, heedless, irresponsible, and selfish persons. But obligations and the requirements of meeting them are so heavily emphasized in discussions of Japanese ethical codes that the essential humanity of the Japanese people often seems to be forgotten. There is, of course, a concept called *ninjō*, usually translated as "human feelings," that ameliorates the code of obligations and duties. This concept has been thoroughly explored in English, but a detailed analysis of it is not necessary for our purposes; I only want to discuss it as it bears on the relations between the living and the dead. Sugi (1963: 268–70) gives an excellent brief description of ninjō:

> The following are some of the characteristics of *ninjō*: (1) Although *ninjō* presumably allows for human desires and individual needs, it does not include the notion of legal or moral "rights." It was primarily a recognition of the demand for emotional outlet—an escape valve in a regimented society. (2) It concerned private, personal relations—not public. (3) *Ninjō* was not institutionalized—that is, embodied in law.
>
> · · ·
>
> *Ninjō* was seen existing between two specific individuals—rarely more than two; the world of *ninjō* was therefore the world of "unpredictable," private relations formed in intimate social intercourse. In relations between groups or between the individual and the group, the principles of *ninjō* were not applicable, and therefore "human" considerations were theoretically divorced from public social action, since by definition, human impulses—*ninjō*—were endlessly variable, unpredictable, "disorderly."

Ninjō has to do with the human emotions of sympathy, kindness, pity, and love. As we shall see in Chapter 6, there are a great many tablets in the domestic altars of Japanese households whose presence can best be explained by this concept. They are expressions of individual emotion and human sympathy, and it is in this spirit that many of the deceased are given offerings and addressed through the rites directed at them.

Although there is this world of personal, private feelings, looming larger in the lives of most people is the world of obligation, which however intermingled with love and affection represents duty still. Japanese ethics defines one's parents as paramount among those very few individuals toward whom one incurs the unrepayable debt of on. There is about on a characteristic not always taken into account but important to an understanding of how it operates (Lebra 1969: 131). "The unilateral, asymmetric obligation imposed by the *on* has been culturally stabilized and reinforced by systematic indoctrination of indebtedness and gratitude for what the individual was hardly free to accept or refuse: he is reminded of the fathomless *on* he owes to his parents, ancestors, country, and countless fellow-human-beings, alive and deceased, known and unknown to him, for his life, and for what he is today." There is also a Buddhist idea of the on that one owes to all beings of the six planes of existence—*shujō no on*. It is in this connection that Anesaki's observation (1930: 69) has special relevance. "Japanese Buddhists even nowadays observe strictly the periodical services in memory of the deceased members of the family. This is a family cult and ancestor-worship, as it is called, but the spiritual communion intended in the cult may be extended indefinitely to the whole cosmos."

It follows that a person's life is an expression of his effort to repay some portion of this boundless debt; he has traditionally been pledged to support his parents in their old age, to honor their memory in death, and to apologize to their spirits for failure and shortcomings. In July 1968, newspapers carried an account of a locomotive engineer who had unaccountably vanished following an accident in which he had obviously been at fault. He had gone to his natal home to report his negligence to his father's memorial tablet and to offer his apologies. Only then did he turn himself over to the authorities.

The Japanese child is taught that it is his duty to provide for his parents in their old age and to care for them in death. A strikingly literal example of the injunction to care for the ancestors is found in the New Religion Tenri-kyō, according to Schinzinger (1963: 34):

> [Tenri-kyō] treats the person of its dead woman founder as if she were still alive. Meals are served to her and taken away, the morning and evening newspapers are brought to her, and a bath is prepared for her every day. This is the classic example, indeed, of what goes on before every house altar. The youth of today in Japan has little feeling for this aspect of ancestor worship, but in every family there is always someone who observes the pious ritual and will take no food until a little bowl of rice has been placed before the house altar.

It is true that many people I asked about this practice derided it as obviously absurd; but it is in fact only an exaggerated version of what many households do in a less dramatically complete form.

As I have already pointed out, it is quite common—at least at the early memorial services for the dead—to include as a central item in the offerings at the altar some prepared food of which the person was particularly fond in life. Perhaps the most appropriate example in the context of this volume involves Hozumi Nobushige, author of the well-known book *Ancestor Worship and the Japanese Law*, which was first published in 1901 and was long the only book in English on the subject. At the end of the revised seventh edition (1943: 194) is a note written in 1938 by Hozumi Shigetō, who identifies himself as "son and successor to the original author." In this note is a very touching passage. "The most everyday form of ancestor-worship in a Japanese home, as is stated in the book, is to offer, on the family altar, the flower or food which the dead ancestors most loved. My father's favourite flower was the rose, and his favourite food grilled sardine à la japonaise. So in my household we never omit to offer this flower and this dish to his spirit from time to time, on due occasions." To cite another example, on the occasion of the first anniversary of the death of their daughter, wife of the former Prince Higashikuni, the emperor and empress were reported in the Japanese press to have gone to her husband's house for the memorial service. They brought with them buckwheat noodles (*soba*), "of which the Princess had been very fond." A third example, and one of my favorites, I have already shared with David Plath (1964: 308–9). An American acquaintance reported that he and his wife were invited by their widowed landlady to a memorial service for her deceased husband. The ceremony, otherwise entirely traditional, featured a chocolate cake—one of her husband's favorite foods—that bore the decorative inscription "Happy Anniversary, Mr. Y——." The first slice was placed before his tablet on the altar; the rest was distributed among the guests.

Even where the relationship between the deceased and the survivor was very bad, the practice of offering favorite foods—and more—may be observed. In Mishima Yukio's 1950 novel *Ai no kawaki* (*Thirst for Love*), Etsuko's husband has died at the height of an affair with another woman. He had cruelly and deliberately tormented his wife with this affair. As she rides in the hearse, sitting behind his casket, she hears a rattling sound that she concludes must be her husband's pipe, put in the casket with his body because he had been so fond of it. And less than a year after his death, at the autumnal equinox, she is in town shopping for "a pomelo to offer before the tablet of her deceased husband, who had loved that fruit" (Mishima 1969: 6).

The food placed on the altar often is eaten later by those attending the ceremony, or later still by members of the household. The food offered to the wandering spirits is neither personalized in this manner nor eaten by the living after its removal from the special altar where it has been placed. It is scarcely necessary to remark that as the individual fades in the memory of his family such personal touches are abandoned, first because no one remembers him or his tastes very clearly, and second because with the passage of time his spirit is thought to have become in some degree purified and no longer very attached to the world he knew. But until this fading occurs, the spirit of the dead is liable to be dealt with in a very literal way, as though he were still alive. One poignant example will suffice.

In 1962, newspapers in Tokyo carried the tragic story of a woman who was killed when a would-be suicide leaped from the roof of a department store and struck her as she walked along the sidewalk by the building. She was the sole support of her four children, whose desperate plight led to their inclusion in the 1962 "Christmas Cheer Fund" drive of the English-language *Asahi Evening News*. The newspaper's issue of December 12, 1962, carried a memorable photograph with the following caption:

NEEDIEST CASE NO. 4: Children of the Suzuki family in Tokyo's Adachi Ward show their Christmas presents, gifts of Asahi Evening News readers through the Christmas Cheer Fund, to their deceased mother, whose photograph is kept in the family's Buddhist shrine. Left to right are Santa Claus (Hidekazu Yamaguchi of the Asahi Shimbun); Kazumi, 11; Toshio, 6; Harumi, 4; and Mieko, 9.

On the altar are a large framed photograph of the mother, with black ribbons across both upper corners; a flower-filled vase; an incense burner; and a small bowl of cooked rice. The children stand facing the altar, each holding an armload of toys and gifts; Santa Claus, complete with fur-trimmed cap and suit, and with flowing white hair and beard, stands holding out toward the altar a large bouquet of chrysanthemums.

It is not only parents and elders who die, and the death of children is an especially painful event. Little evidence can be found that the once general feelings of resentment and frustration directed at the child for this most unfilial of all acts persist. Instead, the sentiments expressed in Mishima Yukio's 1952 story *Manatsu no shi* (*Death in Midsummer*) (1966: 1–29) are much more commonly encountered. Tomoko, mother of two sons and a daughter, has gone to a beach resort with the children and Yasue, the unmarried sister of her husband Masaru. Tomoko has sent Yasue and the children to the beach while she rests. Yasue suffers a fatal heart attack and two of the children drown. "The funeral offerings came to a considerable sum. Funeral offerings are always larger when the head of the family, who can still provide, is a survivor than when it is his funeral" (p. 12). "The forty-ninth-day services were over. Masaru bought a lot in the Tama Cemetery. These were the first deaths in his branch of the family, and the first graves. Yasue was charged with watching over the children on the Far Shore too: by conference with the main family, her ashes were to be buried in the same lot" (pp. 16–17). Tomoko, Masaru, and their surviving son go to visit the cemetery, which Tomoko finds unexpectedly clean, bright, and spacious, with many grassy areas and much cool shade: "What a nice place. They'll have room to play, and they won't be bored. I can't help thinking it will be good for them. Strange, isn't it?" (p. 18). They leave the cemetery and in front of the station encounter a vendor selling a toy that Tomoko remembers from her childhood. She buys one and gives it to her son, and suddenly realizes that she has been looking for something for the two dead children as well, just as though they had been left at home. She mentions this feeling to her husband. " 'Go ahead and buy something. Buy something for them.' Masaru's tone was tense and almost pleading. 'We can put it on the altar.' 'No. They have to be alive' " (p. 20).

I have not yet dealt with another class of occasions, those when the ancestors receive a share of gifts of food received by the family. These informal occasions are not directly concerned with the cycle of memorial services but emphasize the degree to which the ancestral dead are treated as members of the household. A few examples will show how these informal offerings are handled. I was staying at the house of friends, and one day visitors from Tokyo arrived. They had brought the obligatory gift, which in this case proved to be a box of foreign chocolates. It was much admired, but as is the custom no move was made to serve the sweets while the visitors themselves were still there. After they had gone, however, the grandmother of the house took three pieces of the candy, placed them on a small lacquer dish, and, after opening the door of the altar, set them before the ancestors. The children of the house were clamoring for some, but they were told that they must wait. Their disappointment was so manifest that the old lady relented and said that they could have some "in a little while, when the ancestors have finished."

There are many variations on this theme. Sometimes the entire box of candy or cakes or other gifts of food will be set temporarily before the altar, to be removed later and eaten by the family members. This is particularly the custom with what are referred to generically as "unusual things" (*mezurashī mono*), e.g. especially fine cakes, foods from distant places not usually available locally, or the first fruits of the season. (Some old people will not offer pomegranates to the ancestors because the fruit looks so much like bloody meat when cut.) To many people still it is a breach of etiquette to consume gifts of food without first offering them to the ancestors—the more so when the item in question was a favorite of one or another of the people represented in the altar. The currency of this particular kind of offering is shown in Ooms's data from Nagasawa (1967: 240–41). Of eighteen households with ancestral tablets, three reported that they made no daily offerings; but all eighteen said that they invariably shared gifts of food brought to the family.

In the daily offering to the altar, the ancestors are usually given a portion of the meal before the family eats. When the morning rice is cooked, a bit will be taken off the top of the pan and put in a small bowl that will then be placed on the altar, usually with a cup of tea. Such rice, when it hardens in the air, is rarely thrown away (the Japanese are extremely reluctant to throw out rice in any event). Instead, it will be reheated or incorporated in another dish, fed to a pet (Ooms 1967: 241), or eaten by children or by mice (Embree 1939: 238). In many houses, similar offerings of daily fare are made to the god shelf on the first and fifteenth of every month, but this is much less common than the offering of food to the altar. Some households, to be sure, have given up the practice altogether: "Life is too busy, nowadays, one can't spend all one's time running round with offerings of rice and water for the ancestors" (Dore 1958: 144).

I do not know what has happened to the practice of sharing the morning meal now that so many families have shifted to Western-style breakfasts. It is my guess that the following account by my colleague Etsuko Ohnuki-Tierney of the change in her home represents the trend:

> At our household, quite a while ago we changed to Western-style breakfasts with toast and eggs, and since then we've offered the meal at the altar whenever we first cooked rice, sometimes at noontime and sometimes not until the evening meal. Interestingly enough, we've never offered anything that is not a traditional meal. Of course, when it came to something a guest brought that was not in the category of meals, we did offer at the altar such things as Western fruits.

Once I was alerted to this issue, I began to ask many people about it, and they generally have agreed that the preference probably would be to wait until the day's first traditional meal before sharing any portion with the ancestors.

These changes in tradition have not always been made easily, as Sugimoto Etsu relates in her book *A Daughter of the Samurai* (1925: 26). When she was eight years old, around the middle of the Meiji period, she came home one day to discover her grandmother and a maid sealing up the Buddhist altar with white paper. Although perfectly familiar with the custom of sealing the god shelf during illness and death in the house, "I had never known the [altar] to be sealed; and besides, this was the very hour for it to be lighted in readiness for the evening meal. That was always the pleasantest part of the day; for after the first helping of our food had been placed on a tiny lacquer table before the [altar], we all seated ourselves at our separate tables. . . . But the [altar] was closed. What could it mean?" What it meant was that her father, much impressed by a physician's praise of the nutritional value of meat, had to her grandmother's horror ordered the preparation of beef for the family's meal. The grandmother was sealing off the ancestors from the pollution consequent upon this gross violation of the vegetarian rules that had been observed in Japan up to that time. She might well have sealed off the god shelf, too, for although Shinto makes no injunction against the eating of flesh in ordinary circumstances, it abhors as polluting the blood and death implied by the presence of meat near a sacred place. In any event, the grandmother's actions indicated clearly that a momentous event had occurred—this was the first family meal that could not be shared with the ancestors.

This now almost quaint story highlights a difference between the daily offerings and the offerings made at the memorial services for the individual deceased. On the latter occasions, I think it is clear that traditionalism imposes far fewer constraints than it does on the former ones. We have already noted sardines and chocolate cakes figuring in these offerings. I have no information that meat—however fond the deceased may have been of it—is ever offered at an altar, but I can see no reason whatever to think that it does not happen. After all, it is the individual ancestor who is being feted, not the buddhas or the Buddha. Are these offerings really for the sustenance of the ancestors? It may equally well be that "as respected members of the family they should not be left out of anything—the doors of the *butsudan* are opened when, for instance, a marriage is celebrated in the house—and they have a right to the first share in all the delicacies the family enjoys" (Dore 1958: 323–24). But many older people told me that the ancestors had to eat every day "just like anybody else," and an old woman made the same remark to Ooms (1967: 298).

The issue of what kinds of food are offered to the ancestors on a daily basis is no trivial matter, as we have seen in the discussion of patterns of worship in Chapter 3. The central theme of offerings and reports to the spirits of the dead should be clear by now: the aim is to assure the deceased of the continuance of the pleasures and tastes that he enjoyed in life, for he is offered favorite foods, he shares in unusual gifts of food brought to the family, and he is kept posted on family affairs. There is an intriguing parallel here to the manner in which the Shinto gods are dealt with at shrine festivals. Offerings are made, of course, and prayers are addressed to them, but reporting on events of this world is equally common, and many festivals feature a wide range of entertainments held for the diversion of the gods. These include fireworks, archery, horse races, wrestling, and many other sports and events. At the Yasukuni Shrine there is a Nō stage where performances are given at which the sole audience is the spirits of the war dead enshrined there. An actor of my acquaintance, himself a veteran of the China campaign, once told me that when he dances on these occasions, all alone, the sense of the presence of the spirits of the dead is overwhelming and the intensity of the experience almost beyond bearing.

The members of the family do not offer the deceased more than he had in life. There are no paper villas crowded with servants, or model Cadillacs, or fortunes in paper money burned for him. His pleasures lie not in such things but in the knowledge that his descendants have prospered, that they perhaps now have a villa and a fine car, having built on the patrimony bequeathed them by the ancestors. There is no clearer demonstration of the tendency to construe the relationship between the living and their ancestors as one of essential continuity. What pleased a man in life will please his spirit. To offer him more is both unnecessary and inappropriate; to offer him less is to betray his memory and to court danger.

Not even conversion to another religion necessarily interferes with the maintenance of the relationship between the living and the dead through the idiom of ancestor worship. During my interviews I encountered a Christian couple with a single tablet. It was for the wife's grandfather. At the end of World War II, they told me, this elderly man had been gravely ill, but they were unable to do more than care for him in their home, since medicine was unavailable and they could not afford to send him to a hospital. He died and they had a memorial tablet made for him. "We felt that it was the least we could do; we wanted to care for him in death as we simply could not do in life. We had a tablet made, of course. He was a Buddhist, after all."

A colleague, T. J. Pempel, has provided me with a variation on this theme. In the altar of a family of his acquaintance there are photographs of two deceased daughters of the house. Both were Catholic nuns and are shown in their habits. Their father had felt that it would be inappropriate either to have Buddhist tablets made for them or to abandon them altogether. The photographs are his compromise. In his view, his daughters belonged in the altar of their natal house, since they had entered no other as brides or adopted daughters. After all, it is the standard practice to make memorial tablets for unmarried sons and daughters and to place them in the altar of their natal house. Sugimoto (1925: 287–88) gives a moving account of how she, a convert to Christianity, observed the Buddhist rites as required of a filial child on the occasion of her mother's death. Criticized by her Christian friends, she observes drily that she was quite sure that had she predeceased her mother, that devout Buddhist lady would have had Christian rites performed for her daughter.

Thus, on occasion, as a substitute for a tablet some other object will be placed on the altar. Ordinarily it is something closely associated with the deceased. In the 1954 novel by Kawabata Yasunari, *Yama no oto* (*The Sound of the Mountain*) (1970: 47), the old man's wife Yasuko, speaking of a piece of cloth that she has come across in going through some things, says:

> "It was my sister's. When she died they sent it home with a dwarf tree tied up in it. A fine maple."
> Back in the country, his father-in-law's chief extravagance had been dwarf trees. He gave particular attention, it seemed, to maples. Yasuko's elder sister was his assistant.
> Probably her father had given her one when she married. Perhaps she had asked for it. And when she had died her husband's family had sent it back, because it was so important to her father, and because they had no one to look after it. Or possibly her father had gone for it.
> The maple had been on the family altar.

We should note that it may have been there in lieu of a memorial tablet, which would have been in the altar of her husband's house.

Talking with the Ancestors

How do the Japanese address the spirits of the household dead? Do the appeals and vows made to them differ in any way from those made to the gods and buddhas? The anguished mother says to Kannon, Goddess of Mercy, "Please restore my little boy's health. I will make a hundred circuits of the temple reciting the sutra, if only you will make him well." Are there parallels in the prayers to the ancestors? I think that there are, but it seems clear that the circumstances of the appeal are the major determinants of its form, just as the rites for the ancestors seem to take on added significance in times of stress and when important decisions must be made (Dore 1958: 143).

A standard morning prayer at the ancestral altar will go something like this: "Please see the members of the family safely through the day" (*Kyō mo ichinichi minna ga buji ni kurase masu yō ni*). But on special occasions, sometimes depending on the season of the year, other requests will be made. The ancestors will be asked for protection on a trip, a successful job interview, fertility of cattle, a good catch of fish, an abundant harvest, and general assistance in times of crisis. Let us suppose that a young man is about to take the college entrance examinations. He may go to the altar, where his mother's tablet is, and bowing before it say something like this: "Mother, since I am about to take the entrance examinations, please look after me (*Okā san, kore kara nyūgaku shiken o uke masu no de dōzo o-mamori kudasai*). When the results are in he returns to the altar, and if he has passed he may say "Thanks to you, everything went well. Thank you" (*Okage sama de umaku iki mashita. Arigatō gozai-masu*). If he has failed, he will apologize, saying "Please forgive me. I will try to do better from now on" (*Dōzo yurushite kudasai. Kore kara motto shikkari shi masu*). The language is that of normal discourse—perhaps slightly more formal, but not markedly so.

There can be no question that the young man is speaking to his mother. So that there will be no misunderstanding about the nature of the help being requested, let me transpose the action to the world of the living. When a boy is studying for his examinations, it is ordinarily his mother who oversees him. She will strive to provide a place for his desk and books, will sacrifice to hire tutors, and through a variety of devices will keep up the pressure on her son to do well. So well established is this aspect of a modern mother's role that the most aggressive mothers are known as "education mamas" or "dragon mothers." When her son leaves to take the examination she will wish him well, and she will share his anxiety until the results are known. She cannot, of course, actually offer help during the examination itself, but her son's success redounds to her credit and she shares his joy in it. So it is with the world of the spirits as well. The son who addresses his mother's tablet no more expects direct intervention than he would if she were alive. But he does ask for her general oversight of his endeavors, and her spirit joins him in his anxiety and shares his happiness in success.

In the summer of 1968, the immensely popular television drama *Ashita koso*, presented by the NHK (Japan Broadcasting Corporation), featured a sequence that offers considerable insight into this matter. The government network stations, surrounded by the wasteland of Japanese commercial television, hold out for education and the promotion of culture. The dramatic serials are ordinarily designed to show proper people behaving properly and improper people behaving improperly. To many young Japanese the programming is stuffy and the morality not a little anachronistic, but serials like *Ashita koso* nonetheless attract large audiences. This particular serial concerns the everyday joys and cares of a recently widowed woman and her grown children. They live in a residential section of Tokyo, and their relationship is a close one; they have faced up bravely to the unanticipated adversity of the father's death. The daughter is a young woman in her early twenties who has just finished college. She has been looking for a job and has been interviewed by a publishing house that puts out an intellectual magazine. Both mother and daughter have high hopes that she will be hired, and each day they anxiously await the letter carrier. On the day in question he hands over an envelope bearing the name of the firm. Standing at the front door of the house, the daughter opens it while her mother looks on. The young woman's face lights up; she clasps the letter to her breast, beams tearfully at her mother, and hurries into the living room. There she kneels before the altar, opens its doors, holds up the letter to her father's photograph and tablet, and bows low. The camera pans to the mother's tear-streaked face.

What have we seen? Remember that the father has died only recently and that all his hopes and plans for his children are fresh in the memories of his family. Now dead, he is powerless to help them directly, but his spirit can rejoice in their happiness and success. For all the overlay of sentimentality, the representation is essentially accurate. The daughter is saying, in effect, "Thanks to all the love and care you gave me, I have succeeded. I have a good job because I tried hard and did my best, as you always taught me to do. Please do not worry about us. We will be all right now. Rest assured that I will work with all my strength to do well at my job, so that you can be proud of me." How would the scene have been played had the letter been a notification that she had not gotten the job? It would have been quite in character for the daughter to offer abject apologies to her father's spirit for her failure and to vow to redouble her efforts from then on. No blame could fall on him for having made insufficient efforts on her behalf.

Is it all that common for people to report events to their ancestors? In Shitayama-chō in 1951 (Dore 1958: 325), 32 of 100 people said that they had done so, and another nine said that they probably would on an appropriate occasion. Reports had been made on such matters as the status of the family business, the making of changes in the layout of the house, births and marriages, illness, and the successful passing of the entrance examination for college. In addition, apologies had been offered for having let down the ancestors in some way. Some people said that they made these reports to the collectivity of the ancestors; others claimed that they addressed them to specific individuals. On the other hand, in Nagasawa only one case of a report to the ancestors is mentioned (Ooms 1967: 262, 299). A boy in middle school came home with his graduation certificate and held it up to the altar exclaiming, "Grandfather, I got it!" Although the ancestors are thought always to be in the house, apparently the notion that they are really concerned about what is happening there is not at all strongly held.

In my own experience, in Yasuhara, the ancestors were almost invariably informed about births and marriages, but reports on other events were rare because people assumed that the ancestors knew what was going on anyway. In 1958, though, I was myself the occasion of a report to an ancestor. Between my second and third visits to the village, an elderly man with whom I had often passed the time died. I had been told about it before I went to his house, and so I asked if I could burn incense at the family altar. The wife of the house was pleased, and she put one of the cakes I had brought on a small dish and took it to the altar. She knelt and said in a loud voice—the old man had been very hard of hearing—"Grandfather, Mr. Smith is here."

The NHK conducted interviews in the cities of Sendai and Tokyo in 1966 with five hundred apartment-dwellers, asking whether they had ever spoken "in certain ways" to the ancestors. Although the figure is hard to interpret, an astounding 97 percent replied affirmatively (Ooms 1967: 326). Reporting events to the ancestors seemed routine enough to the authors of a popular book on family sociology published in 1962 (cited in Plath 1964: 312). "You probably all have had the experience of having graduated from school and gotten a job, and when you received your first pay your mother took the pay envelope, displayed it on the household shelf, and offered a candle. This probably is a survival of rites to indicate that you have come of age and been added as one link in the social bonds of the household as a unit."

On formal occasions of worship, such as deathday observances and bon, prayers are said for the dead, but specific petitions are not usually addressed to them. These are times when the family gathers before the altar, along with close friends and sometimes neighbors. It is the family members and the friends who light the incense and the candles; priests may be called in to offer up sutras in numbers commensurate with the length and elaborateness of the ritual the family has decided on. But on less formal occasions, when no priestly ritual is required, a family member may address the spirit of the dead directly to ask its help or to thank it for its assistance. In this case there seems to be no question about the character of the relationship between the family member and the ancestral spirit. The person who has seen to the well-being of the spirits of the household dead through observance of the formal ceremonies, and who has caused prayers to be said on their behalf, can now turn to them and seek their support. One prays for the spirits of the dead in part so that one may also pray to them.

There are, to be sure, many people who are utterly unconcerned with all these issues and who never address the ancestors or offer them anything. The Rissho-kosei-kai, which tells the faithful that men often err through ignorance, warns that the most dire consequences flow from such behavior (Norbeck 1970: 188). "One of the common 'ignorances' which cause misfortune and distress is neglect of the ancestors, to whom the living are mystically bound in an endless cycle of transmigration. Those who do not venerate ancestral spirits 'betray a defect of character which can only result in misfortune for themselves and their families, and indescribable unhappiness for those who have left this world.' "

I cannot leave this topic without reiterating what I stated earlier in this chapter: the nature of the prayers addressed to the ancestral spirits is without doubt a function of the identity of those spirits. A couple whose altar contains only the tablets of their infant children will never pray *to* their children's spirits but will only pray *for* them, because the children neither had power in life nor are owed a boundless debt (on) by any member of the house. On the other hand, the tablets of senior ancestors will be the objects of both varieties of prayer, for their spirits both exercise direct tutelary functions by virtue of positions held in life and have a claim on their descendants for comfort and support. In the most general case, prayers are said *for* all the household dead but *to* the senior dead alone.

A person's relationship with a particular spirit of the dead is likely in some degree to derive from and reflect the relationship between them in life. A fine example, and one that illustrates as well how spirits are thought to be present in the house, is found in Mishima Yukio's 1954 novel *Shiosai* (*The Sound of Waves*) (1956: 69). A widow whose husband was killed in an American strafing attack in the last year of World War II sits resting, looking down at her own firm, unwrinkled thighs. " 'Like this, I could still have four or five children more.' But at the thought her virtuous heart became filled with contrition. Quickly tidying her clothing, she bowed before her husband's memorial tablet." However, communications between the living and the dead do not always follow the usual subordinate-superior status patterns that obtained when both were alive. The spirit of a younger brother who was quick and clever in life may well be appealed to by an elder brother facing a hard decision or a difficult choice, just as might have been the case when both were living. But direct personal ties of this intimate sort will not survive the death of the elder brother, and perhaps may fade out even earlier when he marries and moves into adult life. Nevertheless, in cases where the relationship was especially close, as we shall see, the survivor may have a copy of the memorial tablet made to take with him when he sets up his own house.

Other kinds of personal ties are operative as well, and may involve an appeal by a third party. The stepmother may, on behalf of her stepson, supplicate the tablet of his real mother for assistance in seeing him through a grave illness or helping him prepare for the inevitable college entrance examinations. Dore (1958: 143) noted this tendency and wrote that for many people in Shitayama-chō "the cognitive accompaniments of the ritual acts are almost exclusively centered on memories of recently deceased close relatives—children, wives or brothers—as often as on direct ascendants, ancestors in the proper sense of the term." Karen Brazell (personal communication) tells me of a middle-aged woman who for the many months following the death of her husband constantly informed him of things she had done and people she had met, prepared dishes that he had especially liked, and regularly spoke to his tablet in the altar. But once the ties established in life are terminated by the death of both parties, or fade in the memory of the living, the spirits of the dead become indistinguishable. All personal characteristics eventually fade, and the individual spirits merge with the collectivity of the household gods.

Some people are inclined to go much further than others in the observance of rites and ceremonies. For example, the scale of deathday observances and the number of years they are held vary, with the full treatment usually reserved for the major ancestors; however, such full treatment can be extended to all the spirits of the household dead. I was told the following story by a college student whose home is in Takarazuka. "My father is the head of the main house, and one of his duties as a family head and a Buddhist is to take care of the ancestors. Most people observe the anniversaries of death for about two generations, but my father last year [1965] observed the anniversary of a boy who died at the age of seven 127 years ago! Not many people take such good care of the ancestors." They certainly do not, and none of the interviews I conducted in 1963 provided anything to match this story.

We must conclude, I think, that the Japanese have both memorialism and ancestor worship—all in the context of the single domestic altar—by differentiating persons by status and importance in life and then by according them differential ceremonial treatment for longer or shorter periods as seems appropriate. The Family of God may be the family, as Plath (1964) argues; I have no doubt that the family's dead are its gods. Like all gods they are worshiped and petitioned. The failure of a petition cannot be blamed on them, for it is humans who fail, not gods. Accordingly, they are owed a double apology when the living do fail. Not only was the effort evidently insufficient, but the fortunes of the house were not advanced.

Social Control

Are the ancestors a means of social control within the household? I think they are, but primarily in their capacity as extensions of parental authority. It is their very humanity that renders the ancestors formidable. They rejoice or are disappointed in their descendants, and they can be frustrated or angered by events. The authors of a popular sociology book certainly assume that this is the case (cited in Plath 1964: 312). "Or a more extreme situation is when we often are dragged by dad or mom to the front of the household shelf and asked, 'Do you think you can give any excuse to the ancestors for doing that?' The shelf is associated with the household and with society, so that rebelling before it is like rebelling against the whole world; and this is why a lecture in front of the shelf has such potency." A vivid example of the use of the ancestors in this way occurs in Tokutomi Kenjirō's 1900 novel *Hototogisu* (1904: 161). Takeo's widowed mother has been trying to persuade him to agree to divorce his ailing wife, whom he loves. The mother argues that because the wife has tuberculosis, her presence in the family threatens the extinction of the line. Takeo is adamant in his refusal to hear of a divorce. "The widow stood up suddenly, and taking down an ihai from the household shrine, set it in front of Takeo. 'Look here, Takeo. You make light of my words, but repeat what you have been saying before your father. Repeat it. The spirits of your ancestors are looking at you. Say it once more. You disobedient son!' "

This scene does have a somewhat anachronistic air about it, to be sure, but it cannot be said to be entirely foreign to contemporary Japanese attitudes. Today it may well be that the spirits of the dead "serve mainly as moral arbiters and as sources of emotional security" (Plath 1964: 307). The people of Shitayama-chō seem to subscribe to this view in two senses (Dore 1958: 322). Some say that when they worship the ancestors they are pledging themselves to observe certain moral standards in order not to shame the ancestors; others say that because the ancestors are always watching one must behave properly. Norbeck (1970: 141) has this to say on the subject of ancestor worship's moral role:

> Ancestor worship . . . may be seen as an indirect sanction for virtuous behavior. In addition to its role in binding the kin group and reinforcing ideals of filial piety, ancestor worship conceivably sanctions ethical behavior because

any departure from ethical rules reflects unfavorably on the ancestors. . . . Old Buddhist beliefs that misfortune will result if rituals honoring ancestors are neglected reinforce ideas of proper conduct by reminding the living of their forebears and thereby also of their obligations to the entire group of kin, living and dead.

Ooms (1967: 299), on the other hand, finds no reason to think that in Nagasawa the ancestors function as moral arbiters at all—and certainly not in the training of children.

It may well be that the use of the ancestral spirits as agents of social control and as moral arbiters has become less and less common. Indeed, most of the New Religions seem certain that this is what has been happening, and they devote much of their teaching to the importance of ancestral rites and to the central role that reverence for the ancestors will play in a revival of the warm, close-knit, traditional Japanese family (Norbeck 1970: 188). Even if the ancestors are no longer conceived of as moral arbiters, they may perhaps be felt to be continuing to exercise their calm tutelary protection over their descendants. If that is so, then I think it can plausibly be argued that their descendants are obliged to live in such a way as to spare the ancestors pain and disappointment. This idea was put forth by Eto Jun in a talk given at Japan House in New York City in 1971 on recent strains in relations between Japan and the United States:

> According to a Japanese folk belief handed down through the generations, departed souls always watch over the safety of those who still live on earth. There must be millions who died in the past war—both soldiers and civilians—who are watching over our countries at this very moment. All of us who survived bear a responsibility to those souls for maintaining peace in the world. We cannot allow another disaster to rob their sacrifice of its meaning.

Rationales for Ancestor Worship

How shall we sum up all the whys and hows of ancestor worship touched on in the preceding pages? I shall begin by dealing with the reasons given for worshiping the ancestors by the people of Shitayama-chō and Nagasawa. Dore's material (1958: 317–25) reveals a great many reasons for worshiping the ancestors. Sometimes these reasons are mutually exclusive, and sometimes several are given by the same person. Some people seek to benefit the spirits of the dead by comforting or pleasing them or by helping them to enter paradise. Some share this concern but appear also to fear retribution if rites are neglected. Others say that they seek from the ancestors both personal protection and health and happiness for all family members. More commonly, people report that they simply wish to express gratitude to the ancestors for their past favors and for their continuing protection. Some say that they pledge to the ancestors their intention to observe high moral standards so as never to bring shame on them. Some are of the opinion that the ancestors are always watching, i.e. that they are external arbiters. Far less common is an attitude toward the ancestral rites that can only be called mystical, whereby the rites are considered as a kind of training in the same sense that the word is used in contemplative Buddhism. Still others say that they observe the rites out of respect, just as one shows respect to all superiors.

An outstanding feature of most of these reported attitudes is that the referent is always the collectivity of the ancestors, what Dore calls the "ancestor hotoke." But other people spoke with reference to Dore's "close relative hotoke" (called by Plath the "departed"). One man recalled that when he was a boy he used to pay his respects to the tablet of his elder sister; he had been very fond of her, and her face would come floating into his mind's eye. Another person said that "the dead of whom one still has strong personal memories can and should be treated in very much the same way as when they were alive." And finally, some people said (sometimes with reference to the collectivity of the ancestors and sometimes with reference to the individual dead) that reports should be made to them of important household and family events in order to keep them up-to-date on their descendants' situation.

Ooms's (1967: 296–99) approach is somewhat different, in that he seeks to determine what types of encounters there are between the living and the dead. He starts with two questions: are the ancestral spirits present in the house, and are they interested in their descendants? Some people appear to be entirely unconcerned with the first issue, performing the rites out of gratitude and respect. They do not expect to benefit directly from any action on the part of the ancestors. Some revealing comments made in this connection are paraphrased below:

> Performing the rites or not performing them does not result in either good or bad. One does these things naturally. (Female, age 33)

> If I didn't make the offerings my mind would not be at peace. (Female, age 70)

> I do it out of a sense of gratitude; after all, the ancestors looked after us. (Female, age 56)

> It's like one's attitude toward parents and brother—like on. It is because of our ancestors that we can get along today. (Female, age 69, and male, age 54)

> It's dictated by custom; it does not result in either good or evil. (Male, age 45)

Others feel strongly that the ancestors are indeed present in the house and at bon:

> Maybe they come and maybe they don't; I feel that they are here. (Female, age 63)

> I live in their presence and make a welcoming fire early and a sending-off fire late at bon, so that the ancestors will stay longer. (Male, age 67)

When asked if there are days when she omits the offerings of tea and rice, a sixty-three-year-old woman said "People need food every day, don't they? So I offer every day and ring the little bell to notify the ancestors that everything is ready." Still others appear to feel not only that the ancestors are present, but that they protect the living or pose a threat to them, as the case may be. This attitude was apparently not held wholeheartedly by anyone, but few were willing to reject out of hand the possibility that it was true. The overall impression is that the villagers of Nagasawa have little expectation of blessings or punishment; the overriding sentiments are those of gratitude and obligation.

It is precisely that attitude of gratitude and obligation which finds expression in a touching passage from a book by Yanagita (1970: 146) completed during the closing months of World War II: "We believe in the divine protection of our ancestors, we entrust ourselves to their favor, and we think there is no need to demand or worry or suffer concerning their assistance, and thus our festivals become occasions for returning thanks and pouring out our complete joys, and this is due to our knowledge learned from past generations; that is, we know through long experience that our ancestors have the power and pleasure to help us under any circumstances."

Is it then the case that most people still look after the ancestral spirits? Chamberlain (1898: 353), who may be forgiven for the ethnocentrism of his day, had this to say on the subject:

Japanese irreligion differs favorably from the utterly blank irreligion that is flaunted in the modern West. Though they pray little and make light of supernatural dogma, the religion of the family—filial piety—binds them down in truly sacred bonds. The most materialistic Japanese would shrink with horror from neglect of his father's grave, and of the rites prescribed by usage for the anniversaries of a father's or other near kinsman's death. Though unmindful of any future for himself, he nevertheless, by a happy inconsistency, acts as if the dead needed his care.

Sixty years later, writing of the people of Shitayama-chō, Dore (1958: 142–43) found that nearly every family that had an obligation to look after the ancestral tablets (i.e. all except branch families headed by younger sons) was doing so. Although today there is no doubt less of a tendency "to shrink with horror" from a gradual de-emphasis on ancestral rites, the Japanese are a long way from simply disposing of the tablets and abandoning the practice of ancestor veneration altogether. It is not going too far, I think, to say that membership in the household is conceived to be eternal, transcending death, and that for most Japanese the only spiritual community is that of the members of the family, living and dead. "Thus the *ie* is a spiritual community, and ancestor worship is its religion" (Ooms 1967: 288). It follows then that both the eclipse of the household ideal and the increasing tendency to emphasize the nuclear family have had severe repercussions on attitudes toward and treatment of the ancestral dead. This important issue will be taken up again after Chapters 5 and 6, in which the identity of "the ancestors" and the location of the memorial tablets are discussed.

Five. *Who Are the Ancestors?*

> What is termed ancestor worship in Japan ... visualizes and is based on a concrete conception of ancestors in a series of generations going back directly from the dead parent to the founder of the house in which the family is domiciled. The recognized lineage of ancestors is fairly short, hardly going back further than those forefathers who live in the memory as quite concrete personal figures.
>
> —*Nakane 1967: 140*

> Don't waste your time. You won't find any ancestral altars in Tokyo today.
> —*American colleague to the author, 1962*

> Well, you may have found ancestral altars in Tokyo in 1963, but I'll bet there aren't many left there now.
> —*Second American colleague, 1973*

THROUGHOUT the preceding chapters I have repeatedly referred to the memorial tablets. In this chapter I will set out the results of a study that was in fact a "census" of tablets taken in 1963 (see Smith 1966). As far as I know the data are unique, and I must again express my gratitude to the families who so graciously undertook for me a task I had no right to ask of them. Nevertheless, I am bound to report that a great many people seemed to find the enumeration fascinating, for they often discovered tablets for persons they had not even known were represented in the altar, they reminisced about others, and they very often supplied comments and information I had not even asked for. Out of all the personal interviews I conducted, I encountered initial hostility only once—from a woman who was a recent convert to the Sōka Gakkai, the most militant of all the New Religions. Her hostility stemmed not from any unwillingness to give me information about her memorial tablets, but from the fact that I had found that she had any at all, for at that time the Sōka Gakkai insisted that its members destroy both the god shelf and the memorial tablets and substitute for them an approved form of Buddhist altar. She had destroyed the god shelf but had not been able to bring herself to dispose of the tablets and altar, and I had found her out.

TABLE 12

*Distribution of Interviews and Questionnaires by Place
of Residence: The 1963 Tablet Census*

(*N* = 595)

Place of residence	Direct interview	Questionnaire	Total
Urban			
Tokyo	27	156	183
Osaka	11	93	104
Kyoto	6	60	66
Hanshin[a]	16	—	16
Nara	—	30	30
Miscellaneous	12	18	30
TOTAL	72	357	429
Rural			
Sone, Mie Prefecture	113	—	113
Yasuhara, Kagawa Prefecture	20	—	20
Takane, Iwate Prefecture	33	—	33
TOTAL	166	—	166
GRAND TOTAL	238	357	595

[a] Hanshin is used here to mean the heavily urbanized area between Osaka and Kobe.

The data were collected between January and June of 1963 by means of direct interviews and questionnaires I distributed. The interview guide and the questionnaire were identical. Direct interviews were conducted in 238 households. Of the four hundred questionnaires distributed, 32 were never returned and eleven were unusable because they were incomplete. A preliminary analysis of the two sets of data revealed no differences between them; the results are therefore presented here without distinguishing between interview and questionnaire responses. Table 12 presents a breakdown of the two sources of information and the places where the information was gathered.

The three rural communities were chosen because there had been prior ethnographic research conducted in all of them, and because they were assumed to be places of different structural types with very different histories. The community of Sone had been studied by Muratake Seiichi of Tokyo Metropolitan University and his students; later, in 1967–68, Bernard Bernier also conducted field research there (see Bernier 1970). Yasuhara (Kurusu is the name of the hamlet used in most publications) I myself studied in 1951–52 (see Smith 1956), and I revisited it briefly in 1955, 1958, 1963, and 1972. Takane was studied by Keith Brown from 1961 to 1963 (see K. Brown 1964). What kinds of communities were these in 1963?

Sone. Located in Mie Prefecture on the Ise Peninsula, Sone is a community of the type known as *miyaza* (shrine group) villages. (*Miya* is one of the words for Shinto shrine; *za* means group or guild.) There are two kinds of miyaza: one involves all households of the village; the other makes a distinction between the ritually superior households—among whose heads the responsibility for the care of the shrine rotates—and the ritually inferior ones. Sone belongs to the latter category, and until recently the distinction between the *ichizoku* (first families) and the *nizoku* (second families) was sharply drawn. One of the outstanding differences between Sone and the other two rural communities reported on in this study is the very great importance of Shinto shrine affairs here. A second major difference involves Sone's isolation until very recent times. Up to 1959 the only access to the nearest city, Owase, was by boat, and the passage took five hours. Since the opening of the rail line and the highway, Owase is only thirty minutes away. In 1963, the bulk of income of Sone households derived from pearl cultivation, forestry, and fishing; there was virtually no arable land. There were 171 households, representing a total of 26 surnames. Of these 26, only six were in the miyaza, that is, were ichizoku surnames. I was able to collect information about tablets from 113 households, 39 of them ichizoku.

Yasuhara. Located in Kagawa Prefecture on the island of Shikoku, the hamlet of Kurusu in the village of Yasuhara is a community of the type called *kō-kumi* by Japanese sociologists. Communities of this kind are characterized by social and economic equivalence of households. Within the context of this peer relationship, mutual aid and common residence far outweigh considerations of kinship in social organization and community activities. Here there is nothing remotely resembling the shrine group of Sone, and there are no extended groupings of households of the *dōzoku* variety, as are found in Takane. No households hold ritual precedence here; economic differentials among households change over time; there are no main houses with branch houses in the community or nearby. Kurusu lies within easy reach of Takamatsu, the largest city and capital of the prefecture. At an early period a rail line was put through the village, but today a highway and a regular bus service that has operated for the past forty years have replaced the rail-road. Before the land reforms of 1946, Kurusu was known as a tenant hamlet, the bulk of income of its households deriving from agriculture. Supplementary off-season employment has assumed increasing impor-tance over the past several decades, however. In 1963 there were eighteen households in Kurusu. The household census includes two closely con-nected households from elsewhere in Yasuhara, though, and that is why I have used that name. The twenty households, which have twenty dif-ferent surnames, are not linked by any kinship ties.

Takane. Located in Iwate Prefecture, Takane is a community of the dōzoku type. Properly called Takane-*kō*, the community consists of three hamlets of which one, Nakayashiki, was the focus of the tablet census. The dōzoku is a hierarchical grouping of households linked by kinship ties, with a main house from which branch houses derive. The main and branch households recognize connections of varying social and eco-nomic kinds; just how specific these connections are and how they are established have been matters of tremendous interest to Japanese social scientists. Seven different dōzoku are represented in Nakayashiki, of which four have member households in one of the other three constit-uent hamlets of Takane-kō. The community is within easy reach of Mizusawa, a small city on the trunk line between Tokyo and Sendai. Like Yasuhara, Takane is a heavily agricultural community. In 1963 it had 68 households. There were 31 households in Nakayashiki itself.

The questionnaire and the interview guide, which I have mentioned were identical, consisted of two parts: the first inquired about household and family characteristics, the second about each memorial tablet in the domestic altar. In the first part I asked about (1) place of residence; (2) composition of the family (residents only); (3) age and sex of the family head; (4) whether the head identified himself as the successor; (5) the religion of the household; (6) whether the household possessed any kind of domestic altar; (7) whether there were any memorial tablets in one or another of these altars or in any other place in the house; (8) when the memorial tablets were venerated (see the discussion in Chapter 3, pp. 104–14); and (9) which member(s) of the household bore primary responsibility for the care of the tablets (see the discussion in Chapter 4, pp. 117–19). In the second part, about each memorial tablet I asked (1) the date of death of the person represented; (2) the person's age at death;

(3) the relationship of the person to the present household head; and (4) the specific reason for the tablet's being in this altar ("Why do you have this particular tablet?"). The Appendix presents these data in tabular form.

The overwhelming majority (71.4 percent) of the 595 households involved in the study were conjugal families (see Appendix Table A1). Two-generation stem families, with one married couple or at least one survivor of a married couple in each generation, accounted for another 26.1 percent. There were ten unmarried household heads and only five three-generation stem families (the remaining 2.5 percent). In no case did I find two married couples of the same generation living in one household. Appendix Table A2 gives the age and sex of household heads.

Whereas only about three-quarters of the conjugal families had memorial tablets, almost 95 percent of the two-generation and all of the three-generation stem families had them. Overall, 81 percent of the households had memorial tablets (see Appendix Table A3). When I encountered one of the 112 households without tablets I asked why they had none, and in all but a fraction of cases an explanation was offered. These explanations fell roughly into two categories.

By far the more common one was "because this is a new house" or "because we are a branch house," often with the amplification that "no one has yet died here" or "we have no new buddhas [shin-botoke]." This kind of explanation came from what Koyama (1966: 104) has called "created families"—either new branch families or branch families resulting from a neolocal marriage—as opposed to "succeeded families," where the son or adopted husband has succeeded to the headship of the house upon the retirement or death of the preceding head. The second category of explanations, far rarer than the first, will be considered in a moment.

Because there is a special concern about urban households and their alleged tendency to ignore ancestor worship altogether, I have looked closely at the 90 cases of households without tablets in the cities of Tokyo, Osaka, and Kyoto. Table 13 gives the household distribution by age of the head and city of residence. Clearly these are not households headed by very young men; the age range is not markedly different from that of the total number of households surveyed. Of these 90 urban household heads, 79 said that they were nonsuccessors, i.e. they did not

TABLE 13
Households Without Tablets in Three Cities,
by Age of Household Head
(*N* = 90)

Age of household head	Place of residence			Total
	Tokyo	Osaka	Kyoto	
Not known	—	—	1	1
20–29	1	—	—	1
30–39	9	7	2	18
40–49	30	4	3	37
50–59	18	6	6	30
60–69	1	2	—	3
TOTAL	59	19	12	90

succeed to the headship of their natal or adopted families. Eight of these 79 were first-born sons, who might ordinarily have been expected to become successors; thus their reasons for having no tablets are of particular interest. Four said either that their parents were both still living or that their mothers lived in the country and took care of the altars there; one said that he had no tablets but did have photographs of his parents and observed bon; one reported that he had left the altar in the country with a younger brother who lived in the old house; two gave no explanation.

Also of interest among these 90 urban household heads were another nine people who said that they were successors and therefore ought to have tablets. One said that he had a Book of the Past and what he called a temporary altar; a second (age thirty-eight) said that he was not religious; a third (age fifty-two) said "memorial tablets are not necessary"; a fourth (a fifty-five-year-old adopted husband) told me that his wife visited her ancestors' graves four times a year but that they had no tablets for them; a fifth said that his mother was taking care of the altar back in his natal house in the country; a sixth belonged to the Sōka Gakkai and therefore had neither a god shelf nor an altar; a seventh offered an explanation of a sort I was to become very familiar with in the course of my interviews about the tablets themselves: "Although I succeeded my father, his sister looks after the graves and tablets back in the house in the country. He lived with her family—although she married out of our house—until his death." The two remaining successors without tablets offered no explanations. Two of the 90 household heads were widows. One was a member of the Sōka Gakkai; the other had no children and left her husband's tablet in his natal house when she moved to Tokyo.

Of the 90 urban households without tablets, I obtained the following explanations from 69: "This is a branch house or a new house" (43); "We have no new buddhas here" (15); "I am not religious" (9); and "We belong to Sōka Gakkai" (2). Three of the households without tablets said that they did visit the graves, and five said that they worshiped the ancestors at the altar in their natal house. One nonsuccessor did have an altar and a Book of the Past into which he had copied the names from the tablets in the altar of his main house. And one successor said that his apartment in Tokyo was so small that he could not possibly have an altar, so he had copied the names from the tablets into a Book of the Past. It is not clear whether he felt any obligation to observe the rites since the tablets were still being actively cared for by the family members back in the country.

The second, and rather rare, explanation for the absence of tablets was that "I have no interest in such matters" (*mukanshin*), or more simply that "I have no religion" (*mushūkyō*). Such responses are susceptible of several interpretations. Having no religion may often mean that the person has neither interest in nor connection with any form of institutionalized religion, for many people who do have tablets say they have no religion when asked. Or, in the case of a person without tablets to care for, it may mean that he is not concerned—one is tempted to say not yet concerned—with religion; this is the case in the created families. Rarely, it may mean either that the person would call no priest, have no tablet made, and purchase no altar should some member of the family die, or that having both altar and tablets he offers them no care whatsoever.

My question about the possession of domestic altars produced the following results. Of the 112 households with no tablets, only nine (eight percent) reported having an altar. Of the 483 households with memorial tablets, 22 did not say whether they had an altar. The 461 households that did answer the question about possession of an altar responded as follows: 451 (97.8 percent) said that they had an altar, three said that they had an ancestor shelf (*senzo-dana*), one said that it had a god shelf, three said that they had some other unspecified kind of altar, and another three said that although they had tablets they had no altar of any kind to keep them on. Thus the distribution of altars and tablets, although not perfectly complementary, was very nearly so. In my interviews in houses where the tablets showed shallow generational depth, I asked when the household had acquired its altar. Almost invariably the answer was "when someone died and we needed a place to put the tablet for him."

Few of the altars I saw contained either an image or a picture of a Buddha. Dore (1958: 313) reported that just over half of the altars in Shitayama-chō held any symbols of the Buddhist faith. Ooms (1967: 304) seems to have found representations of Buddhas with greater frequency in Nagasawa. On two occasions he asked whom the image represented, expecting to be told that it was Amida, Kannon, Shaka, or another Buddha. Instead, he received the following extraordinarily interesting answers: "It has the shape of Kannon but for us it really represents the ancestors," and "This is not the Buddha: it is a figurative image of the ancestors, while the tablets represent them in a non-figurative way." I can think of no more striking support for the claim that the altar is in fact an ancestor shelf rather than an altar of the Buddhas.

How do my findings on possession of tablets and altars compare with those of other studies? Of the twenty households in Nagasawa (Ooms 1967: 240–41), eighteen had altars containing tablets. The two households that had no tablets were newly established. In 1951, almost every family in Shitayama-chō that had an obligation to care for the ancestral tablets was in fact doing so (Dore 1958: 142–43). Those with no such obligations were what Dore called younger-son branch families (created families), but even among these he found some altars containing copies of tablets for close kin from the main house. But by far the greater part of the 45 percent of younger sons whose houses did have altars had acquired them upon the death of a wife or a child. In 80 percent of the households where at least one ascendant generation was already dead, and where there consequently ought to have been memorial tablets, Dore found them. What kinds of households made up the remaining twenty percent? Some were Christians and Shintoists. A few were headed by eldest sons who had migrated to Tokyo, leaving the tablets in the care of those who remained behind. Others had been bombed out and

TABLE 14
*Possession of Altars: Results of Three
Studies, by Family Type*

Date of study and location	Family type	
	Nuclear	Extended
1963[a]		
Rural	92.8%	100.0%
Urban	70.6	91.5
1964–65[b]		
Rural	82.9	98.3
Urban		
Tokyo blue-collar	50.9	93.2
Tokyo white-collar	31.3	100.0
1966[c]		
Urban apartment dwellers		
Sendai	56.0	91.0
Tokyo	38.0	50.0

[a] Smith (1966).
[b] Morioka (1972).
[c] NHK survey cited by Ooms (1967).

had never replaced the altar, or had the tablets on a temporary shelf of some kind, or had simply put off buying an altar (Dore 1958: 313–14).

In Table 14 I have given the figures on possession of altars from three studies (by Smith, Morioka, and the NHK) done in the 1960's. The general findings reported by Morioka (1972) have already been discussed. The NHK survey was conducted among five hundred apartment-dwellers in Sendai and Tokyo, who were asked whether they had an altar (Ooms 1967: 326). In all three studies noted in Table 14, the percentages given represent "yes" answers to this or a similar question about altar possession. Everywhere a higher proportion of extended families had altars, as was to be expected. But the figure with important implications for the direction that change is taking was the one for the conjugal families of Tokyo white-collar workers. After all, it is just such families that are an ever-increasing proportion of the urban population and of the population of the country at large. Inheriting neither farm nor business from their parents, these people have no link to the ancestors through property; having no deceased family members to care for, they have no occasion to memorialize any spirit. The important decision yet to be made by them is what will be done when the first family member does die.

The full impact of the demographic changes in family composition may for a time be slightly offset by the maintenance of ties between main and branch houses. Until a branch family acquires its own altar, its head may attend the memorial services for his deceased parents back in the main house—now most likely headed by his elder brother. But when the younger son who established the branch family dies, he becomes the object of memorial rites held by his son. As a consequence, by the time of succession in the second generation in both houses, relations between the main and branch families will have become greatly attenuated; by the third generation, when the heads of the two houses are distant cousins, relations will probably have lapsed altogether, for "the individual death-day celebrations for the last common ancestor (the branch head's great-grandfather) have probably ceased altogether (they are continued only for fifty years after death). The ceremonies for all the family ancestors of the main family are the only ones which have any relevance for the branch family and by this time it already has two generations of ancestors of its own to care for." (Dore 1958: 149.) In this regard, Vogel (1963: 134, 179), writing of white-collar families in Mamachi, in Tokyo, as of 1958–60, related that many felt a vague attachment to their (rural or provincial) ancestral homes and said they really ought to go back there at least for bon. Although many had not actually done so for years and did not expect to do so, there did seem to be a willingness to look after the ancestral tablets if the need arose. In one such case, the head of the main family, which had no land, died. The Mamachi branch family became the main family and acquired the heirlooms and ancestral tablets. The graves, of course, remained in the country, and arrangements were made for their care (Vogel 1963: 170–71).

With regard to the number of tablets per household (see Appendix Table A4), the highest proportion of those without tablets occurred among the Tokyo households, which also had the highest proportion of nonsuccessor household heads. In such created households, where no death had yet occurred, there would have been no tablets in "traditional times" as well. Thus the Tokyo figure cannot be taken by itself as an indication of a decline in the practice of ancestor worship. This is, indeed, the great ambiguity that must confound anyone attempting to see what the future holds. There are now more and more conjugal families in Japan, which means that an increasing proportion of all house-

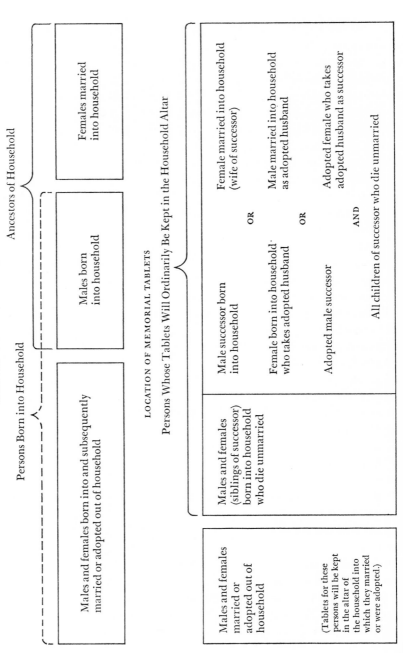

Fig. 2. Reckoning of ancestorhood and location of memorial tablets.

RECKONING OF ANCESTORHOOD

Ancestors of Household

Persons Born into Household

| Males and females born into and subsequently married or adopted out of household | Males born into household | Females married into household |

LOCATION OF MEMORIAL TABLETS

Persons Whose Tablets Will Ordinarily Be Kept in the Household Altar

Males and females (siblings of successor) born into household who die unmarried	Male successor born into household	Female married into household (wife of successor)
		OR
	Female born into household who takes adopted husband	Male married into household as adopted husband
		OR
	Adopted male successor	Adopted female who takes adopted husband as successor
		AND
	All children of successor who die unmarried	

Males and females married or adopted out of household

(Tablets for these persons will be kept in the altar of the household into which they married or were adopted.)

holds will have no tablets. The question is whether such households will continue to have tablets made and conduct rites when a member dies as they now largely seem to do.

It is also apparent from Table A4 that urban households generally have fewer tablets than do households in rural areas. This may indicate either a shallowness of generational depth or a tendency to restrict the range of persons for whom tablets are made, or both. Generational depth is most marked in Yasuhara, where most of the households have existed for a very long time and where there are no branch households. In Sone and Takane, on the other hand, where far fewer surnames are represented, generational depth is nonetheless also marked, if slightly less so in Takane. In the ordinary case, the rules used to decide whether to include a person's tablet in the altar of a given household are very simple. They are shown schematically in Figure 2. At the top of the figure we can see who the ancestors of a house will be, as distinguished from the collateral blood relations.

In every interview I conducted, I found that the ancestors of the house were reckoned from the generation of the founder. That is, each branch house considered its founder to be its senior ancestor. However, I have no evidence to suggest that the founder was venerated separately from all the others. A man takes care of the ancestors of his own house, not those of the house from which he has branched off or in which he was born but with which he no longer has much contact. The major exception to this rule probably was the dōzoku organization when it was still fully functioning; and although it may be true that some dōzoku still operate in the traditional way today, we have no examples of them in our rural communities. In brief, it is usually argued that the dōzoku system draws distinctions among (1) personal kindred and house kin, (2) house ancestors, and (3) the founding ancestor of the dōzoku. The last is said to be the object of separate ceremonies of worship in which the heads of all member houses participate. Insofar as the corporate character of the dōzoku groupings is still in evidence, the deathday rites of the deified founding ancestor will differ from the rites accorded to others (Richard K. Beardsley, personal communication; Nakane 1967: 106–7; Yonemura 1974).

Buddhist sect membership (see Appendix Table A5) appears to bear no relationship to any feature of ancestor worship to be discussed in the following pages. This negative finding serves to confirm the common observation that the emphasis on memorial rites has long since overwhelmed all doctrinal and sectarian diversity among the Buddhists in Japan. Dore (1958: 315) reported that 94 of 100 households in Shitayama-chō were Buddhist. All 94 said that they had a "family temple," often one back in the rural areas they or their families originally had come from. However, sixteen did not know the name of their temple, and seven did not know the name of their sect. More important for our purposes, members of 53 of the 94 households had made 241 visits to temples in the preceding year—206 (85 percent) of these in order to hold memorial services for the dead. In my own survey, the head of the single Christian household said that his family had memorial tablets because "our ancestors were Buddhist and it is only proper that they be venerated in this way"; however, no one in the family was actually willing to arrange Buddhist services for the ancestors.

In collecting these data, I chose to employ a technique that produced a list of egocentric kin terms as identification for each ancestral tablet. The respondent was asked to identify the person represented by the tablet with respect to that person's relationship to the present head of the house (ego). However, these egocentric kin terms are not the ones used in the tables that follow or in the Appendix tables. What I have done is to translate every term—where such translation is required—into another one that places each person represented by a tablet in his relationship to the main descent line of the house. This procedure sounds more cumbersome than it actually is, for the descent rule in Japan is straightforward enough. In every generation the house headship is assumed by a single male heir, and there are four ways to insure this succession: through a son who takes an in-marrying wife; through an adopted son who takes an in-marrying wife; through a daughter who takes an in-marrying adopted husband; through an adopted daughter who takes an in-marrying adopted husband (see Fig. 3). There is even a rather rare fifth alternative available when the succession to a house has lapsed completely: a person will be designated the successor and given the family name, property, and ancestral tablets.

But however the succession is managed, the successor is always male and will refer to the male head he succeeds as "father" (*chichi*), a con-

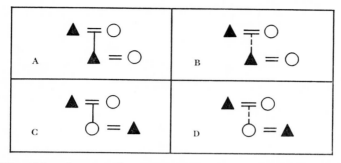

Fig. 3. Ways of insuring succession to the headship of a house. Broken lines indicate adoption; triangles indicate household heads. All symbols to the right of the equals signs represent in-marrying persons. Note that when a Japanese family seeks an adopted son or daughter it prefers a kinsman, either as an adult or as a child. The adopted husband is rarely a kinsman, however; he usually joins his wife's household as an adult at the time of their marriage.

vention I have adopted in the following pages. In the overwhelming majority of cases, a man's "father" is in fact his male progenitor, the head of the household in the preceding generation. The woman called "mother" (*haha*) by the present household head is usually his father's wife, the woman who bore him. Were human affairs so simple, egocentric terminology would serve very well; but as we have seen there are three other regular ways (and a fourth rare way) in which the succession to the house headship may be established, for all predecessors are not "fathers" and all successors are not "sons."

One alternative way to assure the continuation of the family line is for the household head to adopt a son. The adopted son (*yōshi*) takes the family name of his foster father. ("Foster father" is in terms of Japanese descent reckoning the exact sociological equivalent of "father" and is so classified below.) The second alternative involves a daughter's taking an adopted husband (*muko-yōshi*). The in-marrying husband takes his wife's family name and becomes the successor upon the death or retirement of her father. To such an adopted household head, the former household head represented by the memorial tablet is, in egocentric terminology, "wife's father" (*tsuma-no-chichi*); but from the point of view of descent he is simply "father," the first ascending generation household head. The third alternative involves adopting a daughter (*yōjo*), for whom an adopted husband will be found. "Father" in this case is, egocentrically, "wife's foster father," but in terms of the

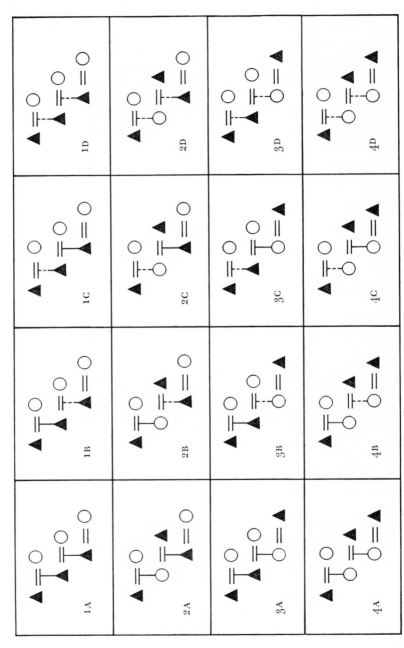

Fig. 4. Ways of insuring succession in a sequence of two generations. Symbols as in Fig. 3.

descent line he is indistinguishable from the others classed as father of the present household head. Thus in the discussion below, "father" comprehends the following relationships: "father," "foster father," "wife's father," and "wife's foster father." Obviously, even the simplest case of succession may involve considerable complexity, though we have thus far restricted our examples to households with male heads. Where the household head is female (a situation always defined as temporary), the term father in our list of kin may refer to the man (1) who was the woman's own father (where she took an adopted husband in order to guarantee the succession), (2) who was her husband's father (in the case of a regular marriage where her husband had predeceased her), (3) who was her own foster father (where she was an adopted daughter), or (4) who was her husband's foster father (where he came as an adopted son and she married in).

As we ascend the generational ladder each kin term embraces a larger and larger number of possible relationships. With each succession to the headship of the house, one of several alternatives may be employed. It follows that for any sequence of two successions in a given house there are sixteen possible ways by which the present household head can have come to his position. These possibilities are shown in Figure 4; all of them result in succession being passed from the present household head's "father's father" to his "father," in our condensed terminology. I have called the senior male shown in each square of Figure 4 "father's father," and I have called his wife "father's mother." Egocentrically, and where ego is male, the sixteen possible succession sequences follow.

1A—father's father (the most ordinary case); 1B—foster father's father (where ego is adopted son); 1C—father's foster father (where father was adopted son); 1D—foster father's foster father (where ego and father were both adopted sons).

2A—mother's father (where father was adopted husband and married in); 2B—foster mother's father (where ego is adopted by widow or divorcée); 2C—mother's foster father (where mother was adopted daughter who took in-marrying adopted husband); 2D—foster mother's foster father (where ego is adopted by widow or divorcée who was herself adopted).

3A—wife's father's father (all of the following cases assume ego to be an in-marrying adopted husband); 3B—wife's foster father's father; 3C—wife's father's foster father; 3D—wife's foster father's foster father.

4A—wife's mother's father; 4B—wife's foster mother's father; 4C—wife's mother's foster father; 4D—wife's foster mother's foster father.

Where ego (the household head) is female, all the above sequences still apply, with the appropriate shift of referent: i.e. 1's and 2's prefix "husband's" and 3's and 4's drop the prefix "wife's." In the first two cases, ego is the in-marrying wife of a husband who has died; in the third and fourth cases, she is the widow or divorcée of an in-marrying adopted husband, where she was either the daughter or the adopted daughter of the house. Thus we can summarize the instances when a woman will occupy the headship of a house: (1) her in-marrying husband has died, or she has been divorced from him, and she remains in her natal home; (2) she is an in-marrying wife whose husband has predeceased her, leaving no child as his designated successor; (3) she is the daughter of the household head, she has never married, and no male successor has been secured by any other means. In all three cases her headship is viewed as temporary; there is always pressure to regularize the situation so that a male can assume the headship.

There is one type of female household head that complicates the range of persons we have called "father's father" in the figures even further. It may happen that a deceased adopted household head (male) has had two wives in succession, and that the house is headed after his death by the widowed second wife, despite the fact that the descent link is through the deceased or divorced first wife. This means that the current female head will offer food and incense for a tablet representing a "father's father" who is in fact her "husband's first wife's father's father." One such case occurred in the households I surveyed. I must emphasize, however, that the intricacies of the linkages outlined above were fundamentally of no concern to most of the people I talked to. Insofar as ancestor worship and the descent line go, the tablet representing the second ascending generation's household head is "father's father," no matter how the succession was arranged. For the sake of convenience, and because it more nearly reflects the psychological reality of kinship reckoning in Japan, I have used this generic phrase throughout.

The principles outlined above are also employed in converting other kin terms into descent-line equivalents. Thus, "father's elder brother"

mother, or (2) his wife's foster father and mother (in this case he would be the adopted husband of an adopted female). Each couple commonly shares a single tablet, but for purposes of enumeration here and elsewhere I have taken each individual name to represent one tablet.

3. Spouses of progenitors are any husbands and wives of a progenitor who were not married to the progenitor at the time succession to the headship in the next generation was secured. Each commonly has a single tablet. If your father's father married early and his young wife died, there will be a single tablet for her; if he remarried and his second wife bore your father (the successor) and other children before she died, then her name will appear on the same tablet with that of your father's father; if he married a third time, whether other children were born or not, his last wife will have a single tablet.

4. Spouse of head means a husband or wife of the present head; tablets for this subgroup are often found even when the present head has remarried.

5. Spouse of spouse means a husband or wife of the spouse of the present head. This subgroup includes the male head's first wife, the adopted husband's first wife, the first adopted husband, etc.

6. Descendants are children of the present head by all marriages.

7. Siblings, their spouses and children, form a subgroup that is self-explanatory. Siblings of the present male head, or of the wife of an in-marrying adopted husband, are clearly Lineals in my sense. These tablets usually represent persons who died before marrying (as we shall see below), or who married out but returned to their natal house. Where a whole family is represented by tablets, this means that a neolocal house has died out (such a house is called *zekke*) and its tablets have reverted to the natal house of the head of the zekke. The presence of tablets for siblings' spouses and children in such cases is one of the very rare exceptions to the rule stated above that Lineals are usually people who have at some time been listed in the household register.

8. Father's siblings, their spouses and children, form a self-explanatory subgroup. "Father" here refers to the next ascendant male household head, irrespective of the derivation of succession in the direct line.

9. Father's father's siblings, their spouses and children, form another self-explanatory subgroup. "Father's father" is the second ascendant male household head.

10. Father's father's father's siblings, their spouses and children, form still another self-explanatory subgroup. "Father's father's father" is the third ascendant male household head.

11. "Other" represents tablets of unclassifiable but presumably Lineal kin ("uncle," "aunt," "cousin," etc.).

Nonlineals. Nonlineals are persons not in the household register or entirely unrelated to the direct line of succession. There are three categories: (1) kin of an adopted child or an adopted husband; (2) kin of the mother of the present household head, where she married in; and (3) kin of the wife of the present head, where she married in. In short, these are the kin of those who either have been adopted in or have married in. All Nonlineals come from the natal house of an adoptee, a mother, or a wife. The subcategories for Nonlineals closely parallel the ones for Lineals.

12. Unidentified means the same thing it meant for Lineals. These tablets are all known to be for Nonlineals.

Yōshi's kin (kin of an adopted child or husband) are broken down into three types.

13. Progenitors are ascendants of the adoptee's natal house.

14. Father's and mother's siblings, their spouses and children, are those of the adoptee.

15. Siblings are the adoptee's own siblings from his or her natal house. Mother's kin are broken down in much the same way.

16. Progenitors are ascendants of the present household head's mother (where she married in) from her natal house.

17. Miscellaneous includes other kin of mother from her natal house.

18. Siblings, their spouses and children, refer to the mother's siblings and their spouses and children. Wife's kin follow the same pattern.

19. Progenitors are ascendants of the present household head's wife (where she married in) from her natal house.

20. Father's and mother's siblings, their spouses and children, are also from the wife's natal house.

21. Siblings are from the wife's natal house as well.

Non-kin. Non-kin are persons entirely unrelated to any past or present Lineal or Nonlineal member of the household. Tablets in this category might include one for a teacher, a stranger, a lover, etc.

Let us now consider some of the outstanding findings from the tablet census. Once again, as with Sone's patterns of worship, we have one unique rural case: in Takane alone I found no tablets at all for Non-lineals and Non-kin (see Appendix Table A6). The implications of the exclusively Lineal character of the tablets in this dōzoku community are highly significant. During my interviews there, I was asked why I was undertaking such an extraordinary census, and when I said that I was trying to see how much diversity there was in holdings of tablets I was not understood. I explained that on the island of Shikoku (where Yasuhara is located) and in the cities I had found many tablets for Nonlineals and even Non-kin in the household altars. This assertion was politely but firmly rejected as reflecting some misunderstanding on my part. The universal opinion was that I must be mistaken because "no household would have tablets for such people in its altar—they belong somewhere else." My own tentative conclusion is that in Takane the principle of lineality is so strongly held and has such vital implications for interhousehold relations and an orderly community structure that dilution of the lineal character of the tablets is simply inconceivable. Indeed, when I unintentionally uncovered an irregularity in tablet possession, it was at once rectified. A branch household actually had some old tablets of senior generations that should have been held by its main house. They had apparently been left with the branch house for safekeeping when the main house emigrated. After the main house returned to the community, however, it somehow neglected to reclaim its senior tablets. When the discrepancy was discovered in the course of my interviews, the main house at once demanded the return of the tablets and quickly got them. It was clear that for years they had been in the wrong household altar.

The Nonlineal tablets were of special interest because in many ways they represent an anomaly. There is absolutely nothing—either in the rationale for ancestor worship or in the principles that most people invoke in explaining what tablets one ought to have in the altar and why they should be there—that explains the presence of tablets for Nonlineals. Certainly none of the communities represented in my census had any of the special features of social organization that produced the bilaterality of tablets found by Ushijima (1966) in the Izu Islands. To be sure, there were only 189 tablets for Nonlineals, representing 6.2

percent of all tablets. Yōshi's (adopted son's) kin accounted for 28.3 percent of the 180 identified Nonlineal tablets, and these were almost entirely the kin of muko-yōshi (in-marrying adopted husbands). Mother's kin accounted for 29.4 percent, and wife's kin for 42.1 percent. All nine unidentified Nonlineal tablets were found in Sone.

What can we conclude from this distribution? I suggest that the practice of placing Nonlineal tablets in the household altar may be a fairly recent and increasingly common one. When we recall that the great majority of households surveyed were conjugal families, and that wife's kin occurred far more frequently among the tablets for Nonlineals than did mother's or yōshi's kin, we realize that here we may have the opening wedge of *family*-centered as opposed to *household*-centered ancestor worship. Those who have studied Japanese society for a long time will be struck by the implications of the following interview I conducted. A couple in their thirties had no tablets but did have photographs (with black bands across the corners) of the husband's mother and of the wife's father and mother. When I asked why they had these photographs, the husband replied "Why, because they are our ancestors." This is quite correct in the sense that they are the ancestors of *family* members; but in the traditional meaning of the term "ancestor" in Japan, not all the people in the photographs are ancestors of the *house*.

A final word on the tablets for Nonlineals. With the interesting exception of Sone, where there were 47, such tablets were rare in the rural cases: three in Yasuhara, and none in Takane, as I have already noted. Indeed, almost three-quarters of all Nonlineal tablets were found in the urban areas (139 of 189). The most common ones were those for progenitors of the wife of the household head (32 households had such tablets, versus 21 households with tablets for the progenitors of yōshi and mothers).

As far as the Lineal tablets are concerned, the materials in Table 15 and Appendix Table A6 are largely self-explanatory. But because the last column deserves special attention I have separated it out into Appendix Table A7. Everywhere more households had tablets for progenitors than for any other category of kin (406 households with such tablets out of 483 households with any tablets). The next most commonly reported tablets were those for siblings and their spouses and children

(174 households); they were followed closely by tablets for children of the present household head (154 households).

Again we have one rural community that presented an unusual situation. Appendix Table A6 shows that in the households of Yasuhara Lineal tablets for progenitors constituted a smaller percentage (38.4) of the identified Lineal tablets than in any other place. Everywhere else such tablets accounted for from 50.8 to 74.1 percent of the identified Lineal tablets held. The explanation behind this situation is that in Yasuhara almost half of all tablets are unidentified, and virtually all of these are for Lineals. This is a community where every household has a different surname, and where interhousehold relations depend on proximity, shared responsibility, and mutual aid. There are a great many very old tablets in Yasuhara, so shallow generational depth is not characteristic of its households. Rather, I think it is a place where lineality as such is simply not an issue to the extent that it is in Takane's dōzoku and Sone's miyaza. The houses in Yasuhara are not bound by ties of kinship, and each household venerates its own ancestors without regard to genealogical concerns other than its own.

Let us shift our attention once again from the tablets to the households. We have seen in Appendix Table A7 the number of households that had at least one tablet for a particular category of relationship to the household head. We can now turn to the larger question of the number of households that had Lineal, Nonlineal, and Non-kin tablets. Of the 483 households with tablets, 409 (84.7 percent) had tablets for only Lineals; 57 (11.8 percent) had tablets for both Lineals and Nonlineals; 8 (1.7 percent) had tablets for only Nonlineals; 7 (1.4 percent) had tablets for Lineals, Nonlineals, and Non-kin; and 2 (0.4 percent) had tablets for both Lineals and Non-kin.

The 57 households with both Lineal and Nonlineal tablets were distributed as follows: 15 were in Tokyo (8.2 percent of 183 households), 7 were in Osaka (6.7 percent of 104 households), 6 were in Kyoto (9.1 percent of 66 households), 5 were in Hanshin (31.3 percent of 16 households), 1 was in Nara (3.3 percent of 30 households), 8 were in miscellaneous households (26.7 percent of 30 households), 13 were in Sone (11.5 percent of 113 households), and 2 were in Yasuhara (10.0 percent of 20 households). The 8 households with tablets for Nonlineals only were distributed as follows: 6 (3.3 percent) in Tokyo, 1 (0.9 percent) in Osaka, and 1 (1.5 percent) in Kyoto. The 7 households with Lineals, Nonlineals, and Non-kin were distributed as follows: 3 were in Sone (2.7 percent), and 1 each was in Tokyo (0.5 percent), Osaka (0.9 percent), Hanshin (6.3 percent), and Yasuhara (5.0 percent). The 2 households with Lineal and Non-kin tablets, but without Nonlineal ones, were found in Nara (3.3 percent) and Sone (0.9 percent).

Among the 409 households having tablets for Lineals only there were some extremely interesting cases: 30 (7.3 percent) had tablets for descendants only, 15 (3.7 percent) had tablets for spouse of head only, and 2 (0.5 percent) had tablets for siblings only. Thus 47 households (11.5 percent of those with Lineal tablets only) had no tablets for any ascendants.

It is usually said that the tablet will be disposed of when the final rites for a person are held on the thirty-third or fiftieth anniversary of death. There obviously is some reduction in the number of tablets, but a great many very old tablets are kept by the household long after the last formal observances for the persons are held. Of all 3,050 tablets, only about half were for persons who had died in the fifty years since 1914. About fifteen percent represented people who had died over a hundred years before I collected my data (see Appendix Tables A8 and A9). It is noteworthy that a few tablets representing persons dead less than fifty years could not be identified by anyone in the household. In every one of these cases some extraordinary turn in the family's fortune—such as the death of the household head at an early age—had left the altar in the care of a person who knew very little about the people represented by the tablets, but who nevertheless continued to perform acts of devotion before them.

Is there a connection between the relationship to the household head and the age of the tablets? Appendix Table A10 gives the breakdown of data on this point and shows that there is a consistency. Particular attention should be directed to the Nonlineals. Of the identified persons who died within the past 33 years, 7.2 percent were Nonlineals; of those who died between 34 and 50 years ago, 4.7 percent were Nonlineals; of those who died between 51 and 100 years ago, 9.8 percent were Nonlineals. It would be tempting to conclude from these figures that there has been little change—perhaps even a slight decline—in the frequency of placing such tablets in the altar. Although we cannot be entirely sure that any given tablet was placed in the altar where it is today at the time of the person's death, the figures do suggest that bilaterality of tablets is by no means an exclusively contemporary phenomenon. In addition, we have one piece of supplementary evidence on this point. In Nagasawa, Ooms (1967) found a Book of the Past that had been made up only two years before. It was based on twenty old tablets that had been in the altar of a second-generation branch house. Three of the names listed could not be identified at all, but the remaining entries were interesting for being so markedly bilateral in character: "Even three rather distant relatives of the two in-married wives were on the list; a nephew of the grandmother and a niece of the wife of the head of the household and her daughter" (Ooms 1967: 256).

We also know that the presence in the altar of tablets for an in-married wife's kin is very much a feature of traditional practice in some kinds of rural communities. As an example, let us take a case reported by Ushijima (1966) from a village in the Izu Islands. Before the local system began to weaken, the ties between a young married couple and the wife's parents were very strong. After marriage, the couple slept at the wife's parents' home but worked in the husband's parents' home for a period of time. If the husband was the successor, when his father retired as household head the couple would take up virilocal residence and the wife would be installed as the head's wife. The bilateral tendencies were reinforced by the young couple's maintaining relations with both sets of parents and visiting both at bon and at the New Year. Ushijima found no trace of unilineal groupings of any kind, not even in terminology. At the death of a parent, sons and daughters (whether married or not) would return to their natal house for the first seven days of mourning. This indicates that the pollution of death is thought to fall only on the residents of the deceased's house and on his or her children, not on their spouses. When the children left the natal house to return home, each bore a copy of the memorial tablet. As a consequence, the tablets in an altar were often bilateral in character. It is worth noting that the special rites of the first bon (here called *ni-bon*) were formerly held at each house with a copy of the tablet for the recently deceased. More recently, all children have assembled at their natal houses for the ni-bon ceremonies.

Ushijima (1966: 176) offered six general rules about tablets in this community: (1) the altar often had tablets for parents of both the husband and the in-marrying wife, or for parents of the in-marrying adopted husband; (2) when parents retired as household head and wife, they took the tablets of both the husband's and the wife's parents, or copies of the tablets, to the retirement quarters if the last individual rites had not yet been held; (3) in the main house, the altar contained a collective tablet for ascending generations of the ancestors (*senzo-daidai*) and the tablets of those for whom the last rites had not yet been held (all of which tablets were patrilineal in character); (4) for two generations bilaterality of the tablets was complete, but three generations back the tablets for the female side had been selected out or "naturally disappeared"; (5) there were no distinctions of age or sex among siblings in the distribution of tablets for a deceased parent; and (6) after the fiftieth anniversary of death there was no longer any individual identity assigned to the tablets, for the persons they represented would have become ancestors. The tablets of such ancestors were sometimes buried at the cemetery or taken to the temple once the priest had written the posthumous name in the household's Book of the Past; or sometimes five or six names might be copied onto a single tablet to be kept in the household altar. Contrary to the usual easy assumptions about the direction of change in Japan, in communities like this one we find an increasing unilineality in the tablets as the traditional norm of bilaterality is obviated by social and economic change.

In Table 15 we found that there were more tablets for the siblings than for the children of the household head. However, we did not take into account the implications of the domestic cycle and the timing of these tablets' placement in the altar. It is obvious that the siblings of the present head are the children of the preceding head, who may very well have placed the tablets there while the present head was still a child. Table 16 shows the extent to which this seems to have been the case. Of the 1,698 Lineals whose age at death was known, 25.5 percent died before they were ten years old. This was far and away the most commonly represented age group, the next most frequently found being persons in their seventies (14.4 percent). Unfortunately, it was impossible to say what the effect on this distribution might have been if we knew the age at death of the very large number (40 percent) of Lineals

TABLE 16

Age at Death and Relationship to Household Head

(N = 3,050)

Age at death	Relationship to household head							
	Lineals		Nonlineals		Non-kin		Total	
	No.	Pct.	No.	Pct.	No.	Pct.	No.	Pct.
Under 10	433	25.5%	5	4.1%	—	—	438	24.0%
10–19	67	4.0	5	4.1	—	—	72	4.0
20–29	158	9.3	8	6.6	1	33.3%	167	9.2
30–39	86	5.1	8	6.6	—	—	94	5.2
40–49	134	7.9	13	10.7	—	—	147	8.1
50–59	196	11.5	16	13.2	—	—	212	11.6
60–69	235	13.8	28	23.1	1	33.3	264	14.5
70–79	244	14.4	26	21.5	—	—	270	14.8
80–103	145	8.5	12	9.9	1	33.3	158	8.6
TOTAL	1,698	100.0%	121	100.0%	3	100.0%	1,822	100.0%
Age unknown	1,138		68		22		1,228	
GRAND TOTAL	2,836		189		25		3,050	

NOTE: Owing to rounding off, percentage figures do not always total exactly 100 percent.

for whom this information was not available. The picture was very different for Nonlineals whose age at death was known. The young were underrepresented, and well over half were persons who died after they had reached the age of sixty.

One further refinement with respect to the analysis of the tablets for siblings and children was possible (see Appendix Table A11). I have taken all the tablets of siblings of the present household head and grouped them by age and sex. Sixty percent (198) were male, forty percent (132) female. The sex differential applied as well to the age at death. Taking all the tablets, 51.5 percent of the female siblings died before they reached the age of ten, whereas only 32.3 percent of the male siblings died so young. The difference is even more marked if we ignore those for whom age at death was not known: of the 105 females whose age at death was known, 64.8 percent died before the age of ten; of the 148 males whose age at death was known, 43 percent died before the age of ten. Clearly, a household is far less likely to make tablets for its older daughters than for its older sons.

We can also say something about the tablets for children of the present household head (see Appendix Table A12). Taking all the tablets, 159 (65.7 percent) died before the age of ten. It should be borne in mind that

TABLE 17
Lineals, Nonlineals, and Non-kin:
Sex of Persons Represented by Tablets and Their
Relationship to Household Head
(N = 3,050)

Type of tablet by relationship to household head	Number of tablets			
	Total	Male	Female	Sex unknown
LINEAL				
1. Unidentified	595			
2. Progenitors	1,284	700	584	—
3. Spouses of progenitors	50	3	47	—
4. Spouse of head	91	47	44	—
5. Spouse of spouse	7	2	5	—
6. Descendants	256	132	98	26
7. Siblings, their spouses and children	358	212	144	2
8. Fa's siblings, their spouses and children	147	77	65	5
9. Fa's fa's siblings, their spouses and children	29	14	15	—
10. Fa's fa's fa's siblings, their spouses and children	10	7	3	—
11. Other	9	4	5	—
TOTAL 2–11	2,241	1,198	1,010	33
NONLINEAL				
12. Unidentified	9			
Yōshi's kin				
13. Progenitors	40	20	20	—
14. Fa's and mo's siblings, their spouses and children	7	2	3	2
15. Siblings	4	3	1	—
Mother's kin				
16. Progenitors	32	15	17	—
17. Miscellaneous	6	3	2	1
18. Siblings, their spouses and children	15	7	8	—
Wife's kin				
19. Progenitors	53	28	25	—
20. Fa's and mo's siblings, their spouses and children	8	4	4	—
21. Siblings	15	7	8	—
TOTAL 13–21	180	89	88	3
NON-KIN	25			
GRAND TOTAL	3,050	1,287	1,098	36

these were children of the household head. There were, once again, more tablets for sons (127 or 52.4 percent) than for daughters (93 or 38.4 percent); for 9.2 percent the sex was unknown. But there is a marked contrast with the data on siblings cited previously. Almost the same percentage (about 65 percent) of both sons and daughters were children who died before the age of ten. There is, however, a jump in the number of tablets for sons who died in their twenties that is not found for daughters in the same age group. These sons were for the most part young men who died before marrying, so that their tablets were in their natal house. Daughters, who characteristically marry at an earlier age, would be represented by tablets in the house into which they had married should they have died at this age. If we take only the 208 children for whom the age at death was known, we find that 76.4 percent of them were under ten years of age at death.

In Table 17 I have presented the aggregated data on the kin relationships of those represented by tablets to the present household head broken down by sex. Among Lineals there was a slight preponderance of males (53.4 percent) over females (45.1 percent). There was no difference for Nonlineals. Unaggregated data appear in Appendix Table A13. The Non-kin listed at the end of Appendix Table A13 deserve some comment, if only because they are a genuinely exotic company. One of them was a teacher of the household head, and probably could be classified with the three *onjin*—persons to whom ego or an earlier household head owed an unrepayable debt. There was one nurse, who came into the house with the present head's father's father's mother when she married in and apparently lived out her life there. One man already had his own tablet in the altar: "Can't be too careful these days," he said, "because young people don't care much about the ancestors any more." Properly, of course, his tablet is, or will become, that of a Lineal; I have put it here only for convenience. The "wife's mother's 'husband' " is a fine example of the skeleton in the family altar, as is "father's lover."

The sixteen tablets in a single altar in a Yasuhara household greatly inflate the total of Non-kin, and they represent a rather special case. A daughter of this house who married out subsequently emigrated to Paraguay with her husband and their two children. These are all the tablets of her husband's household, left where the young couple assumed they would most likely be cared for properly. The husband's unmarried younger brother refused to take them on the grounds that there was no place for the altar in his small room in the city. It is assumed that one day he will marry and come to claim them, or that the young couple will come back and once again care for them. Why were they not taken to Paraguay? The reason is one I met with frequently where migration had been only as far as a nearby city—the tablets would then have been too far from the graves of the people they represented.

Finally, there is one *tanin*—a stranger. This tablet was in an altar in Sone, and the household head told us that he had found it on the beach after a great tidal wave had struck the Ise Peninsula and washed away many houses. I asked why he had kept it rather than turn it over to the temple to look after. His reply was "Because I found it, I felt that I was meant to take care of it."

In Appendix Table A14 I have listed the 22 most common kin relations represented among the Lineal tablets. In all, there were 93 separate kin relations listed in Appendix Table A13; the 22 shown here accounted for 88.6 percent of all identifiable Lineals. The first four in terms of frequency were the first two ascending generations from the present head of the house; they accounted for 44.8 percent of all identifiable Lineals.

Little has been said up to this point about the generational depth of the ancestral tablets. To obtain the figures given in Appendix Table A15 I have defined a generation as 25 years. In Appendix Table A16 I have tried to determine whether or not people could identify the persons represented by older tablets as well as by newer ones. Appendix Table A16 shows the difference, if any, between the number of generations the tablets went back and the number of generations back any household member could identify tablets by kin relation to the present head of the house. Just over 72 percent of the households had from one to three generations of identifiable tablets; about 12 percent had tablets but none for an ascendant; and about 15 percent had from four to fourteen generations of tablets they could identify. Almost 90 percent of the households with any ascendants' tablets could identify all the generations represented, whereas the remaining 10 percent had tablets for one or more generations whose identity was unknown to them. The generational depth of tablets was considerably less in the cities than it was in the three rural communities. It is also clear from Table A16 that few households had more generations of tablets than they could identify (a total of only 46 such households, 26 of which were in Sone). Ten households had at least five generations of tablets beyond the oldest they could identify; five of these were in Sone, two in Yasuhara, and one each in Tokyo, Osaka, and Nara.

The larger issues raised by the results of the tablet census are easily stated. The memorial tablets found in household altars do in part represent people who are ancestors in the strictest sense. But as we have seen, fully one-quarter of all the tablets were for young children, ancestral to no one. Many others—about one-half—were for persons not even in the direct ascent line, that is, not heads and their wives in each ascending generation. It follows that there should be, and are, fairly clear distinctions among those memorialized in terms of the strictness and the duration of the special memorial services for individual death anniversaries, with the chief emphasis on those who have contributed directly to the maintenance of the descent line. It is further apparent that whereas some of the spirits of the dead—the ancestral spirits—are prayed to for guidance and assistance, others are not so petitioned, for they died young or without issue, or are in the altar because it was literally the resting place of last resort and they had no place else to go when they died. These spirits are cared for and comforted, but if they have any role at all in the ongoing life of the household, it is a generalized tutelary one. Although a man may seek assistance in a venture from some of the spirits in the altar, he would never seek such help from many of those whose tablets he possesses. Quite the contrary, he may well conceive of them as unfortunates requiring his assistance. Yet for all these obvious distinctions, the memorialized dead are everywhere referred to as ancestors (senzo), and all share to some degree in the offerings and rites directed at the collectivity. Among the myriad problems remaining to be investigated is whether the differential treatment accorded the spirits of the dead can best be understood in terms of their proximity to the main line of descent and in terms of the length of time that has elapsed since their death. The axis of differentiation is quite likely to turn out to be the contrast between worship of (or reverence for) the ancestors (sosen-sūhai), on the one hand, and consolation of the spirits of the dead (sosen-kuyō), on the other.

Six. *The Realm of Personal Attachments*

To GIVE AN idea of the welter of considerations that affect the decision to place a tablet in a particular altar, I want to share some of the comments about these decisions made during my interviews. Elsewhere I have discussed "unusual" tablets, which I defined as those whose presence in the altar required some explanation (Smith 1966). Most tablets require no such comment, for they are in a given altar for reasons so obvious that it is almost foolish to ask about them. Nevertheless, for every tablet I asked "Why do you have this tablet here?" For the most part the reply was straightforward: "Because this is my father's tablet and I am the successor"; "She was my child"; "He is an ancestor and this is the main house"; "This is my first son's tablet—he died when he was only five"; "My three younger brothers died before they married, and my parents had tablets made for them, of course"; "This is the tablet for my father's father. He was the fourth head of this house, and I am the successor."

But explanations of quite another kind were offered for some tablets that should have been held for the most routine reasons. Some were for people who ordinarily would have been memorialized in a particular household and whose tablets were in fact found there—but for unorthodox reasons. "This is my elder brother's tablet. Actually, he married out rather than take the succession here. When he died I went to that house to ask for his tablet because I knew they would not take proper care of it." "My father ran away after we were all grown. He remarried, and when I heard that he had died I had a copy of his tablet made so that I could venerate it here. After all, he was my father." "This is my elder sister's tablet. My mother had it made and brought it here when she came to live with us. There must be another one in the house that my sister married into, even though she died shortly afterward." All of these explanations were for tablets that under ordinary circumstances should have been where they were. Without the comments made about them the casual observer would never have known that the elder brother and elder sister, and even the father, would normally not have been represented by a tablet in this particular altar. The personal elements involved in the decisions to have tablets made or transferred to their present location were the critical ones. They have altered the normal order of things, for strictly speaking—on the basis of the explanations given—none of these tablets should have been in the altars where I found them.

I also found tablets representing people who normally would have been memorialized in some other household, but who were being looked after by the people to whom I spoke. Dore (1958: 151) related a nice instance of such a situation involving a house in Shitayama-chō. This branch house, headed by a second son, had become much more prosperous than the main house back in the country, whose head was the first son (the successor). The mother was living with her second son and had brought the altar and the tablets with her for the obvious reason that they—like herself—would be better cared for there. But in my interviews far and away the most common comment about such anomalous tablets was "We have this one because there is no other place he could go. We felt so sorry for him." The word which I have translated "to feel sorry for" is *kawaisō*, which means pitiful, pathetic, sad. It is often used in contexts where the most fitting translation is "Oh, the poor thing!" and indicates a degree of compassion.

Human affairs being the tangled things they are, tablets come to rest in altars by a variety of routes. I should like to examine some of these anomalous tablets for the light their stories shed on the more routinely venerated ancestors. Where they have proved to be copies of originals held elsewhere, I have attempted to explore the circumstances behind the decisions to make duplicate tablets and I have also indicated known copies.

Duplicate Tablets

The distribution of duplicate tablets is shown in Table 18. Although some people I interviewed expressed the feeling that there should be only one tablet for any given individual, "lest he become confused and not know where to go at bon," duplicates are not uncommon. The Japanese have no practice comparable to the Chinese one of "dotting" the tablet with red ink; consequently, there is no unambiguously "real" tablet as opposed to a lifeless copy. In Nagasawa slips of paper on which the posthumous name is written are prepared, and one is distributed to each household in the dōzoku at the time of the funeral. In this community the "real" tablet is clearly distinguished from copies (Ooms 1967: 275). Some people I interviewed reported that in the area or district where they were born all sons, and in some cases all children, received a copy of a parent's tablet. For reasons of affection and sentiment, many others had asked to have a copy made of a tablet from their natal house's altar, "to bring here so that I could take care of him too."

Duplication of tablets has sometimes arisen from the specific circumstances of a person's death. About a tablet for an elderly man one household head said, "This is my father's tablet, even though we are a branch house. You see, he lived here with us for many years before he died.

TABLE 18
*Duplicate Tablets and Relationship
to Household Head*
($N = 167$)

Type of tablet	Relationship to household head			All relationships
	Lineals	Non-lineals	Non-kin	
Original, copy known to exist elsewhere	25	1	—	26
Copy, original known to exist elsewhere	72	30	5	107
Duplicate, unknown whether copy or original	17	17	—	34
TOTAL	114	48	5	167
Total as percent of all duplicate tablets	68.3%	28.7%	3.0%	100.0%
Total as percent of all tablets in each category	4.0%	25.4%	20.0%	5.5%

Since he died here we had a tablet made, but there is one in the main house, too, where his first son is now the head." The old man had once been head of the main house, and under normal circumstances he would have lived out his life there. Upon his death a tablet would have been made for him and placed in the altar of the main house, and that would have been the end of it. But for some reason he had moved to the house of one of his younger sons. Now in structural terms it is essential that there be a tablet for him in the main house; in terms of sentiment, however, members of "the house in which he died" will often want a tablet as well. Why? In the first place, those who cared for him in his old age will feel that they should care for his spirit as well. He had, after all, shared in the daily life of the house for some years. But there may be another motive as well. The house in which a person dies is the place his soul will cling to, and it is important that his spirit be shown due respect by that house's living members. The duplicate tablets in cases such as this represent the two faces of the motivation for ancestor veneration in Japanese society—the one structural, the other sentimental.

I did occasionally find younger sons and daughters, married out of their natal houses, who had copies of their parents' tablets. Most reported that they felt such attachment to their parents that they "wanted to have them in the new house" when they married, not only to care for them, but to receive the comfort their presence afforded as well. Sometimes sentiment was the only consideration. Behind one of the more unusual duplicate tablets lay a complex tale of romantic love and conflict between duty and personal desires. Distraught at the unexpected death of a woman with whom he had carried on a long affair, a man had asked a friend to copy the posthumous name from her tablet in the altar of her natal house. He had then written it on a plain wood tablet and had placed it in his own altar, where I found it among all the regular tablets for Lineal kinsmen.

It was difficult to determine for every tablet whether there was a duplicate somewhere else; I am certain only that there were 167 (5.5 percent) in my 3,050 tablets for which there was at least one duplicate elsewhere. The distribution of these among categories of kin was instructive, even though I am convinced that a great many duplicated tablets were not reported as such. Perhaps the most common reason for this was that the present members of the household simply did not know whether one of their older tablets was unique or had been copied. It was extremely unlikely that anyone could be certain that the tablet for his father's father's mother in his altar was the only one in existence, for, as I mentioned, nothing on a Japanese tablet indicates whether it is an original or a copy. For Nonlineals one-fourth and for Non-kin one-fifth of all tablets were duplicates; for Lineals the proportion was only four percent. Of the 167 duplicated tablets, just over two-thirds were for Lineal kin. It is my guess that these were for the most part tablets copied for reasons of affection by children of the deceased to take with them when they married and changed residence. One man put it succinctly when he said "I asked my eldest brother if I could make copies of our parents' tablets, and he said that it would be all right. So I brought them here after I got married because I didn't want to be the head of a house without any ancestors in it."

For the sake of convenience I have divided the cases discussed below between rural and urban households. I have done this not so much because I think the rural-urban distinction important, but because I think that those who know Japanese society and who are of the opinion that there are real differences between city and country in matters such as these will see that my findings provide little support for their assumption. After each kin term or other tablet category (given in italics), I have indicated whether the speaker was a successor or a nonsuccessor, or whether he bore some other relationship to the household head. The tablets roughly follow the order of the categories of terms in Table 15.

RURAL

Father. Successor (adopted husband). "My wife's younger brother has this tablet, too. He wanted a copy of it when he married and moved to Nagoya."

Elder brother. Successor. "He was my elder brother who went to Tokyo and got married there. When my father died he refused to come back and take over the house. His family has his tablet, too; this is a copy of it my mother had made."

Elder brother and his wife. Successor. "He was the first son but did not take the succession. Even after he married and went to Osaka, he always said that he wanted to be looked after by his main house after he died. These two tablets are in his son's house in Osaka, of course.

It was his son who had these copies made for my father and brought them here to put in this altar."

Younger brother. Successor. "He was killed in World War II and one urn of his ashes was sent here. We held a funeral and had this tablet made at that time. His widow in Osaka also received an urn of ashes, and his tablet is there, too."

Father's younger brother and his wife. Successor. "His tablet is also in the house of his daughter, who married out. My father had these two tablets made because this young couple left no successor." (Houses that die out are called zekke; they are discussed more fully in Chapter 5.)

Sister. Adopted couple; husband is successor. "This is actually the daughter of our foster parents. It's a copy of her original tablet, which is in the house she married into in Kyoto. She was forty-two when she died and our foster parents had this tablet made. Probably it was because she was the only one of their nine children who lived to marry." (Had the parents known that only one daughter would live to maturity, they obviously would have tried to find an adopted husband for her and would never have let her marry out. It was only after she was already married that her two younger brothers were killed in World War II and a sister died of tuberculosis.)

Father's younger brother. Successor. "Now that you ask, it seems to me that his married daughter has this tablet, too. I guess my father's father wanted to look after him. This must be a copy he had made."

Mother's mother (Nonlineal). Successor. "This tablet is also in the house where she was born. We have this one because her grave is nearby. She was buried here because she lived in this house for a long time and did not have much to do with any of her children except for my mother."

Mother's younger sister (Nonlineal). Nonsuccessor. "Her child has this tablet, too. I used to know why this one is here, but I don't remember the whole story too well anymore. Mother must have brought it here when she came to live with us."

Mother's brother's kin (four Nonlineals). Widow of adopted husband, successor. "All of these were copied by my uncle because he wanted to venerate them, too. I take care of them because my mother brought them here after her brother died and I took an adopted husband."

Father's lover (Non-kin). Successor. "This tablet is a copy. That is, the original is in her house where it belongs. My father couldn't ask for a copy, so he sent a friend over there to find out what posthumous name she had been given. The friend brought back the information and my father made this tablet. I doubt if her family knows anything about it." (I unwittingly stumbled into this awkward situation when I pressed my questions about a discrepancy between the identification originally offered of this tablet as "father's sister" and the age at death. It is one of three "skeletons" I found in the altars; there were doubtless many more I missed.)

URBAN

Father, mother. Successor. "My younger brothers all have copies of these."

Father, mother. Successor. "My younger brother took copies of these with him when he got married."

Father, mother. Successor. "Since I am the successor, these tablets are here. My younger brother had copies of them made when he got married and was made a branch house."

Father, mother. Successor. "I have these because I am the successor. My younger brother asked for copies of them, which he has in his house in Hagi."

Father, mother. Nonsuccessor. "These are copies made from the originals in the main house."

Father, mother. Nonsuccessor. "These are copies I had made from the ones in the main house after I got married and moved to the city."

Father, mother. Nonsuccessor. "These are copies from the tablets in the main house's altar. Even though I am not the successor I wanted to venerate my parents."

Father, mother. Nonsuccessor. "These were copied from the tablets in the main house."

Father, mother. Nonsuccessor. "There are copies in the altars of all of us brothers. It is the custom in my native district."

Father, mother. Nonsuccessor. "This is a new house, but when I married I asked the main house if I could have these made. I was always very close to our parents."

Father, mother, elder brother. Nonsuccessor. "I have the tablets only because the main house has moved away. They did take a set with them, but I don't know which ones are the copies. It doesn't matter anyway."

Father, mother, younger brother. Nonsuccessor. "These are copies of the tablets in the main house. I had them made when I got married and bought this altar to keep them in."

Father. Nonsuccessor. "All the children have copies."

Father. Nonsuccessor. "This is a copy from the altar in the main house. I pray for good health and my family's happiness before the ancestors. We are in this world because of them. The ancestors are the roots, parents the trunk, and we are the branches and leaves. Therefore I worship them with all my heart." (This is a standard Seichō-no-Ie phrasing of the relationship to the ancestors.)

Father. Successor. "I'm the successor, so I have his tablet. My sister has a copy. She's a member of the Risshō-kōsei-kai." (In this as in some of the other New Religions women are urged to worship the tablets of their own parents as well as those of the house into which they marry.)

Father. Nonsuccessor. "I copied this from the one in the main house, where my elder brother is the successor."

Father. Nonsuccessor. "I made this copy from the one in the altar in the house where I was born. My eldest brother is head there and he said it would be all right."

Father. Nonsuccessor. "This is a copy of the one in the main house."

Mother. Successor. "This is my mother's tablet, but it's really a copy. My father died young and she remarried into another house. They have the original, of course, but I thought we should have her tablet as well, so I asked them if we could make a copy. They were very nice about it."

Mother. Nonsuccessor. "This is a copy I had made from the original in the main house because I wanted to take care of her, too."

Mother. Nonsuccessor. "The main house made one for each of us sons."

(Wife's) mother, (wife's) mother's brother, (wife's) younger brother. Nonsuccessor (adopted husband). "These are all copies from the altar in the main house. My wife wanted them here even though we are a branch house."

Father's father and mother. Successor. "These are copies from the altar in the main house, where my father's elder brother is head. My father actually had these made and brought them to this house when he married and became a branch house."

Father's father and mother. Nonsuccessor. "I had these copies made from the main-house originals. They worship the ancestors, to be sure, but we have no ancestors in this house as yet. To express our gratitude to those to whom we owe our lives, we worship my grandparents' tablets every day."

Husband. Widow, not remarried. "There is a copy in his natal house where his elder brother is head."

Husband. Widow, not remarried. "Our first son, who is the successor, has a copy in his house. I keep this one because I want to take care of his spirit."

Husband's father and mother. Widow of nonsuccessor, not remarried. "My late husband had these made after we were married. They are also in the altar of the house where he was born, of course."

Husband. Widow, remarried. "His father made a copy of this to take back with him to the house where he was born."

Husband, husband's father and mother. Widow, not remarried. "My husband was the successor. His younger brother wanted copies for his altar, so I said he could have them made."

First wife. Successor. "They came from her natal house and asked if they could have a copy made. So they have one, even though she married out."

Elder brother. Nonsuccessor. "He was just like a father to me. I'm the fifth son, so he was much older, you see. I made this copy from his tablet, which is in the house of his first daughter, who took an adopted husband to guarantee the succession."

Younger brother. Successor. "My mother had this tablet made. His widow has the original, of course. I think that mother just wanted to be sure his spirit would be well cared for."

Younger brother. Successor. "This is my younger brother who died just after he got married. Since there were no children and his wife went back to her family, we took his tablet. Our mother, who was living with another of my younger brothers, had a copy made for the altar in that house, too, so that she could take care of him."

Yōshi's father's mother and elder brother (Nonlineals). Nonsuccessor. "These are both copies from my foster father's elder brother's house. That's the main house. My foster father had these made when he set up this house and always regarded them very highly, so we try to look after them because he would want us to."

Yōshi's father and mother (Nonlineals). Adopted son. "I brought these copies of my parents' tablets with me when I came to this house. Why? These people gave me life; they are my ancestors."

Yōshi's father and mother (Nonlineals). Successor (adopted husband). "These are copies of those in the altar of the house where I was born. I wanted them to look after, too."

Yōshi's father and mother; wife's father and mother (all Nonlineals). (This house was headed by the husband of an adopted couple, both of whom wanted to have copies of their respective parents' tablets from their natal houses. They also had all the tablets of the house into which they were adopted, of course. Since these included their foster parents' tablets, this meant that they had three sets of parents' tablets in a single altar.)

Mother's mother (Nonlineal). Successor. "My mother was raised by her mother. There was no successor in that line. This is the original tablet, and my mother's younger sister has a duplicate of it in her altar as well. They were the only two children and both married out, so they had to take responsibility for looking after their mother's spirit."

Mother's father and mother; mother's first husband (Nonlineals). Successor. "My mother lives with us, and when she came she brought a small altar with these three copies of tablets that she had made from those in the main house of her family. That house is headed by her younger brother and he let her make the copies."

Mother's father and mother; mother's father's mother (Nonlineals). Nonsuccessor. "My mother brought all these copies of tablets from her natal house when she came to live with us. She takes very good care of them."

Wife's father (Nonlineal). Nonsuccessor. "All his children have copies of this tablet. The original is in the main house of my wife's family, where he was the head."

Wife's father (Nonlineal). Successor. "My wife had this made and put it here. It's a copy of the one taken care of by her mother back in the house where she was born."

Wife's father (Nonlineal). Nonsuccessor. "My wife had this copy made from the original in her family's altar, where her eldest brother is the head."

Wife's father and mother (Nonlineals). Successor. "My wife wanted these copies of tablets from her natal house, so that she could venerate them along with the ancestors." (Here the speaker made a distinction few others made. The single domestic altar can shelter both ancestors and dead kinsmen of either the husband or the wife.)

Wife's mother (Nonlineal). Successor. "All of her daughters have copies of her tablet. It is the custom in the area she comes from."

Wife's mother (Nonlineal). Successor. "This is a copy of the tablet in my wife's father's house. She wanted to look after her mother, too."

Onjin (Non-kin). "I asked his house if I could make this tablet so that I could venerate it. I always looked upon him as my father, and owe him absolutely everything." (Onjin are those to whom the unrepayable debt of on is owed.)

Teacher (Non-kin). "I admired him enormously and asked his family if I might venerate this copy of his tablet. They gave me permission very graciously."

Each of the above examples came from a different altar. Below I have given several more complex cases, involving altars with great internal variability. All were from urban households. The first case was that of a house whose head was a fourth son and not the successor; only the duplicate tablets in his altar are dealt with.

Wife's father and mother (Nonlineals). "In my wife's native district every child receives a copy of the tablets of the parents. The main house keeps the original ones, of course."

Elder brother's foster father and mother (Nonlineals). "I asked this house if I could copy these tablets and venerate them. This couple adopted my elder brother, but he died shortly afterward. They are my onjin; I owe them everything."

Father, mother, father's father, father's mother, father's father's second wife. "These are copies from the altar in the main house. Actually, all three of my elder brothers died in adulthood and the main descent line there has been continued through an adopted husband. I had these tablets made after the last of my elder brothers died, so that I could be sure that our ancestors would be well cared for."

The second case of a complex altar was that of a house whose head was the successor. Again, only those tablets that were copies or had been duplicated are considered.

Father. "There is a copy of this in the branch house where my father's sister's husband is head. She had it made to care for in her own altar."

Wife's father (Nonlineal). "My wife had this made from the tablet in the main house of her family, where her brother is now the head. She was always very close to her father."

Father's father and mother; father's father's father and mother (Non-lineals). "My father came here as an adopted son when he was young. He brought these copies with him and venerated them regularly. After all, they were his ancestors."

The third example was that of a zekke, which I discuss in this section because all the tablets were copies of the originals.

Father and mother; (mother's) father and mother; (mother's) father's father and mother; (mother's) father's father's father and mother. Non-successor. "My father was an adopted husband. Both of my parents died when all of us were quite small children, so my mother's younger brother took all of these tablets into his altar. He's the head of that main house and still has the tablets. When I got married I had copies made of all of them and brought them here."

The fourth case was a nice instance of bilaterality. The speaker was a nonsuccessor.

Father's father and mother; wife's father and mother (Nonlineals). Of the first pair of tablets, he said, "My wife's elder brother—he's the successor in her house—has the originals. She wanted these made." Of the second pair, "I had these copies made when we got married. The originals are in the house where I was born. Both my wife and I just wanted to look after our parents' spirits."

The fifth example was another where the tangled fortunes of a man's kinsmen resulted in a complicated set of tablets. The speaker was a non-successor.

Father; father's father and mother (Nonlineals). "My father was an adopted husband, and he and my mother were set up as a branch house. My mother died and he remarried. After I was grown, he died and I asked his second wife for the altar and the tablets for him and his father and mother. She refused, so I bought one myself and made copies of these tablets so that I could worship them here."

A similar motivation, much more clearly expressed, led to the development of my sixth example. The speaker was a nonsuccessor.

Father, mother, elder brother, younger brother; mother's foster father (Nonlineals). "These tablets are all copies from those in the main house, where this elder brother was head until his death. We were always very close, and after he died I wanted to look after his spirit, too. The other four tablets? Well, you see, while he was alive he took very good care of them. I am sure that he's happy, all of them being together in this altar." (We shall find that this is not uncommon sentiment. The deceased and the tablets whose care was his responsibility while he lived have an intimate association. The tablets that he cared for are sometimes treated as dependents of the deceased who now need someone else's care.)

The seventh and last case offered an arresting array of duplicated tablets. Both husband and wife were adopted. The household consisted of this adopted couple, their three children, and their foster mother. The altar held thirteen tablets. The speaker was the adopted husband and successor.

Foster mother's father, mother, elder brother (Nonlineals). "All of these are copies my foster mother had made from those in her natal house's altar."

Foster mother's elder sister and her husband (Nonlineals). "This is not a house that died out. My foster mother had these copies made from the tablets in the house into which her elder sister had married."

Foster mother's elder sister (Nonlineal). "This is a copy, too. The original is in the house she married into."

Foster mother's niece (Nonlineal). "This is a copy of the tablet that is in the house where she died. I think it is the child of my foster mother's elder sister, but I'm not sure which one."

Foster father's younger sister (Nonlineal). "He had this made from the original in the house she married into. She died fairly soon after she went there, but they kept her tablet."

Foster father's elder sister's son (Nonlineal). "He had this made, too, because this was the child of a family member who had married out of the house." (This statement was strikingly unorthodox in its implications, for it is far more common not to place tablets of children of one's married-out children in the altar.)

Father, mother, elder brother (Nonlineals). "These are copies of originals in my natal house. I brought them here when I came as an adopted husband."

Elder sister (Nonlineal). "I had this made from the tablet in the house she married into."

By any lights this last household had an unusual assemblage of tablets. The family belonged to the Jōdo-shin sect, too, and not to one of the New Religions that encourage the collecting of as many ancestral tablets as possible.

Tablets for Adult Siblings of the Household Head

A frequently encountered type of anomalous tablet is that for an unmarried or married adult sibling of the household head. Such a tablet requires comment only when there is some unusual reason why it is in the altar, of course. It may have been put there by the present head's father, who would have been looking after his own child. In other cases it may have been placed there by the present head, who had to care for a brother or sister with an irregular life history. As in the preceding section, I have divided the cases between rural and urban, and I have indicated the status of the speaker where it is known.

RURAL

Elder sister. Successor. "She married out into another house, but returned here and died. I remember her very well because she used to sing while she worked. But I was just a boy when she died. My father had this tablet made because she had no other place to go."

Elder sister. Successor. "She married out and went to Osaka, but got tuberculosis and came back here to die. Her tablet is here because she was never registered in her husband's household register." (In other words, the marriage was not legal. The implication is that the man's household therefore had no obligation to make a tablet for her, although it probably would have done so had she died there, legally married or not.)

Elder sister. Successor. "She married out, and when her husband remarried after her death I took her tablet. He said that he'd rather return it to her natal house where he knew we would take good care of her spirit."

Father's sister. Successor. "She married out, and when her husband died she came back here and died many years later. Her father made this tablet."

Father's sister. Successor. "She was a very unfortunate woman. She married out, but returned here and died. There never was any divorce, so that house ought to have a tablet for her, but they were too poor to have one made. Her father had this one made and she is being looked after by the house where she was born rather than by the house that really has the duty to care for her spirit. The poor thing!"

Father's two younger sisters. Adopted son (successor). "My foster father said that these women married out but for some reason came back and died here without ever remarrying." (They were actually members of the house into which he was adopted, of course, so it is hardly surprising that he was not sure of the circumstances that led to their being here.)

Father's father's elder sister. Successor. "I remember being told that she married out, but came home and died after a short time. It was my father who made the tablet; after all, he was the successor and she was his aunt."

URBAN

Elder brother. "After he died his wife remarried. She couldn't take his tablet with her, of course, so she left it with us in the house where he was born."

Younger brother. "He went to another house as an adopted son, but both his foster parents died before he was old enough to marry, and then he died. I brought his tablet back here. There was no one else to care for him."

Elder sister. "I had it made for fear that she would not be well cared for in the house she married into." (Although this was a copy, I have put it in this section because of the reason given for having it. It was obvious from many of the conversations about the tablets of married sons and daughters that people often felt that the individual's natal house would take better care of them than would the houses into which they had married.)

Father's younger sister. "The house she married into died out, and so my father went there to get her tablet. He always said that her family would look after her because there was no one else to do it."

Father's father's elder sister. Successor. "She was divorced and came back here. When she died my grandfather had this tablet made—see, it says 'Ichirō's second daughter, Mon.'"

Father's father's sister. Successor. "There is a copy in her grandson's house, too. She died there. I'm not really sure why she is in this altar, but my grandfather probably wanted to be sure that she'd be well looked after."

Tablets in the House Where the Person Died

People who take up residence in a house and die there are often memorialized in that altar because they once shared in the household's daily life. Ordinarily their tablets would be elsewhere, and sometimes there are duplicates. Because of their patent incongruity, such tablets are almost always commented on.

RURAL

Father's mother. Successor. "I am the successor, so I have her tablet. But my younger brother has one, too, because she lived in his house for a long time and died there."

Yōshi's mother (Nonlineal). "She died here, having come to live with us just after the end of World War II. But this tablet really ought to be in my elder brother's house; he is the successor in our family, after all."

Mother's mother (Nonlineal). Nonsuccessor. "She died here. My wife felt that she should go on looking after her. No, I don't think there is any other copy of her tablet."

Wife's father (Nonlineal). Successor. "He died here after living with us for years. There is another tablet for him in his own house."

URBAN

Father, mother. Nonsuccessor. "My mother died here. While she was with us she always looked after my father's tablet; he had died many years before. Then when she died I had a tablet made for her and put the two together in the altar here. Both are also back in the altar of the main house in the country."

Father. Successor. "They have a copy of this in the branch house, too. That's where he died."

Mother. Nonsuccessor. "I had this copy made from the altar in the main house because my mother lived with us in her last years. The original is in my elder brother's house, of course."

Mother. Nonsuccessor. "We were very fond of each other, and she lived here a long time. I asked my elder brother if I could have a copy made. She didn't actually die here, but fell ill suddenly on a visit to his house and died there. I wanted to continue to take care of her."

Mother. Successor. "I'm the successor, so I have her tablet. My younger brother has one, too. He was adopted into our mother's natal house. After our father died and I became successor, she went to live with my younger brother—who was now the head of her natal house—because she and I never got along."

Father's mother. Nonsuccessor. "She lived here for many years and died in this house. My elder brother has her tablet, too, since he is the successor."

Uncle. "He lived with us here for a while before he died. There is no place else for his tablet to be."

Aunt. Nonsuccessor. "She lived with us for a long time and died here. I don't think anyone else has her tablet. She had a very hard time in life and we always felt sorry for her."

Father's mother (Nonlineal). Successor. "Although my father was adopted, his mother came to live here and died in this house, so he had a tablet made for her. There is probably one back there, too, but I'm really not sure of that."

Wife's mother (Nonlineal). "My wife wanted to take care of her mother's tablet, which is only natural. Her younger brother also wanted one, because the old lady had lived with his family for many years and it was there that she died."

Yōshi's father (Nonlineal). "He lived here a long time and died in this house."

Wife's father (Nonlineal). "He died here after living with us for a long time."

Wife's father (Nonlineal). Nonsuccessor. "He died here. There is another tablet in his main house, where his first son is the successor."

Wife's mother (Nonlineal). Nonsuccessor. "This is the original tablet. We had it made after the funeral because she lived with us for almost twenty years after her husband divorced her. She died here. As far as I can tell, she never got along with any of her other children, but her first daughter does have a copy which she's got in the altar of her grandson's house where she lives now. There is no tablet for her in her late husband's house, I'm sure of that."

Tablets for Members of Households That Have Died Out

Despite the preoccupation with continuing the household line and the range of alternatives available to insure succession, something may go wrong and a house may literally die out (see Dore 1958: 146–47). Such houses are called zekke or *haike.* An extreme case that I found— and there were surely many such—involved a family in Hiroshima that became zekke when the husband, wife, and three of their five small daughters were killed. A more common cause for the termination of a line is death shortly after marriage; in some cases, though, rebellious young people will refuse to keep a house going by taking an adopted husband or by going as one. I found 27 altars in which tablets for members of zekke were kept, accounting for 108 persons in all. The distribution of these altars was as follows: Tokyo, 6; Osaka, 2; Kyoto, 3; Hanshin, 1; miscellaneous urban, 1; Sone, 10; Yasuhara, 2; and Takane, 2. The tablets proved to be divided almost evenly between Lineals (55— 50.9 percent) and Nonlineals (51—47.2 percent), with only 2 (1.9 percent) for Non-kin. The Lineal tablets were almost exclusively those of household heads' siblings and their spouses and children. The Nonlineals were almost exclusively the parents, or the siblings and their spouses and children, of the household head's wife or of adopted husbands whose own families had died out.

RURAL

Father's father and father's mother. Successor. In all my interviews, this was the only unequivocal case I found of a revived zekke, which is why it is included here. "This house had died out and all of its tablets had been deposited with its main house. When it was decided to revive it, with me as the successor, I went to the main house and got these two tablets. One is the grandfather of the head of the main house; the other is his first wife, who ran away and died in another house. They are both now our ancestors."

Sixteen tablets, comprising two zekke. Successor. "My daughter married out and last year she and her husband emigrated to Paraguay. They left all of his household's tablets here—he is the successor—including two sets of zekke tablets they had been taking care of. I really don't know very much about them. If they get settled in Paraguay or Brazil, maybe they will send for them all." (They may well do so. For a unique treatment of the place of ancestor worship among Japanese immigrants in Brazil, see Maeyama 1972.)

Four tablets with a family name different from that of the household head being interviewed. Adopted husband (successor). "I came here as an adopted husband, but before that I had been adopted into this family. But I left that house and when their only daughter married out they became zekke. She came to me and asked if I would take care of their tablets, so I took them. After all, they were once my foster parents and their children were my foster siblings." (Of course, the married daughter could have taken the tablets, for I have recorded many analogous cases where that has happened; something must have prevented her from doing so in this case.)

Wife's mother (Nonlineal). Successor. "My wife is an only child, so when we got married she brought along her mother's tablet; there was no other place for it." (This was a somewhat ambiguous case, although the word zekke was used in conversation about the wife's house. It could well be that her father had remarried and preferred to leave his first wife's tablet to the daughter's care.)

Mother's mother's father and mother (Nonlineals). Nonsuccessor. "Because my mother's mother was an only child, she brought her parents' tablets with her when she came to live in this house."

URBAN

Fifteen tablets, comprising two zekke. Nonsuccessor. "My elder brother—he is the successor in the main house—did not want these tablets, so I took them all. There are two zekke here, both of them my father's elder brothers and their families. His third elder brother died without marrying, and so my father—the fourth son—became successor. These really ought to be in the main house, but my elder brother just won't hear of it. I could not bear to see them neglected, so I am taking care of them."

Aunt, uncle, aunt's father and mother (Nonlineals). Successor. "This is a zekke. My father died young and when my mother remarried I went to live with this aunt, but she never adopted me legally. When she died

I had a tablet made for her and now I keep it with the other three that she had looked after for such a long time. She and my uncle had no children."

Father's younger brother and his wife. Successor. "They both died, leaving no children. It is zekke, so naturally we have their tablets here in the main house. There is no other place they could go."

Father's younger brother and his wife and son. Successor. "My father's younger brother and his wife were quite young when they died and their son was too small to take care of their tablets. He came to live here and my father put his parents' tablets in this altar. Then the little boy died, too, so we put his tablet here with those of his father and mother."

Elder brother, his wife, and their three daughters. "They were all killed in Hiroshima. The two surviving daughters were too young to take the tablets, so I look after them here."

Father's younger brother and his child. "There was no other place for them to go. This man's wife remarried, so it is a kind of zekke."

Two sets of tablets, comprising two zekke. "Originally I married into my wife's house as her adopted husband (we are first cousins), but her parents threw me out. My wife ran away from there and followed me to the city. Now they are all dead, and we have the tablets for both our natal households because neither of them could find a successor."

Eight tablets of husband's mother's foster family. Successor's widow. "My husband's mother was adopted by that house and was supposed to take an adopted husband and continue the line. But when the time came she refused and married out instead. They could not find a successor, so when they died she felt an obligation to care for their tablets and took all that were in the altar. As long as she lived here she looked after them very conscientiously. I never knew any of them."

Father, father's mother, elder brother (Nonlineals). Widow. "I take care of them because they have no other place to go. After I married here, my house died out."

Wife's father and mother; wife's elder brother (Nonlineals). Nonsuccessor. "This is a zekke. My wife took the tablets because there was no one left to look after them."

Wife's father and mother (Nonlineals). Nonsuccessor. "My wife had no brothers or sisters, so she had to bring her parents' tablets here."

Wife's father and mother; wife's elder sister (Nonlineals). Nonsuccessor. "They all died and no one was left to carry on their house, so my wife brought their tablets here to care for them."

Wife's mother; wife's two younger brothers; wife's younger sister (Nonlineals). Successor. "My wife has all these tablets because her family died out."

Wife's father (Nonlineal). Successor. "My wife's natal house was a branch house, and when her father died she took his tablet. Her mother married into another house, so my wife's family is zekke."

Wife's father and mother; wife's younger brother (Nonlineals). Successor. "My wife's younger brother was supposed to be the successor, but he died unexpectedly. There was no other place for them to go, so my wife has their tablets here."

Eight tablets of wife's foster kin (Nonlineals). Nonsuccessor. "My wife took all of these when the successor to her house died leaving no one to take over. She had been adopted into that family, but had married out."

Seven tablets of yōshi's kin (Nonlineals). The speaker in this case was the son and successor of this adopted husband. "My father came here as an adopted husband. When his family unexpectedly died out, he took all the tablets and the altar from his natal house and brought them here. There was nothing else to do."

Other Tablets in the Care of Houses Not Their Own

For a variety of reasons, tablets for some people are kept in the altars of houses where they really do not belong. At least some of the people I talked to felt that they were in some senses being imposed upon by having tablets left with them that they ordinarily would not have. It sometimes happened that apparently routine tablets were in a given altar for a variety of very complex and very human reasons.

RURAL

Six tablets of the main house. The speaker was the sixth son, and not the successor. "My eldest brother is the successor, but he moved to the city with his family. They left the tablets here with me near the family graves, but when they get a larger apartment I plan to take the tablets to them."

Five tablets of wife's mother's family (Nonlineals). "These tablets are here only temporarily. My wife's brother is in Kobe. He's the successor in that house, and he asked us if we would keep them here until he got settled and sent for them."

Father's younger brother's wife and daughter. "They are here because the one surviving daughter was very young when her mother died. My father's younger brother remarried and left these tablets with us when he moved out for the second time. He did not want these tablets in the altar of his new house."

Father's father and mother. Successor. "These ought to have been taken by my father and mother to the altar in their retirement quarters. I don't know why they are here." (The practice referred to here—where a retired couple assumes full responsibility for the worship of the ascendants of the previous generation—is very common in certain areas of the country.)

Elder brother's child. Nonsuccessor. "My elder brother died in Tokyo, and this little boy's tablet was sent down here to the main house. I don't know why they did that; his tablet should be with his father's."

Husband's younger brother's son. Widow of successor. "My late husband's younger brother died very young. We take care of his little boy's tablet because his wife remarried. She must have taken her husband's tablet with her."

Elder sister's son. Successor. "My elder sister brought this tablet to us just after the war ended. She left it when she went back to the city and never came back for it."

Father's younger sister's son. Successor. "This boy's mother brought him back to this house with her when her husband died. The boy died a few years later and shortly after that she remarried. She left the tablet here. But she is dead now, too, and her tablet is in the house of her second husband. We look after this one because there is no one else to look after it. She often said that she would come back for it, but she never did."

First son's son and daughter. Nonsuccessor. "We have the tablets here because it seemed better to have them near the family temple. Their parents live in Kyushu and seldom visit here."

Wife's mother's husband. Adopted husband. "This man was my wife's mother's second husband, but their marriage was never registered. They had no children, and he asked my wife to care for his tablet when he died. She does so. There really was no place else for him, although by rights his main house ought to have taken it."

Mother's younger sister (Nonlineal). Successor. "Before she died this woman asked my mother to care for her tablet, so it is here. They were always very close."

Mother and mother's daughter. Successor. "My mother married again after my father died, but she fell ill almost at once and came back here with this tablet. After she died we had a tablet made for her, too, and venerate them together." (By rights both should be in the house of her second husband; the informant did not know if they were there or not.)

Three unidentified tablets. Successor. "Why, these have a different surname! I have no idea who they are or why they are here." (They were dated 1811, 1821, and 1838.)

Seven unidentified tablets. Successor. "These were all in the altar when I came back from Kobe to take over the succession after my elder brother's death. I never thought to ask who they are." (They were dated from 1818 to 1873.)

Three unidentified tablets. Nonsuccessor. "When I was made a branch house, I didn't want to have a house with no ancestors, so I took these tablets from the altar in the main house." (The man was a fifth son. The tablets were dated 1828, 1837, and 1861.)

Stranger (tanin) (Non-kin). Successor. "I found this on the beach after the great tidal wave some years ago. I thought that since I found it, I was meant to care for it."

URBAN

Father, mother. Nonsuccessor. "These really ought to be in my elder brother's house, but I took them when I found out that no one there was willing to take care of them."

Father, two elder brothers, younger sister. Nonsuccessor. "I took these because the main house was not taking proper care of them."

Fifteen tablets of main house. Nonsuccessor. "I'm not the successor, but my elder brother just did not want to be bothered with the tablets, and since there was no one else to take them, they are here in our altar."

Elder brother. Nonsuccessor. "I had this made out of affection; I miss him very much."

Father's elder brother. Successor. "This man was the first son, but he had a terrible row with his father—my grandfather—and was expelled from the house." (The term is *kandō*, meaning to be physically driven out and to have one's name removed from the household register.) "But my father always had the highest regard for his brother and when he became head of this house he had a tablet made for him. My grandfather would have been furious."

Cousin (itoko). Successor. "We all grew up together like brothers and sisters because her parents died young and she lived here as a child. When she died I had a tablet made for her because there was no one else in the world to care for her, and I loved her like a sister."

Mother's father and mother (Nonlineals). Successor. "My mother had these and venerated them while she lived with us. It's a bit unusual because actually her father just disappeared and we never found out what happened to him. It was several years later that she made this tablet, assuming that he was dead."

Some Curiosities

A few people commented on the absence of tablets that they felt they ought to have had but did not. I have given several instances below.

RURAL

The speaker was the daughter of the house, who had taken an adopted husband. "We should have my grandfather's tablet, but we don't. What happened is that my father came here as an adopted son and sometime later his family seemed on the verge of dying out. When they took another man as their adopted successor, he came to us and asked if he could have grandfather's tablet to give some 'depth' to his altar, so we let him have it. I doubt if anyone in that house has any idea whose tablet it is. Poor thing! I don't even know where they live now. We should at least have kept a copy of it."

The speaker was a man who succeeded his grandfather rather than his father, as would normally have been the case. "I don't have my father's tablet. He was adopted into this house, but after we children were born he went back to his natal house. I was told that they have his tablet there, but I've never seen it."

The widow of a successor told me, "My husband's father's mother married again after he died, so we have his tablet, but not hers. It's in the second house she married into."

URBAN

The speaker was a successor. "This altar used to have many other tablets in it, but now there are only those for my father and mother. My mother took very good care of the tablets, which included some for her relatives as well as some for my father's. Just before she died, she asked me to have all the tablets placed in her coffin and cremated with her. She said 'No one will really look after them when I am dead, and it would be better not to leave them behind only to have them neglected.' I kept only my father's tablet and had one made for her."

A widow, who had neither tablets nor an altar, told me, "I used to have a small altar and my husband's tablet. As long as I lived in our house I kept them, but when I moved to this city and got this room, I did not want to bring the tablet here. I thought that he'd find the surroundings disagreeable—he liked our house very much—and I know he wouldn't like being cared for by his lonely widow. He'd hate being reminded every morning that I'm still a widow, still all alone, and getting old. He always wanted me to look young. So I took his tablet back to the house where he was born, where I'm sure they take good care of him."

In addition to all the other kinds of anomalous tablets, there were three cases of false identification. One, the case of the father's lover identified as "father's sister," has been discussed already. The other two were from rural households as well. One tablet bore the information that it was for the second son of the former household head; it was in fact a tablet for an illegitimate son of the present head of the house. The second indicated that it was the tablet of the present household head's second son, who was in fact so registered in the household register in the village office. However, internal evidence revealed that the boy was actually the illegitimate son of the household head's unmarried sister.

In two rural households I found multiple copies of certain tablets.

In neither case was the household head aware of the situation, nor could either one think why they should be there. The best guesses were either that multiple copies had been made but not distributed to those who were supposed to receive them at the time of the funeral, or that a child who had received a tablet later returned it to his natal house for some reason. A third possibility, of course, was that the second copy was the tablet intended for the temple but never delivered. In one of the cases I found two copies each of tablets for "mother," "father's father," and "father's mother." The head of the house was an adopted husband, and all three of these people were in his wife's descent line. His reaction was one of puzzlement. "That's odd. There are two of each of these. I wonder why? I never noticed that before." In the second case, the speaker was again an adopted husband, referring to multiple copies of tablets for "father's first wife" and "father's half brother," again in his wife's descent line. "For some reason there are two of each of these. Why would anyone have two copies of the same tablet in the altar? I wonder if my wife knows anything about this?" (She did not.)

Lacking a lineage system, the Japanese are not preoccupied with the issue of the presence in a single altar of multiple descent lines. I found only two cases of anything even bordering on concern for the problem— each case representing quite a different situation. The first was from a rural household, the second from an urban one. In the first instance, the altar had tablets for the household head's father and mother. "Both my father and mother were *ato-tsugi* (that is, each was the link through which their respective houses were carried on). I succeeded my mother and my younger brother succeeded my father, who was an adopted husband. Both he and I have tablets for both our parents." Now occasionally when an adopted husband marries in, it will be agreed that children of the couple will take the surnames of wife and husband alternately. The first two sons, with different surnames, will be designated as successors, respectively, in the mother's and father's lines. But note that in this case both sons had both parents' tablets.

In the second case, the altar had full sets of tablets for both husband's and wife's families. "My wife and I are both ato-tsugi, so we have both sets of tablets here. Each of us will have a successor, of course; mine will take my family's tablets and hers will take the tablets of her family."

(Will both successors have both your tablet and hers?) "Of course! We are their ancestors!"

In this chapter I have dealt with a great variety of circumstances and situations that affect decisions to make tablets for given persons and to place them in given altars. It is appropriate to conclude with a small hint of the very great variability in the reasons that people give for having tablets for the deceased members of the household at all:

So that I can pray for the health and happiness of my family every day.

It's an old Japanese custom.

Conclusion

How often one hears "It's an old Japanese custom" as an explanation for why a thing is done, or for why it is done in a certain way. The implication usually is either that the Japanese have been doing this for a very long time (and so continue to do it), or, more likely, that back in some unspecified traditional time almost everyone did this, or did it in this way. History is always present in such explanations of behavior, but in the flat sense of "traditional times." Tour guides used to start their lectures on almost every temple and shrine with the stock phrase "About three hundred years ago . . . ," as though time began with the establishment of the Tokugawa shogunate. Although there is a certain validity to this bit of folk insight (for many twentieth-century Japanese institutions did indeed originate at about that time), it affords too short a perspective on the practice of ancestor worship in Japan. We shall begin, then, with history.

Since at least the seventh century some elements of the population have conducted ceremonies designed specifically to benefit the souls of the dead, to seek their benign protection and assistance, to secure the intercession on their behalf of one or another of the compassionate Buddhas, or to share with them the pleasures and sorrows of the living. More accurately, what our long journey from the time of the Nara court to contemporary Japan has unequivocally shown is that ancestral rites of some description have served all of these aims throughout recorded

Japanese history in different ritual contexts and among a wide range of social groups.

Two principal features of what the Japanese call ancestor worship or ancestor veneration stand out. The first is a property of the ancestors themselves—a property the Japanese are well aware of: the ancestors are, above everything else, a category of dead who exercise tutelary powers over some social group (be it household, dōzoku organization of linked families, hamlet or village, professional or trade guild, or nation) to whose members they are thought to be ancestral. The second feature of ancestor worship, less commonly perceived and extrinsic to the phenomenon itself, is that its practice at all levels of Japanese society has for centuries been shaped in form and defined in content by larger political and administrative imperatives. Whether as an aspect of the sixth- and seventh-century promotion of Buddhism, as a leading element of the seventeenth-century suppression of Christianity, or as a pillar of the nineteenth- and twentieth-century revival of (a largely fictive) tradition, the veneration of the ancestors has served the purposes of great religious bodies, dissenters from orthodoxy, powerful authoritarian governments, and faltering, uncertain reformers. To many special interest groups throughout the country's history, the devotion of the Japanese to their dead kinsmen has provided a reservoir of fidelity that when successfully tapped has greatly benefited its exploiters. But this has in no way seemed to lessen the people's propensity to pay homage to and to seek to care for the ancestral spirits, toward whom they have for centuries given evidence of feelings of respect, gratitude, and pity.

None of this discussion will have surprised the historians among my readers, but I hope that it will have given pause to the anthropologists. For it is my conviction that the anthropologist who willfully chooses to remain ignorant of the historical materials on ancestor worship at even the lowliest level of household usages simply will not know how to interpret what he sees on the ground, for as Macfarlane has said (1973: 322):

Historical material, once invoked, requires a new explanatory framework. Such sources wreak a peculiar destructive magic, turning to dust the beautiful but insubstantial functional and structural models. It is arguable that it was only by excluding historical material that anthropologists were able to simplify the complexity of human life to a level where it seemed possible to achieve a new synthesis. By delimiting in time, as they did in space, they seemed able to achieve an overview of *all* thoughts and actions. They could then show how these were linked. We now know that this was largely a deception, but in the agony of destruction it is uncertain how much can be saved from the wreck.

I do not want to be misunderstood. There is no doubt whatever in my mind that at the heart of anthropology must lie our long-standing commitment to the observation of people's behavior as they live out their daily lives, coupled with a respect for the supremely intriguing variability of their interpretations of what they themselves call their customs. Yet these people exist in a flow of history whose minimum duration is the length of a person's life at the time we encounter him. Some people know something of past events beyond their personal experience, others know very little. But outside them all is what we may call extrinsic history; in Japan this is the record of imperial edicts, theological treatises, legislative codes, shrine and temple registers—documents of all kinds, each devised in its day to initiate, confirm, extol, prohibit, register, or require behavior of some sort.

How does familiarity with this record alter our perception of what we have observed? When we discover that in 1640 the extremely effective central government of Japan required that all persons register as parishioners of Buddhist temples, we have not unlocked the secret of the universalism of temple affiliation in the nineteenth century. But we have learned why (given the evidence for the efficient enforcement of the law in the seventeenth century) the household rather than the individual became the unit of temple affiliation. It had not been so before that time; it has been the rule for the past 300 years. Further acquaintance with the historical materials will also reveal the origins and continued reaffirmation of the principle that all men owe reverence to both the gods and the buddhas. This principle has held solidly into the present, with the result that most households are at once Buddhist and Shintoist. An obvious alternative path of development might well have led to a situation in which each household was either Buddhist, Shintoist, Confucianist, or even pagan. We can also learn from the historical record something very important about the reasons why Buddhism developed in the particular direction it did in Japan over the centuries. It is too easily forgotten that religious policy has repeatedly played a vital role at the level of state policy. All the faiths blended into popular Japanese religion today have at one time or another been promoted, downgraded, or suppressed by the state. These efforts have not always met with complete success, of course, but I must emphasize that nothing inherent in any of the religions or in the nature of Japanese society or psychology has led inevitably to the situation that obtains today. Historical evidence alone can help us explain why ancestor worship in Japan has assumed the form it has—and why Buddhism has become almost totally dependent upon it for its continued existence. Perhaps more important still, we can know why Buddhism has not become something else entirely or died out.

Recognition of the importance of history in this sense may also aid us in dealing with a problem of a somewhat different sort posed by the study of Japanese society—a society presenting us with a host of phenomena that at once resist tidy exposition and appear always to lie just outside ready comparative frameworks. It is difficult to characterize the contribution that students of Japan have made to the comparative enterprise of anthropology except perhaps in their role as "spoilers." For example, a colleague said to me in some exasperation when one of his rather neat cross-cultural generalizations had foundered once again on the Japanese data, "But Japan never *fits!*" What we are dealing with in the case of Japan is a society where official history until recently claimed that the imperial institution antedated the founding of the state, and where the present emperor is said to be the 124th in an unbroken dynastic succession; where ethnic homogeneity is so great that all Japanese actually have Japanese names (setting it apart from all other nation-states, surely), yet where one to three percent of the population of what is otherwise essentially a system of social classes is accorded the status of an untouchable caste; where the prime corporate entity is the household; where what at first seems to be a patrilineal system turns out to be something else; and finally—because genealogical connection is far from the primary determinant of ancestral status—where practices resembling ancestor worship do exist but the ancestral cult does not.

In part, no doubt, the peculiarly indeterminate concepts and terms pose the major obstacle to clear exposition. Precision of definition and explicitness of formulation are not highly valued in Japan; the Japanese have perhaps more than most peoples explored to the fullest the uses and delights of ambiguity. One consequence of their way of handling the world is a tendency to leave unresolved apparent contradictions that would in other world views seem to cry out for resolution. The reader may recall that throughout the foregoing chapters the words "multilayered" and "coexistent" have been used in discussing Japanese religious beliefs and practices. They are entirely apt, for there is less blending than one might expect, and more willingness simply to add new and appealing propositions and concepts to the inventory of those already current.

Anyone who has tried to understand Japanese society and culture must at some point have had the feeling either that there is something rather special about them, or that we have not been fully informed about the complexities of other societies, which somehow always seem more orderly in the way they appear in our colleagues' analyses. In one of the best books ever written by anyone on any aspect of Japanese life, Ronald Dore's *City Life in Japan*, there is a hint of why this feeling is so common. Dore gives us a picture of a Tokyo ward and its people shortly after the end of World War II. Until I reread it recently, I had not focused on how thoroughly historical it is in orientation. In particular, I was struck by the device Dore uses to illuminate social and attitudinal changes: he contrasts contemporary urban society not with its rural counterpart but rather with Tokugawa society. In passing he makes an observation of profound significance for our understanding of ancestor worship (Dore 1958: 88). "The changes in attitudes and behavior which are taking place are often discrete and unrelated to each other—unrelated both in the sense that they have different immediate causes, and in the sense that they are not related in the minds of the people who experience them."

I submit that this has been so for a long time. For example, the conception of the destination of the soul will serve as a good illustration of the way this kind of "discrete and unrelated" change has evolved in the context of ancestor worship. Leaving aside those who said that there was no soul and therefore no afterworld (many of whom nonetheless had ancestral tablets to which they made offerings), I found a multiplicity of views of the matter. A few represented the teachings of specific religious groups; others existed side by side in the same small community; many were held simultaneously by the same person. And all of this occurs in the context of a population possessing a rare degree of cultural and linguistic homogeneity and shared historical experience. In the 1930's the villagers of Suye told John Embree that a man's spirit goes to the afterworld in which he had believed when he was alive. In the course of my interviews in 1963, I was often told that Buddhist rites should be held for Buddhists whether or not their descendants were of that religion or of any religion at all. This is a genial kind of tolerance—the despair of Christian missionaries, who find firm commitment a more satisfactory target. But surely, we say, the same person cannot hold contradictory views about the fate of the soul. Such a protest misses the point that ideas will be seen to be contradictory only if they are considered simultaneously, compared and contrasted, and ultimately chosen among. These are steps not taken by a great many Japanese, apparently, for people I know remain receptive to all sorts of new concepts and accord many of them some respect, however unlikely a combination may result. The exotic and the novel still exert a formidable appeal in contemporary Japan, just as they have for centuries. Not many Santa Clauses have offered flowers to the memorial tablets in a Buddhist domestic altar, but it is an engaging scene, the perfect exemplification of the "fluidity and suppleness peculiar to Japanese ways of life" (Singer 1973: 86).

That suppleness and fluidity are everywhere in evidence in the key decisions that must be made in ancestor veneration—the choices of the objects of worship and of the occasions of worship. Beyond these very basic and easily determined issues lies the fundamental one of attitude toward the objects of the rites. Let us review what we know about these matters. There are several rules governing the inclusion of memorial tablets in a particular altar. In general it may be said that a household will have at a minimum tablets (either temporary or permanent) for all persons who were living in the household at the time of their death. Such people are most often kinsmen, of course, but not exclusively in the direct descent line. Thus sons and daughters who have married or been adopted out into other houses, as well as those who have established neolocal residence, will not be represented by tablets in the altar of their natal house. The only exceptions to that rule are when a disaster overwhelms a neolocal house or it becomes zekke. In those events all the tablets of the created house will be taken in by another house.

Should a child of the house return to it as the result of a broken marriage or a broken adoption and not leave it again, his tablet will be placed in its altar. In general, it may be said that all of these tablets are where they properly belong. But there are some that have come to rest in altars for reasons of sentiment and affection alone. Most commonly they represent decisions made by the living to afford the souls of the deceased an extra measure of care or the certainty of care if it is suspected that proper care will not be forthcoming in the houses where the tablets ought to be. In a few cases such an anomalous tablet is in a given altar because the person it represents requested this final favor. The grounds for a request of this nature are usually those of personal affection or a desire to return to one's natal house after death.

Heirs alone do not venerate the ancestors; ancestors are not defined solely as those who have left property to their descendants. Anyone may venerate the tablets, and the altars are filled with tablets of people who have left no property to anyone. It is true that the successor acquires both property and ancestral tablets, but any other child may make copies of the tablets if he or she wishes. My findings show that duplicated tablets are not uncommon and that there is only marginal concern for which is the original and which the copy, despite the fact that the tablet is thought of as the locus of the soul and every effort is made to save it from fortuitous destruction. Tablets are rarely "ranked" in the altar by status, the only exception being that a tablet is placed in the center and to the front of the altar when it is the object of veneration. To be sure, there is some tendency to make larger tablets with more exalted posthumous names for senior ancestors, and to hold rites for them on a larger scale and for a longer period.

As far as occasions of worship are concerned, they seem to be an area of almost free variation of behavior. Contrary to the expected standard response to questions about when people made offerings or prayed at the altar, I found that the Japanese seem to do either or both of these things in anything but patterned ways. All members of the household have access to the ancestors and may approach them for a wide variety of purposes. Food may be served to them by anyone, without regard to age, sex, or status in the household, although women usually perform the task, which may be seen as an extension of their duty to serve the family's meals. Men appear to take the lead in more formal rites. Today, with very rare exceptions, all ancestral rites are domestic observances participated in chiefly by members of the household. Priests—Buddhist or Shinto—are not essential, although they usually officiate at the funeral and at such of the memorial services as the family wishes to schedule. There being no geomancy of graves, save for a general feeling that they ought to face not north but rather west (the direction in which paradise lies), the services of a specialist are not required in the laying out of plots and stones.

What are the needs and capabilities of the ancestors, be they deemed buddhas or gods? At the most immediate level, relations between them and their descendants involve the sharing of daily fare and special gifts of food received by the family from visitors. The ancestors are thought to take pleasure in this, as well as in other activities of the house. In this way they are not excluded from the world of the living, over whom they exercise benign tutelary power. On more formal occasions family members offer them ceremonial foods and say prayers on their behalf.

Here we have come to the crux of the matter. It cannot be said either that the Japanese pray *to* the ancestors or, alternatively, that they pray *for* them. In fact they do both or either, depending on the category of the deceased and on the ritual context. What is more, they do all of this at the single domestic altar. All spirits of the dead may be prayed for collectively and welcomed back into their homes, as is done at the midsummer Festival of the Dead. At other times the collectivity of ancestors may be prayed to, especially during personal and family crises. Spirits of the recently dead are often prayed to individually; long-dead ancestors who are no longer remembered as persons are not addressed as individuals but rather are collectively asked for guidance and assistance. Some souls are never directly petitioned, but are instead ever the objects of solicitude. Among these are the spirits of deceased children, spouses, and siblings, none ancestral to those caring for their tablets. Some categories of the dead are for a time treated as though they were still alive; in the belief that they continue to enjoy the things of this world, they are offered favorite foods and addressed by name or familiar kin term. Nevertheless, despite all these distinctions, the word ancestor (senzo) is in general use as a generic term for the dead of the house—whether an ascendant, a member of the speaker's own generation, or a descendant. Above all, it should be clearly understood that there is no distinction between ancestor and forebear in the Japanese view.

Ancestral spirits are thought to be generally protective and benign, and are rarely reported to be punitive. The only exception is that whereas they ordinarily do not cause misfortune, they may fail to act to prevent it. Once they seem to have been strong agents of social control within the household, but today they are more likely to serve as sources of emotional support for its members. The weakening of their disciplinary power can only be attributed to the weakening of the authority of the senior members of the social groups that once defined the range of their capacities. Heads of households; main houses of the dōzoku, hamlet, village, and guilds; and even the emperor himself as head of the nation no longer wield the kind of power they did until fairly recent times. Yet it would be a mistake to conclude that the power of the ancestors was ever merely a heightened version of the formidable authority of the household head. Ancestor veneration has also a dimension of mutual dependency perhaps even more effective than authority alone in guaranteeing continuity of the rites. There was a time when the boundary between descendant and ancestor was blurred, for the young were in a sense conceived to be in the process of becoming ancestors (Lebra 1974; Maeyama 1972: 177–78; Yanagita 1970: 27–28). Further, the complete dependence of the junior members of the household on their seniors inevitably culminated in a reversal of the relationship, for when the elders died they became at once entirely dependent on their descendants, whose right and duty it was to venerate their spirits.

In a remarkable book on the importance of dependency relationships in Japanese life, Doi (1973: 62–63) has taken up a question that is basic to our discussion. Is there, he asks, a connection between the pattern of dependency—the desire to be the passive object of love, summed up by the word *amae*—and the Japanese conception that by dying one becomes a buddha or a god? He thinks there is, and offers a personal experience and a generalization (*ibid.*):

> Following the death in rapid succession of both my parents and the consequent severing of my bonds with them, I became aware of them for the first time as independent *persons*, where hitherto their existence was real to me only insofar as they were my own parents. This made me wonder whether to become a god or a buddha for the Japanese might not mean that [the] human personality of the individual concerned, which during his lifetime had frequently been lost sight of, buried beneath formal relationships or plas-

tered over with the cares of everyday life, was accorded new attention and respect. This in no respect contradicts the traditional belief that considered the emperor the embodiment of satisfied *amae*, as a god incarnate. Indeed, one might well see ancestor worship as existing in a mutually complementary relationship with emperor worship, since both use the term "god" in referring to those who lie beyond the anguish of unsatisfied *amae*—which is where, this suggests, the essence of the Japanese concept of divinity lies.

Finally, we come to the matter of the household and its precipitate decline in recent decades. Since about the sixteenth century, the corporate household has been the principal context within which ancestral rites have been observed and the unit to which successive central governments have directed their attention as the ideal locus for implanting attitudes of obedience and loyalty—the ultimate virtues of the subject —through the promotion of ancestor worship. But the household has to all intents and purposes been so completely eroded in the past generation that even its shadow cannot long endure. In the past if one encountered a conjugal family composed of a couple and their children it was best understood as a temporary condition rather than a family type, for the vast majority of conjugal families were in fact only stages in the domestic cycle, on their way to becoming three-generation extended (but never joint) households. This is no longer true. The family is in the ascendancy as the dominant type of domestic kin unit, and what remains now is to see to what extent this new entity in Japanese society is likely to continue practices resembling ancestor worship. In my interviews in Tokyo I found one family that may well represent the wave of the future, a wave that will carry the veneration of the ancestors very far indeed from the world of priests, temples, altars, and tablets. As I mentioned in an earlier chapter, I encountered a young couple in their early thirties living with their two small children in an apartment complex. On a shelf containing some souvenirs of their travels in Japan and a few books there were three photographs that proved to be of her parents and his mother, all deceased. Neither husband nor wife had any interest in the Buddhist or Shinto forms of ancestor worship, and theirs was a neolocal house. In explanation of the photographs, they provided a patently viable and almost revolutionary alternative to traditional concepts. "We have their photographs here so that we will keep their memory. They are, after all, our ancestors." They were indeed, in the familiar Western sense, the ancestors of the couple, but in the older Japanese sense they were not. At least one of the New Religions, Reiyūkai-kyōdan, has caught the mood of the times and urges women to worship their own parents' tablets as well as those of their husbands. This is a very contemporary attitude that may well become increasingly evident in the teachings of other religious groups.

But if this young urban couple is the wave of the future, how are we to explain the "butsudan boom" reported in the Japanese press in the late 1960's? Sales of altars had risen, it was suggested, because consumption-oriented newly affluent families—having secured all the obligatory electrical appliances, an automobile or two, and other durable goods—had got down the list to domestic altars. This is surely too facile an explanation, and the real reason is more likely to lie in the nature of the family cycle (Morioka 1970: 157). There were simply more families. Neolocal residence had become increasingly the rule following the end of World War II, and the death of any member called for the purchase of an altar in which to place the memorial tablet. The heads of these families, raised in a society in which ancestor worship had been the rule, were carrying forward a traditional pattern of behavior. Men and women now in their thirties may well buy altars when their parents die or have tablets made to put in existing altars, but it is far less certain whether those now in their twenties or younger will do so in turn. If they make no tablets or buy no altar, it will not be through what many Japanese feel is the simple perversity of today's young. Far more important is what has happened to the household; since it was deprived of its legal standing a generation ago, it has become increasingly devoid of economic importance and has almost entirely ceased to be the focus of family relations.

The changes in family composition in the postwar period—marked by a rapid shift to neolocal residence resulting in the creation of ever larger numbers of conjugal families—have set the stage for fundamental changes in the character of memorialism. It seems clear from all available evidence that transmission of the attitudes supporting ancestor worship formerly occurred almost exclusively in the household and in the schools. Neither now functions in this fashion. In the household, training proceeded by encouraging children to participate in the rites along with adults, especially grandparents. The first son, as putative successor, was apparently more deeply involved than his siblings in the rites for the obvious reason that the right and duty to conduct them would eventually devolve on him. In the course of his childhood he would observe and be taught by his grandparents at the altar; in his youth and young adulthood his parents would serve as models; when he reached his late forties or early fifties, and his wife had perhaps been married into his house for twenty years, he would with her take over the rites upon the death of his parents (see Ooms 1967: 264). The successor, then, had a lifetime of direct and indirect involvement and experience in ancestor veneration. However, nonsuccessors have always had a different career, for they have generally been less involved in the rites during childhood.

Let us take as an example a young man who finds employment in the city, marries, and has children. His will be a created conjugal family with no ancestors of its own and no altar. Indeed, it will probably not have an altar for a very long time. This is particularly true today, for before the sharp decline in infant mortality following World War II such a family might experience the death of an infant or small child and thereby secure a tablet toward which some rites would be directed (Morioka 1970: 152). Today children in families of this kind are likely to live to adulthood, which means that there is no occasion for them to become socialized to the practices of veneration of the dead. Only if the family returns to the country to the father's natal house for bon or important periodic anniversary rites will the child have any direct experience of the matter at all. To put it in the simplest possible terms, there are a great many young adults in Japan today who have reached maturity in families where there have never been any ancestors.

To make the change even more far-reaching, in the postwar period the successor has joined his younger siblings in the move to the city, leaving his parents in the country to carry on as best they can with some financial support from him. Almost invariably the tablets are left in their care. When they die the successor will probably have tablets made for them and bring the altar to the city. His own children may then have their first direct experience of the ancestral rites, and as a consequence may have tablets made for him and his wife when the time comes. Nevertheless, there remains one signal difference between the older household and the newer family—inheritance of property built up and transmitted by the ancestors was a feature of the former, but figures hardly at all in the latter. As we have seen, although memorial tablets have long been made for people from whom one inherited no property, it was the case nonetheless that the head was expected to nurture and expand the household's holdings. Having received these holdings from the ancestors, he was responsible for passing them on to his descendants. The farmer and the white-collar worker are, in that sense at least, poles apart. One obvious possible outcome is that veneration of the known "departed" (Plath 1964) will supercede veneration of the "ancestors" (see Ooms 1967: 263–65).

There has been another major shift in behavior since the end of World War II. Today people exercise more selectivity in their relations with kinsmen than they ever did before, simply avoiding those with whom they do not get along, and without any great fear of social censure (Morioka 1970: 159). The corollary in the ancestral rites is that there is less and less emphasis on the observances for the remote dead, which were essentially concerns of the household, and an increasing tendency to demonstrate affection for recently deceased kinsmen only, in the form of simplified memorialism. Certainly the fear of social censure is much reduced for the urban family, for neither neighbors nor temple will know whether or not deathday observances are being held punctiliously. I was told by a man in Tokyo that as the eldest son who had moved to the city, he did have his family's altar and that he kept it in the closet of his small apartment. "I get it out and put it on the television set when I'm expecting relatives from the country. They'd be very upset if they knew that I keep the ancestors in a closet!" Another man told me, "We put the altar away when the war ended and have done nothing about the ancestors since. Who among our friends would care?"

Among the institutions feeling the impact of the decline of household-centered ancestral rites most directly are the Buddhist temples. Indeed, as the agricultural villages have emptied out the rural temples have been especially hard hit, but urban ones have been facing severe financial strains as well. In Yokohama there is a public cemetery that was founded in 1874 (see Fujii 1970). Around it were built fourteen temples representing seven major Buddhist sects. The records of one of these temples of the Jōdo sect reveal that between January 1949 and July 31,

1969, 1,064 households registered deaths there. Of these, almost exactly half have had no subsequent contact with the temple or have never called on its priests to perform memorial rites. Lest we jump to the conclusion that this is a phenomenon of the past 25 years only, consider Fujii's report on another Jōdo temple in Osaka. Great numbers of migrants from rural areas flooded into that city at the end of the Tokugawa period, and many joined this Jōdo temple. By 1887 there were so many abandoned remains of those whose relatives had never come back to the temple after the funeral to collect the ashes that an image of the Buddha was fashioned from them, and in every decade since that time another has been made. So the urban populations have apparently for some time enjoyed a somewhat tenuous connection with institutionalized Buddhism.

In 1973 a large newspaper advertisement suggested that at least one major sect was not giving up without a fight, though.

The "Cemetery" in a Dignified Contemporary Building
Completion expected at the end of March. Higashi Honganji, The Higashi-yama Garden of Purity. Shinshū, Ōtani Sect, Main Mausoleum Maintenance Foundation. The image of the cemetery has changed. Complete air regulating system and radiant lighting—an unprecedented new type of sanitary cemetery.

Located at the foot of Higashiyama, Kyoto, a grand and sacred area suitable for the eternal repose of the ashes.

Buddhist altar and urn repository provided separately. Assignment of the altar and repository will be made in the order in which applications are received. Those wishing to secure specific locations should make application early.

Thorough Maintenance. In the event of your departure from the area owing to job transfer or change of residence we, the Main Mausoleum Foundation, will in your stead exercise responsible perpetual care. During the period for reserving space we can make a contract for 380,000 yen [about $1,400 in 1973]—300,000 for the altar and 80,000 for perpetual care. Convenient bank loans available.

Contracting Company, Itōman K.K.
Real Estate and Construction, Main Office

The illustration shows a large, brightly lighted room with rows of double-tiered cabinets. Each upper tier contains an altar very like any domestic butsudan; each lower tier, with a separate door, appears to have six sections to hold urns of ashes. With a minimum of transposition of the funereal language, we could easily make the advertisement read very much like any other prospectus that the Itōman real estate people might put out for condominium apartments or suburban housing developments.

One should perhaps applaud the Ōtani sect's decision to remain in the mortuary business, for many temples faced with declining revenues have resorted to even more worldly enterprises, converting part of their compounds into parking lots or building high-rise apartments on them, capitalizing on real or imagined historical importance by contracting with tour-bus companies and then building snack bars on the temple grounds to feed the tourists, and pioneering in funeral services and mausoleums for house pets. Buddhism has paid a high price for its conversion to so exclusive a concern with ancestor worship, for it was a commitment inextricably bound up with the household; once that institution is swept away, Buddhism's hold on the population will be irrevocably lost.

What of the future? Those who have predicted the future course of events in Japan over the past century have generally been wrong. However, they are not an unworthy group, and I have little hesitation in joining such good company. What I believe will happen is that observances on behalf of the spirits of the dead (in an increasingly bilateral mode, and for one or two generations of parents and grandparents) will become the dominant form of Japanese ancestor worship before the century is out. The temples and municipal mortuary facilities will continue as they have done for decades to adapt their services to a very large and highly mobile population. Altar and tablets alike have already been scaled down in size and cost to be almost perfectly suited to a mobile world of nuclear families and small dwellings, and they have been made completely portable. The altar has in any event long been an ancestral altar rather than a specifically Buddhist one, and to a remarkable extent, even in conjugal families today, where there is cause to have one—which is to say, where some member of the family has died—one will ordinarily be found.

There are in my opinion two keys to the future. One is held by those young married couples still in their twenties who have not yet faced the question of what treatment to accord their immediate kin when they die. The other key is in the hands of those responsible for formulating national policies; but the time remaining for its use is short. In another generation it will be too late even to think of using many of the old customs as a basis for a nativist culturalism designed to stabilize the domestic scene. Nevertheless, given the past history of exploitation by the state of the idiom of ancestor worship, it is not inconceivable that the ancestors could once again be pressed into service.

Appendix Tables

TABLE A1

Household Type by Place of Residence

(N = 595)

Place of residence	Household type				Total (595)
	Head unmarried (10)	Conjugal (425)	Two-generation stem (155)	Three-generation stem (5)	
Urban					
Tokyo	6	147	30	–	183
Osaka	–	68	36	–	104
Kyoto	1	48	16	1	66
Hanshin	–	15	1	–	16
Nara	–	20	10	–	30
Miscellaneous	–	19	11	–	30
Rural					
Sone	2	85	25	1	113
Yasuhara	1	11	8	–	20
Takane	–	12	18	3	33

TABLE A2

Age and Sex of Household Heads

(N = 595)

Age	Sex						
	Male		Female		No answer	Total	
	No.	Pct.	No.	Pct.		No.	Pct.
20–29	18	3.4%	–	–	–	18	3.0%
30–39	73	13.7	5	8.6%	–	78	13.1
40–49	149	27.9	23	39.7	2	174	29.3
50–59	180	33.6	14	24.1	–	194	32.6
60–69	82	15.3	7	12.1	–	89	15.0
70–79	24	4.5	6	10.3	–	30	5.0
80–89	5	0.9	1	1.7	–	6	1.0
No answer	4	0.7	2	3.5	–	6	1.0
TOTAL	535	100.0%	58	100.0%	2	595	100.0%

TABLE A3

Possession of Memorial Tablets, by Household Type

(N = 595)

Household type	Do you have memorial tablets?		Total (595)
	Yes (483)	No (112)	
Head unmarried	8	2	10
Conjugal	324	101	425
Two-generation stem	146	9	155
Three-generation stem	5	—	5

TABLE A4
Number of Memorial Tablets per Household, by Place of Residence
(N = 595)

Number of tablets	Urban households						Rural households			Total	
	Tokyo (183)	Osaka (104)	Kyoto (66)	Han-shin (16)	Nara (30)	Misc. (30)	Sone (113)	Yasu-hara (20)	Ta-kane (33)	No.	Pct.
None	59	19	12	3	9	3	3	–	4	112	18.8%
1	34	15	15	2	5	2	10	1	2	86	14.5
2	28	15	15	2	1	2	9	1	2	75	12.6
3	20	18	4	2	5	7	5	1	1	63	10.6
4	13	14	3	2	1	2	8	1	1	45	7.6
5	8	10	5	1	1	3	8	–	4	40	6.7
6	5	1	2	–	2	–	3	–	2	15	2.5
7	2	2	2	1	–	2	9	2	4	24	4.0
8	3	2	2	1	1	–	11	1	1	22	3.7
9	2	2	2	–	1	–	4	2	3	16	2.7
10	2	–	–	–	1	1	6	–	–	10	1.7
11–19	5	5	4	1	3	6	30	1	7	62	10.4
20–29	2	1	–	–	–	2	6	5	2	18	3.0
30–39	–	–	–	1	–	–	1	3	–	5	0.8
40–57	–	–	–	–	–	–	–	2	–	2	0.3

TABLE A5
Religion of Household
(N = 595)

Religious affiliation	Households	
	Number	Percent
Buddhist		
Jōdo-shin sect	170	28.6%
Zen sect	155	26.1
Jōdo sect	98[a]	16.5
Shingon sect	49	8.2
Bukkyō (Buddhism)	39[b]	6.6
Nichiren sect	31	5.2
Nichiren-shō sect	18	3.2
Tendai sect	3	0.5
TOTAL	563	94.6%
Other		
Shinto	3	0.5%
Tenri-kyō	3	0.5
Seichō-no-Ie	1	0.2
Christian	1	0.2
TOTAL	8	1.3%
None	23	3.9%
No answer	1	0.2%
GRAND TOTAL	595	100.0%

[a] Includes two responses "Jōdo sect and Seichō-no-Ie."
[b] Includes one response "Bukkyō (Buddhism) and Shintō."

TABLE A6

Type of Tablets Held by Relationship to Household Head,
and Number of Tablets by Place of Residence

(N = 3,050)

Type of tablet	Tokyo			Osaka			Kyoto		
	No. of tab-lets	Pct. of grand total	H'hlds w/1 or more tabs.	No. of tab-lets	Pct. of grand total	H'hlds w/1 or more tabs.	No. of tab-lets	Pct. of grand total	H'hlds w/1 or more tabs.
LINEAL									
1. Unidentified	43	9.2%	5	26	7.4%	6	18	8.3%	2
2. Progenitors	208		92	205		78	102		44
3. Spouses of progenitors	4		3	6		5	2		2
4. Spouse of head	17		17	12		11	13		11
5. Spouse of spouse	—		—	—		—	—		—
6. Descendants	52		39	18		13	20		12
7. Siblings, their spouses and children	56		32	47		28	31		13
8. Fa's siblings, their spouses and children	27		11	4		3	7		4
9. Fa's fa's siblings, their spouses and children	2		2	2		2	1		1
10. Fa's fa's fa's siblings, their spouses and children	—		—	—		—	—		—
11. Other	6		3	3		3	—		—
TOTAL 2–11	372	79.5		297	84.9		176	81.1	
NONLINEAL									
12. Unidentified	—	—	—	—	—	—	—	—	—
Yōshi's kin									
13. Progenitors	11		6	8		3	3		2
14. Fa's and mo's siblings, their spouses and children	—		—	—		—	4		1
15. Siblings	2		1	—		—	—		—
Mother's kin									
16. Progenitors	4		3	6		4	3		3
17. Miscellaneous	2		1	2		1	—		—
18. Siblings, their spouses and children	5		1	1		1	—		—
Wife's kin									
19. Progenitors	21		14	7		4	8		3
20. Fa's and mo's siblings, their spouses and children	—		—	—		—	4		1
21. Siblings	7		5	2		1	1		1
TOTAL 13–21	52	11.1		26	7.4		23	10.6	
NON-KIN	1	0.2	1	1	0.3	1	—	—	—
GRAND TOTAL	468	100.0%		350	100.0%		217	100.0%	

NOTE: For the aggregated data from this table see Table 15.

TABLE A6 (continued)
Type of Tablets Held by Relationship to Household Head,
and Number of Tablets by Place of Residence
$(N = 3,050)$

Type of tablet	Hanshin No. of tablets	Pct. of grand total	H'hlds w/1 or more tabs.	Nara No. of tablets	Pct. of grand total	H'hlds w/1 or more tabs.	Misc. No. of tablets	Pct. of grand total	H'hlds w/1 or more tabs.
LINEAL									
1. Unidentified	12	13.5%	1	16	14.8%	5	16	7.6%	3
2. Progenitors	46		12	66		19	122		26
3. Spouses of progenitors	2		2	2		2	7		5
4. Spouse of head	1		1	4		4	4		4
5. Spouse of spouse	—		—	—		—	—		—
6. Descendants	3		3	8		5	4		3
7. Siblings, their spouses and children	14		4	3		3	21		10
8. Fa's siblings, their spouses and children	—		—	4		2	5		4
9. Fa's fa's siblings, their spouses and children	—		—	2		2	1		1
10. Fa's fa's fa's siblings, their spouses and children	—		—	—		—	4		1
11. Other	—		—	—		—	—		—
TOTAL 2–11	66	74.2		89	82.4		168	79.6	
NONLINEAL									
12. Unidentified	—	—	—	—	—	—	—	—	—
Yōshi's kin									
13. Progenitors	2		1	—		—	8		3
14. Fa's and mo's siblings, their spouses and children	—		—	—		—	—		—
15. Siblings	—		—	—		—	1		1
Mother's kin									
16. Progenitors	—		—	2		1	7		4
17. Miscellaneous	—		—	—		—	—		—
18. Siblings, their spouses and children	—		—	—		—	1		1
Wife's kin									
19. Progenitors	7		5	—		—	6		3
20. Fa's and mo's siblings, their spouses and children	—		—	—		—	1		1
21. Siblings	—		—	—		—	3		1
TOTAL 13–21	9	10.1		2	1.9		27	12.8	
NON-KIN	2	2.2	1	1	0.9	1	—	—	—
GRAND TOTAL	89	100.0%		108	100.0%		211	100.0%	

NOTE: For the aggregated data from this table see Table 15.

TABLE A6 (continued)

Type of Tablets Held by Relationship to Household Head,
and Number of Tablets by Place of Residence

(N = 3,050)

Type of tablet	Sone No. of tablets	Sone Pct. of grand total	Sone H'hlds w/1 or more tabs.	Yasuhara No. of tablets	Yasuhara Pct. of grand total	Yasuhara H'hlds w/1 or more tabs.	Takane No. of tablets	Takane Pct. of grand total	Takane H'hlds w/1 or more tabs.
LINEAL									
1. Unidentified	249	26.0%	42	188	47.4%	12	27	10.7%	7
2. Progenitors	334		89	73		20	128		26
3. Spouses of progenitors	10		10	3		3	14		9
4. Spouse of head	32		31	4		4	4		4
5. Spouse of spouse	6		6	1		1	—		—
6. Descendants	93		53	29		13	29		13
7. Siblings, their spouses and children	117		56	43		13	26		15
8. Fa's siblings, their spouses and children	53		29	25		9	22		11
9. Fa's fa's siblings, their spouses and children	8		5	11		4	2		2
10. Fa's fa's fa's siblings, their spouses and children	5		3	1		1	—		—
11. Other	—		—	—		—	—		—
TOTAL 2–11	658	68.7		190	47.8		225	89.3	
NONLINEAL									
12. Unidentified	9	0.9	4	—	—	—	—	—	—
Yōshi's kin									
13. Progenitors	8		6	—		—	—		—
14. Fa's and mo's siblings, their spouses and children	3		2	—		—	—		—
15. Siblings	1		1	—		—	—		—
Mother's kin									
16. Progenitors	9		5	1		1	—		—
17. Miscellaneous	2		2	—		—	—		—
18. Siblings, their spouses and children	7		3	1		1	—		—
Wife's kin									
19. Progenitors	3		2	1		1	—		—
20. Fa's and mo's siblings, their spouses and children	3		1	—		—	—		—
21. Siblings	2		1	—		—	—		—
TOTAL 13–21	38	4.0		3	0.8		—	—	
NON-KIN	4	0.4	4	16	4.0	1	—	—	—
GRAND TOTAL	958	100.0%		397	100.0%		252	100.0%	

NOTE: For the aggregated data from this table see Table 15.

TABLE A7

*Number of Households with at Least One Tablet of Each Type,
by Relationship to Household Head*

(*N* = 483)

Type of tablet	Households with 1 or more tablets No.	Pct. of *N*	Type of tablet	Households with 1 or more tablets No.	Pct. of *N*
LINEAL			**NONLINEAL**		
1. Unidentified	83	17.2%	12. Unidentified	4	0.8
2. Progenitors	406	84.1	Yōshi's kin		
3. Spouses of progenitors	41	8.5	13. Progenitors	21	4.3
4. Spouse of head	87	18.0	14. Fa's and mo's siblings,		
5. Spouse of spouse	7	1.5	their spouses and		
6. Descendants	154	31.9	children	3	0.6
7. Siblings, their spouses and children	174	36.0	15. Siblings	3	0.6
8. Fa's siblings, their spouses and children	73	15.1	Mother's kin 16. Progenitors	21	4.3
			17. Miscellaneous	4	0.8
9. Fa's fa's siblings, their spouses and children	19	3.9	18. Siblings, their spouses and children	7	1.5
10. Fa's fa's fa's siblings, their spouses and children	5	1.0	Wife's kin 19. Progenitors	32	6.6
			20. Fa's and mo's siblings, their spouses and children	3	0.6
11. Other	6	1.2	21. Siblings	9	1.9
			NON-KIN	9	1.9

TABLE A8

*Death Dates of Identified and Unidentified Persons
Represented by Memorial Tablets*

(*N* = 3,050)

Death dates	Identified No.	Pct.	Unidentified No.	Pct.	Total No.	Pct.
Unknown	168	6.9%	102	16.9%	270	8.9%
1600–1863 (over 100 years before study)	138	5.6	344	56.9	482	15.8
1864–1913 (51 to 100 years before study)	594	24.3	133	22.0	727	23.8
1914–30 (34 to 50 years before study)	464	19.0	18	3.0	482	15.8
1931–63 (within 33 years before study)	1,082	44.2	7	1.2	1,089	35.7
TOTAL	2,446	100.0%	604	100.0%	3,050	100.0%

TABLE A9
Death Dates of Persons Represented by Tablets:
Cumulative Totals
(*N* = 2,780)

| | Identified persons | | | | All persons | | | |
| | | | Cumulative | | | | Cumulative | |
Death dates	No.	Pct.	No.	Pct.	No.	Pct.	No.	Pct.
1931–63 (within 33 years before study)	1,082	47.5%	1,082	47.5%	1,089	39.2%	1,089	39.2%
1914–30 (50 to 34 years before study)	464	20.4	1,546	67.9	482	17.3	1,571	56.5
1864–1913 (100 to 51 years before study)	594	26.0	2,140	93.9	727	26.2	2,298	82.7
1600–1863 (over 100 years before study)	138	6.1	2,278	100.0	482	17.3	2,780	100.0

TABLE A10
Death Dates of Persons Represented by Tablets:
Relationship to Household Head
(*N* = 3,050)

| | Relationship to household head | | | | | | | |
| | Unidentified | | | Identified | | | Total | |
Death dates	Lineal	Non-lineal	Non-kin	Lineal	Non-lineal	Non-kin	No.	Pct.
Unknown	100	2	–	151	15	2	270	8.9%
1600–1863	339	5	–	128	7	3	482	15.8
1864–1913	131	2	–	529	58	7	727	23.8
1914–30	18	–	–	439	22	3	482	15.8
1931–63	7	–	–	994	78	10	1,089	35.7
TOTAL	595	9	–	2,241	180	25	3,050	100.0%

TABLE A11
Age at Death: Siblings of Household Head
(*N* = 331)

Age	Brothers					Sisters				
			Inde-termi-	Total				Inde-termi-	Total	
	Elder	Younger	nate	No.	Pct.	Elder	Younger	nate	No.	Pct.
Unknown	36	14	–	50	25.3%	11	10	6	27	20.5%
Under 10	25	31	8	64	32.3	15	51	2	68	51.5
10–19	14	6	1	21	10.6	9	4	–	13	9.8
20–29	18	28	–	46	23.2	4	10	–	14	10.6
30–39	5	2	–	7	3.5	3	–	2	5	3.8
40–49	3	2	–	5	2.5	1	–	–	1	0.8
50–59	3	2	–	5	2.5	3	1	–	4	3.0
TOTAL	104	85	9	198	99.9%	46	76	10	132	100.0%

TABLE A12
Age at Death: Children of Household Head
(*N* = 242)

Age	Son	Daughter	Child	Total	
				No.	Pct.
Unknown	14	16	4	34	14.1%
Under 10	82	61	16	159	65.7
10–19	6	8	1	15	6.2
20–29	20	5	1	26	10.7
30–39	4	2	–	6	2.5
40–49	1	–	–	1	0.4
50–59	–	1	–	1	0.4
TOTAL	127	93	22	242	100.0%

TABLE A13
Lineals, Nonlineals, and Non-kin: Their Relationship to
Household Head (Unaggregated Data)
(*N* = 3,050)

Relationship to household head	Number of tablets	Relationship to household head	Number of tablets
LINEAL		4 father	33
1. Unidentified (595)		4 mother	32
2. Progenitors (1,284)		5 father	10
Father	351	5 mother	10
Mother	264	6 father	5
Fa's father	204	6 mother	5
Fa's mother	184	7 father	5
Fa's fa's father	79	7 mother	5
Fa's fa's mother	73	8 father	4

TABLE A13 (continued)
*Lineals, Nonlineals, and Non-kin: Their Relationship to
Household Head (Unaggregated Data)*
(*N* = 3,050)

Relationship to household head	Number of tablets	Relationship to household head	Number of tablets
8 mother	4	Elder sister	46
9 father	2	Elder si's husband	1
9 mother	2	Elder si's son	2
10 father	2	Elder si's child	1
10 mother	2	Younger sister	76
11 father	1	Younger si's husband	1
11 mother	1	Sister	10
12 father	2	Nephew	1
12 mother (missing)		8. Fa's siblings, their spouses and children (147)	
13 father	1	Fa's elder brother	18
13 mother	1	Fa's elder br's wife	3
14 father	1	Fa's elder br's son	3
14 mother	1	Fa's younger brother	30
3. Spouses of progenitors (50)		Fa's younger br's wife	4
Father's wife	21	Fa's younger br's son	1
Mother's husband	1	Fa's younger br's daughter	1
Fa's fa's wife	14	Fa's younger br's child	4
Fa's mo's husband	2	Fa's brother	23
Fa's fa's fa's wife	11	Fa's elder sister	10
4 fa's wife	1	Fa's elder si's son	1
4. Spouse of Head (91)		Fa's younger sister	24
Wife	44	Fa's younger si's son	1
Husband	47	Fa's younger si's child	1
5. Spouse of spouse (7)		Fa's sister	23
Husband's wife	5	9. Fa's fa's siblings, their spouses and children (29)	
Wife's husband	2	Fa's fa's elder brother	5
6. Descendants (256)		Fa's fa's younger brother	1
Son	127	Fa's fa's brother	7
Daughter	93	Fa's fa's br's son	1
Child	22	Fa's fa's br's daughter	1
Son's son	4	Fa's fa's elder sister	7
Son's daughter	5	Fa's fa's younger sister	3
Son's child	3	Fa's fa's sister	4
Child's child	1	10. Fa's fa's fa's siblings, their spouses and children (10)	
Daughter's son	1	Fa's fa's fa's brother	7
7. Siblings, their spouses and children (358)		Fa's fa's fa's br's wife	1
		Fa's fa's fa's sister	2
Elder brother	105	11. Other (9)	
Elder br's wife	7	Cousin	1
Elder br's son	5	Aunt	3
Elder br's daughter	5	Uncle	3
Elder br's child	1	Aunt's father	1
Younger brother	85		
Younger br's son	3		
Brother	9		

TABLE A13 (continued)
Lineals, Nonlineals, and Non-kin: Their Relationship to
Household Head (Unaggregated Data)
($N = 3,050$)

Relationship to household head	Number of tablets	Relationship to household head	Number of tablets
Aunt's mother	1	Mo's younger brother	3
TOTAL 2-11	2,241	Mo's elder sister	3
		Mo's elder si's husband	1
NONLINEAL		Mo's younger sister	5
12. Unidentified (9)		Mo's younger si's husband	1
Yōshi's kin (51)		Wife's kin (76)	
13. Progenitors (40)		19. Progenitors (53)	
Father	9	Wife's father	24
Mother	8	Wife's mother	21
Fa's father	3	Wife's fa's father	2
Fa's mother	6	Wife's fa's mother	2
Fa's fa's father	2	Wife's mo's father	2
Fa's fa's mother	1	Wife's mo's mother	2
Fa's mo's father	5	20. Fa's and mo's siblings, their	
Fa's mo's mother	4	spouses and children (8)	
Fa's mo's fa's father	1	Wife's fa's younger brother	1
Fa's mo's fa's mother	1	Wife's fa's younger br's wife	1
14. Fa's and mo's siblings, their		Wife's fa's younger sister	1
spouses and children (7)		Wife's fa's sister	1
Fa's elder sister	1	Wife's fa's fa's younger br	1
Fa's elder si's child	2	Wife's mo's elder sister	1
Fa's younger sister	1	Wife's mo's elder si's hus	1
Fa's brother	1	Wife's mo's elder si's son	1
Fa's mo's brother	1	21. Siblings (15)	
Fa's mo's br's wife	1	Wife's elder brother	3
15. Siblings (4)		Wife's younger brother	4
Elder brother	3	Wife's elder sister	3
Elder sister	1	Wife's younger sister	3
Mother's kin (53)		Wife's sister	2
16. Progenitors (32)		TOTAL 13–21	180
Mo's father	13		
Mo's mother	15	NON-KIN	
Mo's fa's father	1	Teacher	1
Mo's fa's mother	2	*Onjin*	3
Mo's fa's mo's father	1	Fa's fa's mo's nurse	1
17. Miscellaneous (6)		Ego	1
Mother's husband	2	Wife's mo's "husband"	1
Mother's daughter	1	Father's lover	1
Mother's uncle	1	Family into which	
Mother's niece	1	daughter married	16
Mother's child	1	*Tanin*—stranger	1
18. Siblings, their spouses		TOTAL NON-KIN	25
and children (15)			
Mo's elder brother	2	GRAND TOTAL	3,050

TABLE A14

Tablets for Lineals: Frequency of Occurrence by Relationship
to Household Head

Rank	Relationship to household head	No. of tablets	Pct. of identified Lineals (N=2,241)
1	Father	351	15.7%
2	Mother	264	11.8
3	Father's father	204	9.1
4	Father's mother	184	8.2
5	Son	127	5.7
6	Elder brother	105	4.7
7	Daughter	93	4.1
8	Younger brother	85	3.8
9	Father's father's father	79	3.5
10	Younger sister	76	3.4
11	Father's father's mother	73	3.3
12	Husband	47	2.1
13	Elder sister	46	2.1
14	Wife	44	2.0
15	Fa's fa's fa's father	33	1.5
16	Fa's fa's fa's mother	32	1.4
17	Father's younger brother	30	1.3
18	Father's younger sister	24	1.1
19	Father's brother	23	1.0
20	Father's sister	23	1.0
21	Child	22	1.0
22	Father's wife	21	0.9
	TOTAL	1,986	88.6%

NOTE: Unidentified Lineals and tablets occurring twenty times or less are excluded.

TABLE A15

Generational Depth of Tablets per Household, by Place of Residence
(N = 483)

Place of residence	Generational depth							Total
	None	1	2	3	4	5	6–14	
Urban								
Tokyo	25	64	25	6	2	–	2	124
Osaka	6	37	33	4	3	–	2	85
Kyoto	9	24	16	4	1	–	–	54
Hanshin	1	6	3	1	1	–	1	13
Nara	2	6	5	4	3	–	1	21
Miscellaneous	–	10	8	3	2	2	2	27
Rural								
Sone	15	18	22	24	14	7	10	110
Yasuhara	–	6	3	–	2	4	5	20
Takane	3	6	7	3	5	3	2	29
TOTAL	61	177	122	49	33	16	25	483
Percent	12.6%	36.6%	25.3%	10.2%	6.8%	3.3%	5.2%	100.0%

TABLE A16

*Difference Between Generational Depth of All Tablets and of
Identified Tablets per Household, by Place of Residence*

(*N* = 422)

Place of residence	Degree of difference, by generations							Total
	None	1	2	3	4	5	6–14	
Urban								
Tokyo	95	1	–	2	–	–	1	99
Osaka	77	–	1	–	–	1	–	79
Kyoto	45	–	–	–	–	–	–	45
Hanshin	12	–	–	–	–	–	–	12
Nara	17	1	–	–	–	1	–	19
Miscellaneous	25	1	1	–	–	–	–	27
Rural								
Sone	69	3	8	5	5	3	2	95
Yasuhara	11	–	2	3	2	–	2	20
Takane	25	–	–	1	–	–	–	26
TOTAL	376	6	12	11	7	5	5	422
Percent	89.1%	1.4%	2.8%	2.6%	1.7%	1.2%	1.2%	100.0%

NOTE: The total of 422 excludes 61 households with no ascendants' tablets.

Glossary

akitsu-kami Manifest god. A term first applied to the emperor in the seventh century.

amae The desire to be loved. A word used to express passive, unconditional dependency.

ato-tsugi Successor. The person through whom the succession in a household is assured.

bon Festival of the Dead. Usually observed today on August 13–15, it is the time when ancestral spirits return to their homes. See *urabon-e*.

bon-hajime Alternate term for Tanabata (the Star Festival), the seventh day of the seventh month, when *bon* observances are begun in some parts of Japan.

bosatsu The Japanese form of the Sanskrit word *bodhisattva*.

bunke Branch house. A "created" house often started by a sibling of the successor. It will have no ancestors of its own until the death of the founder, and members may return to the main house (*honke*, q.v.) at *bon* and other occasions of worship.

butsu The Japanese word for a buddha.

butsudan The Buddhist altar. This is the domestic altar in which the memorial tablets for the dead are kept.

chinju Tutelary deity (Shinto).

choku-gan-sho Place for offering imperial prayers.

chōnan First son. The preferred heir and successor.

chū Loyalty to a superior.

chū-in Mourning period. For men, the first 49 but sometimes the first 100 days after death. For women, usually 35 days.

chūkō-no-taigi "The great principle of loyalty and filial piety."

dai-myōjin A title, Shinto in its implications, bestowed posthumously on powerful persons.

dō Small chapel (Buddhist).

dōzoku A group of households linked by real or fictive genealogical ties. Also used to label a type of hierarchical community organization contrasted with the *kō-kumi* type (q.v.).

engumi A colloquial word for marriage.

eta-hinin The untouchables of Japan.

furu-senzo A term used in the Izu Islands to refer to ancestors whose tablets are on the altar. Its literal meaning is "old ancestors."

gaki Hungry ghost (Sanskrit *preta*).

gaki-dō Plane of the Hungry Ghosts (Sanskrit *preta-loka*).

giri Reciprocal obligations. See *ninjō*.

gokuraku-maru Paradise boat. Words written on the sails of miniature boats used to send off the spirits of the dead at their first *bon*. See *jōdo-maru*.

goryō-shin Vengeful gods (Shinto).

-gū Shrine (Shinto).

haike A household that has died out. See *zekke*.

hatsu-bon The first *bon* after death. See *nī-bon*.

higan Equinoxes. On the middle days of both equinoxes offerings are made to the ancestral spirits.

hitodama Spirit, soul (Shinto).

hōmyō The Jōdo-shin sect's term for *kaimyō* (q.v.).

honji-suijaku Archetype–transient manifestation. A Buddhist theory promoting the unification of the gods (the transient manifestations) and the buddhas (the archetypes).

honke Main house.

hōon Return of *on* (q.v.).

hotoke Buddha. In Japanese it means "the dead."

hotoke-ni-naru To become a buddha. "To die."

ichi-jitsu-shintō One-reality Shinto. The syncretic amalgam of Shinto and Buddhism promoted by the Tendai sect of Buddhism.

ie Household.

ihai Memorial tablet (Buddhist).

ikigami Living god. Apotheosized men and women accorded such status either before or after death.

ikimitama Living spirit, in contrast to the spirit of the dead.

ikiryō Malevolent spirit of the living.

iki-sotōba Living stupa. A tree branch planted on the grave during the last memorial rites for the individual. See *tomurai-age*.

imi-ake Lifting of pollution. The end of the mourning period. See *chū-in*.

innen Karma.

isan-sōzoku Inheritance of goods and property.

-ji Temple (Buddhist).

jichin Tutelary deity (Shinto).

ji-gami Tutelary deity (Shinto).

jikka Natal house, a term usually used by women.

jingū-ji Shrine temple. Place of worship of a syncretic character. See *honji-suijaku*.

jinja Shrine (Shinto).

jōdo-maru Paradise boat. An alternative for *gokuraku-maru* (q.v.).

kachō Household head.

kaimyō Posthumous name. It is inscribed on the memorial tablet (Buddhist). See *ihai*.

kakochō Book of the Past. A record of deathdays (Buddhist).

kami God (Shinto).

kamidana God shelf. A domestic shrine for the gods (Shinto).

kami-fuda Amulet of a god (Shinto).

kampei-sha Shrine where members of the imperial family worship (Shinto).

katoku-sōzoku Inheritance of the headship of a house.

kawa-segaki-e River *segaki* rite held for victims of drowning.

kimon Devil or demon gate. The geomantic northeast where the deity Konjin resides.

kō Filial piety.

kōden Incense money, offering of cash made at a funeral.

kōkeisha Successor. Obsolete term from the old Civil Code. See *ato-tsugi*.

kokka The family-state. The national household.

kokubunji Protector temple of the land.

kokugakusha National studies scholars. Men who in the eighteenth and nineteenth centuries initiated the revival of the native (Shinto) tradition.

kō-kumi A type of rural community characterized by social and economic equivalence of households, in contrast to the *dōzoku* type (q.v.).

kokutai The Japanese polity. An emotive term used to describe Japan's national essence.

kōrei-sai Ceremony for the imperial ancestors held at the equinoxes. It is now the holidays of *shūbun-no-hi* and *shumbun-no-hi* (q.v.).

koseki-chō Household register. The legal document in which the vital statistics of all household members are recorded.

ko-shōgatsu Little New Year. The middle of the first month.

kuri-ihai Memorial tablets. Slips of wood kept in a small box. They can be rearranged to suit the memorial occasion being observed (Buddhist). See *ihai*.

mai-tsuki-meinichi Monthly deathday rite (Buddhist).

mamoru To look after, to care for.

matsuri-jimai The end of ritual, alternate term for *tomurai-age* (q.v.) (Buddhist).

misaki Messenger of a god (Shinto).

mitama Spirit or soul (Shinto).

mitama-dana Spirit shelf (Shinto).

mitama-shiro Spirit substitute. The Shinto equivalent of the *ihai* (q.v.).

mitama-ya Spirit house. The Shinto equivalent of the *butsudan* (q.v.).

miya Shrine (Shinto).

miyaza Shrine group. A term used to describe a village where responsibility for the care of Shinto shrine affairs rotates among the households.

mizu-gami Water god.

muen-botoke Wandering spirit of the dead. A *hotoke* (q.v.) without ties to a household or altar. See also *gaki*.

muen-sama Same as *muen-botoke* (q.v.).

mukae-bi Welcoming fire lighted for the ancestral spirits at *bon* (q.v.).

mukanshin To have no interest in, not to believe in.

muko-yōshi Adopted husband.

mushūkyō Not religious.

nagare-botoke Floating buddha. A term applied to the spirit of a person drowned at sea.

nehan Nirvana. In Japanese, specifically the death of the Buddha.

nenki Periodic anniversaries of death (Buddhist).

nenki-age Same as *tomurai-age* (q.v.).

ni-bon The first *bon* after a person's death. At the end of this *bon* his spirit joins those of the ancestors.

ni-botoke New buddha. A term used to describe the spirit of the dead until the first *bon*.

ninjō Human feelings, in contrast to *giri* (q.v.).

ni-senzo A term used in the Izu Islands to refer to an ancestor whose tablet has just been placed in the altar. The literal meaning is "new ancestor."

nyorai Tathāgata. In the Kegon sutra, the seventh of the bodies of the Buddha is *nyorai-shin* (Sanskrit *Tathāgata-kāya*). The Great Sun Buddha is a *nyorai*.

ogamu To pray to, to venerate, to worship, to pay respects to, to bow before.

o-kyaku-botoke The souls of near kin and of children who have married into other families. Sometimes an alternative term for *muen-botoke* (q.v.).

okuri-bi Sending-off fire lighted to see off the ancestral spirits at the end of *bon*.

on Obligation incurred from a superior. An unrepayable debt.

oni Demon or devil. The *ki* of *gaki* (q.v.).

onjin A person to whom one owes an unrepayable debt.

rokudō The Six Planes of Existence (Sanskrit *kama-loka*).

ryō-bosei Double-grave burial system.

ryōbu-shintō Dual Shinto. The syncretic amalgam of Shinto and Buddhism promoted by the Shingon sect of Buddhism.

sakaki Evergreen ordinarily offered to the gods (Shinto).

sakoku Seclusion policy. The closing of Japan to foreign intercourse from 1639 to 1868.

segaki-e A *segaki* rite designed to quiet wandering spirits. See *gaki* and *muen-botoke*.

seirei-dana Spirit shelf.

seki-shi Child (of the emperor). That is, his subject.

senzo Ancestor.

senzo-daidai Ascending generations of the ancestors. Commonly inscribed on a memorial tablet for the collectivity of the ancestral dead.

senzo-dana Ancestor shelf.

shaku Tablet carried by Shinto priests and members of the nobility on ceremonial occasions.

shin-botoke. New buddha. A recently deceased member of the household.

shinbutsu-bunri Separation of Shinto and Buddhism. A policy of the early Meiji government.

shinbutsu-shūgō Unification of gods and buddhas. See *honji-suijaku*.

shirei Spirit of the newly dead. Not yet an ancestral spirit. See *sorei*.

shitsuke Training, as in the raising of children.

shōgatsu The New Year.

shōkon-sha Shrine for invoking the spirits of those who have died for the country (Shinto).

shōrō-bune Miniature boat for the spirits of the dead, set afloat at the end of *bon* to carry them to paradise.

shōrō-okuri To send off the spirits of the newly dead at the end of their first *bon*. See *hatsu-bon*.

shō-tsuki-meinichi Annual deathday rite (Buddhist).

shūbun-no-hi The middle day of the autumnal equinox. See *higan*.

shugendō A sect of esoteric Buddhism developed in the medieval period.

shūki The Jōdo-shin sect's term for *nenki* (q.v.).

shumbun-no-hi The middle day of the vernal equinox. See *higan*.

shutsuji-no-senzo Ancestor of origin. The god from whom the founding ancestor of a line derives.

sō-kokubunji Principal protector temple of the land.

sonnō-ron Theory of reverence for the emperor. Late Tokugawa slogan of those favoring restoration.

sorei Ancestral spirit.

sosen-kuyō Comforting the ancestors with offerings and prayers.

sosen-sūhai Ancestor worship.

sotōba See *tōba*.

suiga-shintō An amalgamation of Shinto and Confucianism that originated in the seventeenth century.

tama-matsuri Spirit festival (Shinto).

tamashī Spirit, soul.

tanin Stranger.

tatari-gami Vengeful, retributive god (Shinto).

tennō The emperor.

tennō-heika The contemporary term for the emperor.

tennō-sūhai Emperor worship.

tenshi-sama The emperor. A largely obsolete term.

tera Temple (Buddhist).

tōba Stupa. A thin wood slat placed on the grave (Buddhist).

tomurai-age Last of the periodic anniversary rites for the individual, usually held on the thirty-third or fiftieth, but occasionally as late as the one-hundredth, anniversary of death (Buddhist).

toshi-gami Year-god. The deity, perhaps originally conceived to be the ancestor, who comes to the household at the New Year (Shinto).

ubusuna-gami Tutelary deity (Shinto).

uji Extended kinship group of early Japan. Often mistranslated "clan," it was probably a group of families who traced real or fictive descent to the *uji-gami* (q.v.).

uji-dera Temple of the *uji*.

uji-gami Tutelary deity. The god of the *uji*.

uji-no-kami Head of the *uji*. The intermediary between its people and the *uji-gami*.

urabon-e Festival of the Dead (Sanskrit *Ullambana*). See *bon*.

urabon-kyō The *Ullambana* sutra that forms the basis of the *urabon-e*.

urami Bitterness, ill will, enmity, spite, malice.

yōjo Adopted daughter.

yonaoshi-kami-sama Millennial deities. "World-improving gods." Usually apotheosized human beings.

yōshi Adopted son.

yui-gon Last words of a dying person.

yui-itsu-shintō Primal Shinto. A fifteenth-century syncretic thesis developed by Yoshida Kanetomo making the gods the archetypes and the buddhas the transient manifestations. See *honji-suijaku*.

yūrei Ghost.

zekke A household that has died out. That is, one which could not arrange a succession to its headship. Also called *haike*.

Bibliography

Only works actually cited in the text are listed in the following pages. For each novel or short story I have, where possible, given in parentheses the Japanese title, the date of first publication, and the translator. Thus Akutagawa's short story "Ikki no tsuchi," which originally appeared in 1924, was translated by Richard N. McKinnon and published in 1957 as "A Clod of Earth." Japanese-language articles in academic journals often have titles and short summaries in English. I have given the original titles in both languages, rather than my own translation of the Japanese.

Agency for Cultural Affairs. 1972. Japanese Religion: A Survey. Tokyo: Kodan-sha.

Akutagawa, Ryūnosuke. 1957. A Clod of Earth. (Ikki no tsuchi. 1924. Translated by Richard N. McKinnon.) In Richard N. McKinnon, comp. and ed., The Heart Is Alone: A Selection of 20th Century Japanese Short Stories. Tokyo: Hokuseido Press.

Anesaki, Masaharu. 1930. History of Japanese Religion. London: Kegan Paul, Trench, Trübner.

————. 1938. Religious Life of the Japanese People: Its Present Status and His-torical Background. Tokyo: Kokusai Bunka Shinkōkai.

Anonymous. 1954. The Prophet of Tabuse. Tabuse: Tenshō-kōtai-jingū-kyō.

————. 1966. Risshō Kōsei-Kai. Tokyo: Risshō Kōsei-Kai.

————. 1971. Japan Observes "O-Bon," The Feast of Lanterns. *Japan Report* 17 (14): 6–7.

Ariga, Kizaemon. 1959. Nihon ni okeru senzo no kannen—ie no keifu to ie no hommatsu no keifu to (The Conception of the Ancestors in Japan—House-hold Genealogies and the Genealogies of Main and Branch Households). In Kitano Seiichi and Okada Yuzuru, eds., Ie—sono kōzō bunseki (Household—Analysis of Its Structure). Tokyo: Sōbunsha.

————. 1967. Senzo to ujigami (Ancestors and Tutelary Deities). *Minzokugaku kenkyū* 32 (3): 175–84.

Asakawa, Kan'ichi. 1903. The Early Institutional Life of Japan: A Study in the Reform of 645 A.D. Tokyo: Shūeisha.

Ashikaga, Ensho. 1950. The Festival of the Spirits of the Dead in Japan. *Western Folklore* 9 (3): 217–28.

———. 1951. Notes on Urabon. *Journal of the American Oriental Society* 71: 71–75.

Aston, W. G. 1896. Nihongi: Chronicles of Japan from the Earliest Times to A.D. 697. London: Allen and Unwin.

Beardsley, Richard K., John W. Hall, and Robert E. Ward. 1959. Village Japan. Chicago: University of Chicago Press.

Beckmann, George M. 1971. The Radical Left and the Failure of Communism. In James W. Morley, ed., Dilemmas of Growth in Prewar Japan. Princeton: Princeton University Press.

Bellah, Robert N. 1957. Tokugawa Religion: The Values of Pre-Industrial Japan. Glencoe, Ill.: Free Press.

———. 1962. Values and Social Change in Modern Japan. *Asian Cultural Studies* 3: 13–56.

Benedict, Ruth F. 1946. The Chrysanthemum and the Sword. Boston: Houghton Mifflin.

Bernier, Bernard. 1970. The Popular Religion of a Japanese Village and Its Transformation. Unpublished doctoral dissertation, Cornell University.

Bownas, Geoffrey. 1963. Japanese Rainmaking and Other Folk Practices. London: Allen and Unwin.

Boyer, Martha. 1966–67. Ancestor Worship in Contemporary Japan. *Folk* (Copenhagen) 8–9: 37–54.

Brown, Delmer M. 1968. *Kami*, Death, and Ancestral *kami*. In Proceedings of the Second International Conference for Shinto Studies. Tokyo: Kokugakuin nippon bunka kenkyūsho.

Brown, Keith. 1964. Dozoku: A Study of Descent Groups in Rural Japan. Unpublished doctoral dissertation, University of Chicago.

Bukkyō dai jiten (Dictionary of Buddhism). 1960. Vol. I. 3d ed.

Caiger, John. 1968. The Aims and Content of School Courses in Japanese History, 1872–1945. In Edmund Skrzypczak, ed., Japan's Modern Century. Tokyo: Sophia University.

Chamberlain, Basil Hall. 1898. Things Japanese. Tokyo: Shūeisha, 3d ed., rev.

Ch'en, Kenneth K. S. 1964. Buddhism in China: A Historical Survey. Princeton: Princeton University Press.

———. 1973. The Chinese Transformation of Buddhism. Princeton: Princeton University Press.

Chinnery, Thora E. 1971. Religious Conflict and Compromise in a Japanese Village. Vancouver: University of British Columbia, Department of Asian Studies. Publication in Anthropology No. 5.

Cooper, Michael. 1965. They Came to Japan: An Anthology of European Reports on Japan, 1543–1640. Berkeley and Los Angeles: University of California Press.

Coville, Cabot. 1948. Shinto, Engine of Government. *Transactions of the Asiatic Society of Japan* (3d Series) 1: 1–24.

Creemers, Wilhelmus H. M. 1968. Shrine Shinto after World War II. Leiden: E. J. Brill.

De Visser, M. W. 1935. Ancient Buddhism in Japan: Sutras and Ceremonies in Use in the Seventh and Eighth Centuries A.D. and Their History in Later Times. Leiden: E. J. Brill.

Doi, Takeo. 1973. The Anatomy of Dependence. ("Amae" no kōzō. Translated by John Bester.) Tokyo: Kodansha.

Dore, Ronald P. 1958. City Life in Japan: A Study of a Tokyo Ward. Berkeley and Los Angeles: University of California Press.

———. 1964. Education: Japan. In Robert E. Ward and Dankwart A. Rustow, eds., Political Modernization in Japan and Turkey. Princeton: Princeton University Press.

Dorson, Richard M. 1963. Bridges Between Japanese and American Folklorists. In Richard M. Dorson, ed., Studies in Japanese Folklore. Bloomington, Ind.: Indiana University Press.

Durt, Hubert. 1971. La Fête des Morts à Kyoto. *Message d'Extrême Orient* 1: 15–20.

Duyvendak, J. J. L. 1926. The Buddhistic Festival of All-Souls in China and Japan. *Acta Orientalia* 5 (1): 39–48.

Earhart, H. B. 1970. A Religious Study of the Mt. Haguro Sect of Shugendō: An Example of Japanese Mountain Religion. Tokyo: Sophia University.

Earl, David M. 1964. Emperor and Nation in Japan: Political Thinkers of the Tokugawa Period. Seattle: University of Washington Press.

Eder, Matthias. 1956. Totenseelen und Ahnengeister in Japan. *Anthropos* 51 (1–2): 97–112.

———. 1957. Familie, Sippe, Clan und Ahnenverehung in Japan. *Anthropos* 52 (5–6): 813–40.

Ellwood, Robert S. 1973. The Feast of Kingship: Accession Ceremonies in Ancient Japan. Tokyo: Sophia University.

Embree, John Fee. 1939. Suye Mura: A Japanese Village. Chicago: University of Chicago Press.

Eto, Jun. 1971. Japan and the United States: A Personal Reflection. *Japan House Newsletter* 19 (4).

Fortes, Meyer. 1961. *Pietas* in Ancestor Worship. *Journal of the Royal Anthropological Institute* 91 (2): 166–91.

Fridell, Wilbur M. 1972. Notes on Japanese Tolerance. *Monumenta Nipponica* 27 (3): 253–71.

———. 1973. Japanese Shrine Mergers 1906–1912: State Shinto Moves to the Grassroots. Tokyo: Sophia University.

Fujii, Masao. 1970. Un Temple de Grande Ville et la Population Religieuse Flottante. *Social Compass* 17 (1): 67–96.

Fukutake, Tadashi. 1962. Democracy and the Japanese Background. *Orient/West* 7 (3): 33–42.

Gabriel, Theodor. 1938. Das Buddhistische Begräbnis in Japan. *Anthropos* 33: 568–83.

Hall, John W. 1955. Tanuma Okitsugu, 1719–1788: Forerunner of Modern Japan. Cambridge: Harvard University Press.

————. 1968. A Monarch for Modern Japan. In Robert E. Ward, ed., Political Development in Modern Japan. Princeton: Princeton University Press.

Hall, Robert King. 1949a. Kokutai no Hongi: Cardinal Principles of the National Entity of Japan. (Translated by John Owen Gauntlett.) Cambridge: Harvard University Press.

————. 1949b. *Shūshin*: The Ethics of a Defeated Nation. New York: Bureau of Publications, Teachers College, Columbia University.

Hanayama, Shoyu. 1969. Buddhist Handbook for Shin-Shu Followers. Tokyo: Hokuseido Press.

Harada, Toshiaki. 1959. The Origin of Community Worship. In Japanese Association for Religious Studies and Japanese Organizing Committee of the Ninth International Congress for the History of Religions, eds., Religious Studies in Japan. Tokyo: Maruzen.

Harootunian, Harry D. 1970. Toward Restoration: The Growth of Political Consciousness in Tokugawa Japan. Berkeley and Los Angeles: University of California Press.

Hashimoto, Tatsumi. 1962. Ancestor Worship and Japanese Daily Life. (Sosen sūhai to nichijō seikatsu. 1958. Translated by Percy T. Luke.) Tokyo: Word of Life Press.

Hayami, Akira, and Nobuko Uchida. 1972. Size of Household in a Japanese County Throughout the Tokugawa Era. In Peter Laslett, ed., Household and Family in Past Time. Cambridge: Cambridge University Press.

Hepner, Charles W. 1935. The Kurozumi Sect of Shintō. Tokyo: Meiji Japan Society.

Herbert, Jean. 1967. Shintō at the Fountain-Head of Japan. London: Allen and Unwin.

Hildreth, Richard. 1905. Japan as It Was and Is. Tokyo: Sanshūsha. 2d ed.

Hirai, Atsuko. 1968. Ancestor Worship in Yatsuka Hozumi's State and Constitutional Theory. In Edmund Skrzypczak, ed., Japan's Modern Century. Tokyo: Sophia University.

Hirayama, Toshijirō. 1949. Kamidana to butsudan (God-Shelf and Buddhist Altar). *Shirin* 32 (2): 204–32.

————. 1959. Ie no kami to mura no kami (Household Gods and Community Gods). *Nihon minzokugaku taikei* 8: 39–74.

————. 1963. Seasonal Rituals Connected with Rice Culture. In Richard M. Dorson, ed., Studies in Japanese Folklore. Bloomington, Ind.: Indiana University Press.

Hori, Ichirō. 1951. Minkan shinkō (Folk Religion). Tokyo: Iwanami shoten.

————. 1953. Wagakuni minkan shinkō no kenkyū (Studies in Japanese Folk Religion). Tokyo: Sōgensha.

————. 1959a. Japanese Folk Beliefs. *American Anthropologist* 61 (3): 405–24.

————. 1959b. The Phenomenological Development of the Pure Land School in Japan. In Japanese Association for Religious Studies and Japanese Organizing Committee of the Ninth International Congress for the History of Religions, eds., Religious Studies in Japan. Tokyo: Maruzen.

————. 1963. Manyōshū ni arawareta sosei to takai kan reikon kan ni tsuite (Concerning Funeral Customs, Conceptions of the Other World and Souls of the Dead as Found in the Manyōshū). *Nihon shūkyō kenkyū* 2: 49–93.

———. 1966. Mountains and Their Importance for the Idea of the Other World in Japanese Folk Religion. *History of Religions* 6 (1): 1–23.

———. 1967. The Appearance of Individual Self-Consciousness in Japanese Religion and Its Historical Transformations. In Charles A. Moore, ed., The Japanese Mind: Essentials of Japanese Philosophy and Culture. Honolulu: East-West Center Press and University of Hawaii Press.

———. 1969. Hitotsu-mono: A Human Symbol of the Shinto kami. In Joseph M. Kitagawa and Charles H. Long, eds., Myths and Symbols: Studies in Honor of Mircea Eliade. Chicago: University of Chicago Press.

Hori, Ichirō, and Yoshio Toda. 1956. Shinto. In Hideo Kishimoto, compiler and ed., Japanese Religion in the Meiji Era. (Translated and adapted by John F. Howes.) Tokyo: Obunsha.

Hozumi, Nobushige. 1912. Lectures on the New Japanese Civil Code. Tokyo: Maruzen.

———. 1943. Ancestor Worship and the Japanese Law. Tokyo: Hokuseido Press. 7th ed., rev.

Iisaka, Yoshiaki. 1972. The State and Religion in Postwar History. *Japan Interpreter* 7 (3–4): 306–20.

Ikegami, Hiromasa. 1959a. Rei no kami no shurui to arawarekata (Varieties of Spirits and kami and Their Manner of Appearance). *Nihon minzokugaku taikei* 8: 15–38.

———. 1959b. The Significance of Mountains in the Popular Beliefs in Japan. In Japanese Association for Religious Studies and Japanese Organizing Committee of the Ninth International Congress for the History of Religions, eds., Religious Studies in Japan. Tokyo: Maruzen.

Inoguchi, Shōji. 1954. Bukkyō izen (Before Buddhism). Tokyo: Kokon shoin.

———. 1959. Sōshiki (Funerals). *Nihon minzokugaku taikei* 4: 291–329.

Ishii, Ryōsuke. 1958. Japanese Legislation in the Meiji Era. (Translated and adapted by William J. Chambliss.) Tokyo: Pan-Pacific Press.

Iwamoto, Yutaka. 1968. Mokuren densetsu to urabon (The Legend of Mokuren and Urabon). Kyoto: Hōzōkan.

Jansen, Marius B. 1965. Changing Japanese Attitudes Toward Modernization. In Marius B. Jansen, ed., Changing Japanese Attitudes Toward Modernization. Princeton: Princeton University Press.

Kaempfer, Engelbert. 1906. The History of Japan Together with a Description of the Kingdom of Siam 1690–1692. Glasgow: James MacLehose.

Kamstra, J. H. 1967. Encounter or Syncretism: The Initial Growth of Japanese Buddhism. Leiden: E. J. Brill.

Kawabata, Yasunari. 1970. The Sound of the Mountain. (Yama no oto. 1954. Translated by Edward M. Seidensticker.) New York: A. A. Knopf.

Kawakoshi, Junji. 1957. Kazoku ni okeru dentōteki kihan to sono hōkai (The Family: Its Traditional Norms and Their Collapse). *Aichi daigaku bungaku ronsō*, Tenth Anniversary Issue, 95–122.

Kazama, Toshio, and Kazuyoshi Kino. 1965. Ancestor Worship: II. India. In George P. Malalasekera, ed., Encyclopaedia of Buddhism. Colombo: Government of Ceylon. Vol. 1, Fasc. 4: 590–93.

Keene, Donald (translator). 1961. Major Plays of Chikamatsu. New York: Columbia University Press.

————. 1967. Essays in Idleness: The Tsurezuregusa of Kenkō. New York: Columbia University Press.

Keene, Donald (editor). 1970. Twenty Plays of the Nō Theatre. New York: Columbia University Press.

Keenleyside, Hugh L., and A. F. Thomas. 1937. History of Japanese Education and Present Educational System. Tokyo: Hokuseido Press.

Kerner, Karen. 1974. The Malevolent Ancestor: Ancestral Influence in a Japanese Religious Sect. In William H. Newell, ed., Ancestors. The Hague: Mouton.

Kiley, Cornelius J. 1973. State and Dynasty in Archaic Yamato. *Journal of Asian Studies* 33 (1): 25–49.

Kishimoto, Hideo, and Tsuneya Wakimoto. 1956. Introduction: Religion During Tokugawa. In Hideo Kishimoto, compiler and ed., Japanese Religion in the Meiji Era. (Translated and adapted by John F. Howes.) Tokyo: Obunsha.

Kitagawa, Joseph. 1965. The Buddhist Transformation in Japan. *History of Religions* 4 (2): 319–36.

Koyama, Takashi. 1966. The Significance of Relatives at the Turning Point of the Family System in Japan. In Paul Halmos, ed., Japanese Sociological Studies. *The Sociological Review*, Monograph No. 10: 95–114.

Lay, Arthur Hyde. 1891. Japanese Funeral Rites. *Transactions of the Asiatic Society of Japan* 19: 507–44.

Lebra, Takie Sugiyama. 1969. Reciprocity and the Asymmetric Principle: An Analytical Reappraisal of the Japanese Concept of *on*. *Psychologia* 12: 129–38.

————. 1970. Logic of Salvation: The Case of a Japanese Sect in Hawaii. *International Journal of Social Psychiatry* 16 (1): 45–53.

————. 1974. Ancestral Influence on the Suffering of Descendants in a Japanese Cult. In William H. Newell, ed., Ancestors. The Hague: Mouton.

McCullough, Helen. 1968. Tales of Ise: Lyrical Episodes from Tenth-Century Japan. Stanford: Stanford University Press.

Macfarlane, Alan. 1973. Review of David C. Pitt, Using Historical Sources in Anthropology and Sociology. *Man* 8 (2): 321–22.

Maeda, Takashi. 1965. Sosen sūhai no kenkyū (A Study of Ancestor Worship). Tokyo: Aoyama shoin.

Maeyama, Takashi. 1972. Ancestor, Emperor, and Immigrant: Religion and Group Identification of the Japanese in Rural Brazil (1908–1950). *Journal of Interamerican Studies and World Affairs* 14 (2): 151–82.

Mason, J. W. T. 1935. The Meaning of Shinto. Port Washington, N.Y.: Kennikat Press (1967 reprint).

Masutani, Fumio, and Yoshimichi Undō. 1956. Buddhism. In Hideo Kishimoto, compiler and ed., Japanese Religion in the Meiji Era. (Translated and adapted by John F. Howes.) Tokyo: Obunsha.

Matsudaira, Narimitsu. 1936. Les Fêtes Saisonnières au Japon (Province de Mikawa): Étude Descriptive et Sociologique. Paris: G.-P. Maisonneuve.

————. 1963. The Concept of Tamashii in Japan. In Richard M. Dorson, ed., Studies in Japanese Folklore. Bloomington, Ind.: Indiana University Press.

Matsumoto, Shigeru. 1970. Motoori Norinaga 1730–1801. Cambridge: Harvard University Press.

Matsunaga, Alicia. 1969. The Buddhist Philosophy of Assimilation: The Historical Development of the Honji-Suijaku Theory. Tokyo: Sophia University.

Minear, Richard H. 1970. Japanese Tradition and Western Law: Emperor, State, and Law in the Thought of Hozumi Yatsuka. Cambridge: Harvard University Press.

Ministry of Justice (Japan) and the Codes Translation Committee. 1966. The Civil Code of Japan (as of 1966). Tokyo: Eibun-horei-sha.

Minzokugaku kenkyū sho (editors). 1952a. Butsudan (Buddhist Altars). In Minzokugaku jiten (Dictionary of Folklore). Tokyo: Tōkyō-dō.

———. 1952b. Ihai (Memorial Tablets). In Minzokugaku jiten (Dictionary of Folklore). Tokyo: Tōkyō-dō.

Mishima, Yukio. 1956. The Sound of Waves. (Shiosai. 1954. Translated by Meredith Weatherby.) New York: A. A. Knopf.

———. 1966. Death in Midsummer. (Manatsu no shi. 1952. Translated and abridged by Edward G. Seidensticker.) In Death in Midsummer and Other Stories. New York: New Directions.

———. 1969. Thirst for Love. (Ai no kawaki. 1950. Translated by Alfred H. Marks.) New York: A. A. Knopf.

Miyata, Noboru. 1963. "Ikigami" shinkō no hatsugen (The Origins of Belief in "Living Gods"). Nihon minzokugaku kaihō 28: 1–11.

Mogami, Takayoshi. 1959. Shigo no matsuri oyobi bosei (Rituals Following Death and the Grave System). Nihon minzokugaku taikei 4: 331–61.

———. 1963. The Double-Grave System. In Richard M. Dorson, ed., Studies in Japanese Folklore. Bloomington, Ind.: Indiana University Press.

Morioka, Kiyomi. 1966. Christianity in the Japanese Rural Community: Acceptance and Rejection. In Paul Halmos, ed., Japanese Sociological Studies. The Sociological Review, Monograph No. 10: 183–97.

———. 1968. Religious Behavior and the Actor's Position in His Household. In Kiyomi Morioka and William H. Newell, eds., The Sociology of Japanese Religion. Leiden: E. J. Brill.

———. 1970. Ie to no kanren de no shakaigakueteki bunseki (A Sociological Analysis Relating to the Household). In Fujio Ikado and Mitsukuni Yoshida, eds., Nihonjin no shūkyō (Religion of the Japanese). Kyoto: Tankōsha.

———. 1972. Kazoku pattern to dentōteki shūkyō kōdō no kunren (Family Pattern and Child Training in Traditional Religious Behavior). Kokusai kirisutokyō daigaku shakai kagaku journal (International Christian University Social Science Journal) 11: 71–97.

Morrell, Robert E. 1973. Mujū Ichien Shinto-Buddhist Syncretism: Shasekishū, Book 1. Monumenta Nipponica 28 (4): 447–88.

Muraoka, Tsunetsugu. 1964. Studies in Shinto Thought. (Translated by Delmer M. Brown and James T. Araki.) Tokyo: Japanese National Commission for UNESCO.

Nakai, Kate Wildman. 1965. Hakuseki on Spirits: An Analysis of Arai Hakuseki's Essay "Kishinron." In Papers on Japan, Volume 3. Cambridge: East Asian Research Center, Harvard University.

Nakamura, Hajime. 1964. Ways of Thinking of Eastern Peoples. (Revised English translation edited by Philip P. Wiener.) Honolulu: East-West Center Press.

———. 1967. Basic Features of the Legal, Political, and Economic Thought of Japan. In Charles A. Moore, ed., The Japanese Mind: Essentials of Japanese Philosophy and Culture. Honolulu: East-West Center Press and University of Hawaii Press.

Nakane, Chie. 1967. Kinship and Economic Organization in Rural Japan. London: Athlone.

———. 1970. Japanese Society. Berkeley and Los Angeles: University of California Press.

———. 1972. An Interpretation of the Size and Structure of the Household in Japan over Three Centuries. In Peter Laslett, ed., Household and Family in Past Time. Cambridge: Cambridge University Press.

Naoe, Hiroji. 1963. A Study of *Yashiki-gami*, The Deity of House and Grounds. In Richard M. Dorson, ed., Studies in Japanese Folklore. Bloomington, Ind.: Indiana University Press.

Natsume, Sōseki. 1969. Grass on the Wayside. (Michikusa. 1915. Translated by Edwin McClellan.) Chicago: University of Chicago Press.

Niwa, Fumio. 1966. The Buddha Tree. (Bodaiju. 1955–56. Translated by Kenneth Strong.) Tokyo: Charles E. Tuttle.

Noguchi, Takenori. 1966. Mortuary Customs and the Family-Kinship System in Japan and Ryūkyū. In Folk Cultures of Japan and East Asia. *Monumenta Nipponica* Monograph No. 25.

Norbeck, Edward. 1952. Pollution and Taboo in Contemporary Japan. *Southwestern Journal of Anthropology* 8 (3): 269–85.

———. 1954. Takashima: A Japanese Fishing Community. Salt Lake City: University of Utah Press.

———. 1970. Religion and Society in Modern Japan: Continuity and Change. *Rice University Studies* 56 (1).

Oguchi, Iichi, and Hiroo Takagi. 1956. Religion and Social Development. In Hideo Kishimoto, compiler and ed., Japanese Religion in the Meiji Era. (Translated and adapted by John F. Howes.) Tokyo: Obunsha.

Ooms, Herman. 1967. The Religion of the Household: A Case Study of Ancestor Worship in Japan. *Contemporary Religions in Japan* 8 (3–4): 201–333.

———. 1974. Japanese Ancestor Worship as the Religion of the Household. In William H. Newell, ed., Ancestors. The Hague: Mouton.

Osaragi, Jirō. 1960. The Journey. (Tabiji. 1960. Translated by Ivan Morris.) New York: A. A. Knopf.

Ōshima, Tatehiko. 1959. Shinkō to nenjū gyōji (Beliefs and Annual Observances). *Nihon minzokugaku taikei* 7: 67–116.

Ōtō, Tokohiko. 1963. The Taboos of Fishermen. In Richard M. Dorson, ed., Studies in Japanese Folklore. Bloomington, Ind.: Indiana University Press.

Passin, Herbert. 1965. Society and Education in Japan. New York: Bureau of Publications, Teachers College, Columbia University.

Pelzel, John C. 1970. Human Nature in the Japanese Myths. In Albert M. Craig and Donald H. Shively, eds., Personality in Japanese History. Berkeley and Los Angeles: University of California Press.

Pittau, Joseph. 1967. Political Thought in Early Meiji Japan 1868–1889. Cambridge: Harvard University Press.

Plath, David W. 1964. Where the Family of God Is the Family: The Role of the Dead in Japanese Households. *American Anthropologist* 66 (2): 300–317.

Ponsonby Fane, R. A. B. 1962. Sovereign and Subject. Kyoto: Ponsonby Memorial Society.

———. 1963. The Vicissitudes of Shinto. Kyoto: Ponsonby Memorial Society.

———. 1964. Visiting Famous Shrines in Japan. Kyoto: Ponsonby Memorial Society.

Pyle, Kenneth B. 1973. The Technology of Japanese Nationalism: The Local Improvement Movement, 1900–1918. *Journal of Asian Studies* 33 (1): 51–65.

Reichelt, Karl Ludwig. 1934. Truth and Tradition in Chinese Buddhism: A Study of Chinese Mahayana Buddhism. Shanghai: Commercial Press. 4th ed., rev.

Reischauer, Robert Karl. 1937. Early Japanese History. Princeton: Princeton University Press. Part A.

Reitz, Karl. 1939. Totenriten des Shintō. *Annali Lateranensi* 3: 61–89.

Sakamaki, Shunzō. 1967. Shintō: Japanese Ethnocentrism. In Charles A. Moore, ed., The Japanese Mind: Essentials of Japanese Philosophy and Culture. Honolulu: East-West Center Press and University of Hawaii Press.

Sano, Chiye. 1958. Changing Values of the Japanese Family. Washington, D.C.: The Catholic University of America, Anthropological Series No. 18.

Sansom, Sir George B. 1958. A History of Japan to 1334. Stanford: Stanford University Press.

Satō, Takashi. 1964. Higashi Kyūshū no ryōbo iseki ni tsuite (Vestiges of the Double-Grave System in Eastern Kyushu). *Nihon minzokugaku kaihō* 34: 42–43.

Scheiner, Irwin. 1973. The Mindful Peasant: Sketches for a Study of Rebellion. *Journal of Asian Studies* 32 (4): 579–91.

Schinzinger, Robert. 1963. Peculiarities of the Japanese Character. *Orient/West* 8 (5): 30–41.

Schneider, Delwin B. 1962. Konkokyo: A Japanese Religion. Tokyo: International Institute for the Study of Religions Press.

Sebald, William J. (translator). 1934. The Civil Code of Japan. Kobe: J. J. Thompson.

Shibata, Minoru. 1959. Sosen sūhai no genryū (The Origins of Ancestor Worship). In Nihon shūkyō shi kōza, Vol. III. Tokyo: San-ichi shobo.

Shioiri, Ryōdō. 1965. Ancestor Worship: I. China. In George P. Malalasekera, ed., Encyclopaedia of Buddhism. Colombo: Government of Ceylon. Vol. 1, Fasc. 4: 583–90.

Shively, Donald H. 1959. Motoda Eifu: Confucian Lecturer to the Meiji Emperor. In David S. Nivison and Arthur F. Wright, eds., Confucianism in Action. Stanford: Stanford University Press.

Singer, Kurt. 1973. Mirror, Sword, and Jewel: A Study of Japanese Characteristics. New York: George Braziller.

Smith, Robert J. 1956. Kurusu: A Japanese Agricultural Community. In John B. Cornell and Robert J. Smith, Two Japanese Villages. Ann Arbor: University of Michigan, Center for Japanese Studies, Occasional Papers No. 5.

————. 1966. *Ihai*: Mortuary Tablets, the Household and Kin in Japanese Ancestor Worship. *Transactions of the Asiatic Society of Japan* (3d Series) 9: 1–20.

————. 1972. Small Families, Small Households, and Residential Instability: Town and City in "Pre-modern" Japan. In Peter Laslett, ed., Household and Family in Past Time. Cambridge: Cambridge University Press.

————. 1974. Who Are "The Ancestors" in Japan? In William H. Newell, ed., Ancestors. The Hague: Mouton.

Sono, Ayako. 1966. The Environs of Seiganji Temple. (Translated by Kazue Kume). In Maurice Schneps and Alvin D. Coox, eds., The Japanese Image, Volume II. *Orient/West* 10, 1: 145–54.

Spae, Joseph J. 1968. Christianity Encounters Japan. Tokyo: Oriens Institute for Religious Research.

————. 1971. Japanese Religiosity. Tokyo: Oriens Institute for Religious Research.

Steiner, Kurt. 1950. Revisions of the Civil Code of Japan: Provisions Affecting the Family. *Far Eastern Quarterly* 9 (2): 169–84.

Sugi, Masataka. 1963. The Concept of *ninjō*. In John W. Bennett and Iwao Ishino, Paternalism in the Japanese Economy: Anthropological Studies of Oyabun-Kobun Patterns. Minneapolis: University of Minnesota Press.

Sugimoto, Etsu Inagaki. 1925. A Daughter of the Samurai. Garden City, N.Y.: Doubleday, Page and Company.

Suzuki, Jirō. 1961. Burakumin: Japan's "Untouchables." *Orient/West* 6 (7): 9–13.

Suzuki, Mitsuo. 1972. Bon ni kuru rei—Taiwan no chūgensetsu o tegakari to shita hikaku minzokugakuteki shiron (Midsummer Ghost Festival in East Asia—A Comparison of Japan's *bon,* Taiwan's *poto,* and Korea's *manghonil*). *Minzokugaku kenkyū* 37 (3): 167–85.

Takayanagi, Shun'ichi. 1972. Review of Ogata Tomio, Nihon ni okeru Hippocrates sanbi. *Monumenta Nipponica* 27 (3): 352–53.

Takeda, Chōshū. 1959. Ancestor-Worship in Japanese Folklore and History. The Japan Science Review, Volume 10: Abstracts and Reviews of Dissertations. Tokyo: Union of Japanese Associations of Humanistic Studies.

————. 1961. Sosen sūhai (Ancestor Worship). Kyoto: Heirakuji shoten. 2d ed.

————. 1965. Ancestor Worship: III. Japan. In George P. Malalasekera, ed., Encyclopaedia of Buddhism. Colombo: Government of Ceylon. Vol. 1, Fasc. 4: 593–600.

Takeda, Chōshū, and Masao Takatori. 1957. Nihonjin no shinkō (Religious Beliefs of the Japanese). Tokyo: Sōgensha.

Takenaka, Nobutsune. 1955a. Butsudan (Buddhist Altar). *Nihon shakai minzoku jiten* 3: 1260–61. 2d ed.

————. 1955b. Kakochō (Book of the Past). *Nihon shakai minzoku jiten* 1: 158–59. 2d ed.

Tamamura, Taijo. 1963. Sōshiki bukkyō (Funeral Buddhism). Tokyo: Daihōrinkaku.

Tanaka, Shinjirō. 1961. San'in no sōsei (Funerals in the San'in District). *Nihon minzokugaku kaihō* 22: 37–38.

Tanizaki, Jun'ichirō. 1963. The Bridge of Dreams. (Yume no ukihashi. 1959. Translated by Howard Hibbett.) In Seven Japanese Tales. New York: A. A. Knopf.

Tokutomi, Kenjirō. 1904. Nami-Ko: A Realistic Novel. (Hototogisu. 1900. Translated by Sakae Shioya and E. F. Edgett.) Boston: Herbert B. Turner.

Toland, John. 1970. The Rising Sun: The Decline and Fall of the Japanese Empire, 1936–1945. New York: Random House.

Tomaru, Tokuichi. 1967. Jōshū ni okeru o-mitama-sama ni tsuite (Concerning the Spirits in Jōshū). *Nihon minzokugaku kaihō* 49: 17–21.

Tsunoda, Ryusaku, William Theodore de Bary, and Donald Keene (editors). 1958. Sources of the Japanese Tradition. New York: Columbia University Press.

Tsuyuki, Tamae. 1967. Morinoyama kuyō (Memorial Services at Morinoyama). *Nihon minzokugaku kaihō* 49: 30–33.

Ueda, Makoto. 1967. Literary and Art Theories in Japan. Cleveland: Press of Western Reserve University.

Ushijima, Iwao. 1966. Ihai saishi to nihon no kazoku. shinzoku: Izu hantō. Toshima o chūshin to shite ("Ihai" Cult in Relation to Japanese Kinship and Family—Ancestor Worship in Toshima Island, Izu Archipelago). *Minzokugaku kenkyū* 31 (3): 169–78.

Varley, H. Paul. 1971. Imperial Restoration in Medieval Japan. New York: Columbia University Press.

Vogel, Ezra. 1963. Japan's New Middle Class: The Salary Man and His Family in a Tokyo Suburb. Berkeley and Los Angeles: University of California Press.

Waley, Arthur. 1921. The Nō Plays of Japan. London: Allen and Unwin.

Watanabe, Shoko. 1950. The Decline of Japanese Buddhism. *Today's Japan (Orient/West)* 3 (9): 23–28.

———. 1968. Japanese Buddhism: A Critical Appraisal. Tokyo: Kokusai Bunka Shinkōkai.

Watanabe, Yozo. 1963. The Family and the Law: The Individualistic Premise and Modern Japanese Family Law. In Arthur Taylor von Mehren, ed., Law in Japan: The Legal Order in a Changing Society. Cambridge: Harvard University Press.

Weeraratne, W. G. 1965. Anumodanā. In George P. Malalasekera, ed., Encyclopaedia of Buddhism. Colombo: Government of Ceylon. Vol. 1, Fasc. 4: 747–50.

Wimberley, Howard. 1969. Self-realization and the Ancestors: An Analysis of Two Japanese Ritual Procedures for Achieving Domestic Harmony. *Anthropological Quarterly* 42 (1): 37–51.

———. 1972. The Knights of the Golden Lotus. *Ethnology* 11 (2): 173–86.

Wright, Arthur F. 1959. Buddhism in Chinese History. Stanford: Stanford University Press.

Yanagida, Kunio (compiler and editor). 1957. Japanese Manners and Customs in the Meiji Era. (Translated and adapted by Charles S. Terry.) Tokyo: Obunsha.

Yanagita, Kunio. 1970. About Our Ancestors. (Senzo no hanashi. 1946. Translated by Fanny Hagin Mayer and Yasuyo Ishiwara.) Tokyo: Japan Society for the Promotion of Science.

Yonemura, Shoji. 1974. Lineage and Ancestor Worship. In William H. Newell, ed., Ancestors. The Hague: Mouton.

Yoshida, Teigo. 1967. Mystical Retribution, Spirit Possession, and Social Structure in a Japanese Village. *Ethnology* 6 (3): 237–62.

Zürcher, E. 1959. The Buddhist Conquest of China: The Spread and Adaptation of Buddhism in Early Medieval China. Leiden: E. J. Brill.

Index

DATE DUE

DEMCO 38-297